# Country Kitchen Cookbook

➤➤ by ◀◀
Wes & Lois Bauman
and
Friends

Tyndale House
Publishers, Inc.
Wheaton, Illinois

Fourth printing, June 1984

Deepest thanks to the women
of the Old German
Baptist Brethren Church
in California and Oregon.
Their delicious recipes are
treasured family favorites,
each reflecting the
joys of cooking!

*The Cookbook Committee*
Modesto, California
Naomi Barton
Mina Benedict
Bonnie Jamison
Mary D. Miller
Suzanne Overholtzer
Connie Reece
Janet Rumble
Linda Thompson

*Linoleum cut
illustrations by*
Laura Alvord

Library of Congress
Catalog Card Number 81-50541
ISBN 0-8423-0448-7
Copyright © 1981 by
Wes & Lois Bauman.
All rights reserved.

Printed in the
United States of America.

DEDICATED TO

*The Christian Home*

# CONTENTS

## HINTS FOR USING THIS BOOK

Welcome to the *Country Kitchen Cookbook*! May it be a feast for the whole person. To help you make the most of it, please remember the following:

The bits of Dutch and German folk wisdom are accompanied by Scripture verses which illuminate or contrast with the sayings. *Chew them over.*

In the recipes themselves, *unless otherwise specified,*

1. Always preheat oven.
2. Oven temperatures are in Fahrenheit degrees.
3. "Flour" refers to regular, all-purpose flour.
4. "Sugar" or "white sugar" refers to white, *granulated* sugar.
5. "Hamburger" refers to regular ground beef or ground chuck.
6. "Canned creamed soup" is the condensed variety.
7. "Sauté" means fried lightly in very little fat.
8. Abbreviations:
   tsp. = teaspoon
   Tbsp. = Tablespoon
   oz. = ounce
   lb. = pound
   qt. = quart
   pkg. = package

# On the Appetizer Tray

*God tries you
with a little
to see what you'd do
with a lot.*
ANONYMOUS

*My son,
honey whets the appetite,
and so does wisdom!*
PROVERBS 24:13

# Appetizers

## Curry Hors D'Oeuvres

white bread, thinly
  sliced
butter
mayonnaise
curry powder
cucumber slices
shrimp

Cut small bread
rounds from the
bread; butter, then
spread with mayon-
naise and curry pow-
der. Add a slice of
cucumber and put a
dab of curried mayon-
naise on top. Add a
shrimp. Chill.
*Lois Bauman*

## Cheese Hors D'Oeuvres

white bread, thinly
  sliced
grated sharp Cheddar
  cheese
small red onion,
  chopped
mayonnaise

Cut small bread
rounds from the
bread and butter
them. Add grated
cheese and chopped
onion. Spread mayon-
naise on top. Cover
bread rounds and
broil in oven a few
minutes.
*Lois Bauman*

## Cheese Ball 1

1 8-oz. pkg. cream
  cheese
1 16-oz pkg. Cheddar
  cheese
2 Tbsp. green pepper,
  chopped
2 Tbsp. green onion,
  chopped
1 tsp. lemon juice
2 tsp. Worcestershire
  sauce
1 tsp. prepared
  mustard
1/8 tsp. salt
1 pinch of cayenne
  pepper

Whip together cream
cheese and Cheddar
cheese; then add
remaining ingredients.
Chill for 2 hours or
until firm. Roll into a
ball and then in nuts
or parsley.
*Mary D. Miller*

## Cheese Ball 2

1 8-oz. pkg. cream
  cheese, room temper-
  ature
1 jar sharp cheese
  spread
1/4 pkg. dry onion
  soup
dash of Worcestershire
  sauce
dash of parsley flakes
finely chopped nuts, or
  parsley flakes

Beat ingredients to-
gether and form into
ball. Roll in nuts or
parsley flakes. Chill.
Good with crackers
or apples.
*Virginia Skiles*

## Cheese Ball 3

2 lbs. cream cheese,
  softened
2 cups pecans,
  chopped
1/4 cup green pepper,
  finely diced
1/4 cup onion,
  finely diced
2 Tbsp. seasoned salt
1 8 1/2-oz. can
  crushed pineapple

Combine all ingredi-
ents well and shape
into ball. Save 1 cup
chopped pecans to
roll ball in when
finished.
*Mina Benedict*

## Cheese Ball 4

1 small jar pimiento
  cheese
1 small jar cheese
  spread
1 small jar Blue cheese
2 8-oz. pkgs. cream
  cheese
dash of Worcestershire
  sauce
1/2 onion, very finely
  chopped

Mix at room temperature 1 hour before eating. Roll into ball; cover with chopped nuts. After mixing cheese, set in refrigerator to chill so it will stay in ball form. Serve with crackers.
*Jill Bauman*

## Rye and Blue Cheese

1/2 cup butter
1/2 lb. Blue cheese
1/4 cup sour cream
rye crackers
thinly sliced radishes

Cream butter and cheese together. Blend in sour cream. Chill, covered, up to 1 week. Serve with crackers and radishes.
*Eileen Barton*

## Guacamole

2 large avocados,
  mashed
1/2 small tomato,
  peeled and chopped
1/4 tsp. onion salt
1/4 tsp. garlic salt
1/4 tsp. chili powder
1/4 tsp. ground cumin

Combine ingredients well. Chill.
Variation:
Add 2 Tbsp. sour
  cream.
*Dovella Boyd*

## Melon Ball Cocktail

2–4 cups mixed melon
  balls
1 cup sugar
2 cups water
juice of 3 oranges
juice of 1 lemon

Boil sugar and water 5 minutes; then cool. Add the juices. Pour over melon balls. Let marinate several hours.
Variation:
Use frozen concentrate to taste, approximately 4 Tbsp. orange juice and 3 Tbsp. lemon juice.
*Eunice Grover*

## Rumaki Appetizers

dates, pitted
walnuts, quartered
bacon, uncooked

Fit a quarter of a walnut inside a pitted date. Wrap with a 1/3 slice of uncooked bacon. Spear with a toothpick to hold the bacon on date. Bake slowly until golden brown, about 45 minutes at 350°. Cool slightly before serving.
*Suzanne Layman*

## Mexicali Appetizers

Dough:
3 cups flour
2 tsp. chili powder
1 1/2 tsp. salt
1 cup shortening
1/2–3/4 cup cold
  water

Beef Filling:
1 Tbsp. butter
1/4 cup green pepper,
  chopped
1/4 cup onion,
  chopped
1 clove garlic, crushed
1/2 lb. ground beef
1/3 cup catsup
2 Tbsp. flour
1 tsp. chili powder

Stir together flour, chili powder, and salt. Cut in shortening until mixture resembles coarse crumbs. Sprinkle with water until dough begins to stick together. Press into ball; divide in half. Roll out on lightly floured surface to circle 1/16 inch thick. Cut 60 circles with floured 2-inch cutter; place on ungreased baking sheet. Prepare filling. Melt butter in skillet. Cook onion, green pepper, and garlic until soft, about 5 minutes. Add beef and brown. Combine catsup, flour, and chili powder. Blend into mixture and cook, stirring constantly, until mix-

ture thickens. Remove from heat. Spoon 1 tsp. of filling in center of each circle. Roll out remaining dough and cut; place on top of filled circles. Seal edges securely with fork. Bake in oven at 400° for 15 to 18 minutes or until lightly browned.
*Anita Angle*

## Cha-Shew
(Chinese Red Pork)

2 lb. whole pork tenderloin or spare-ribs
1 tsp. red food coloring
1 1/2 tsp. seasoned salt
1/2 cup sherry, (optional)

1/2 cup pineapple juice
1/2 cup honey
1/4 cup soy sauce
1/3 cup ginger
2 Tbsp. cornstarch

Brush pork tenderloin or spareribs with red food coloring. Sprinkle seasoned salt evenly over meat. Place on rack in shallow roasting pan. Roast in 325° oven until tender, about 1 1/4 hours. Combine remaining ingredients in saucepan; cook, stirring constantly, until thick and clear. Brush meat lightly with sauce 10 minutes before end of baking time. Remove from oven; cool

slightly. Cut into pieces or slice. To serve, spear meat with wooden picks, cocktail forks, or chopsticks. Dip into sauce. Garnish with thin slices of fresh or canned pineapple, papaya, or honeydew melon, or sprigs of watercress, if desired. Yields about 40 to 50 appetizer servings.

---

*TAKE TIME FOR TEN THINGS*

1 *Working: The price of success*

2 *Thinking: The source of power*

3 *Playing: The secret of youth*

4 *Reading: The foundation of knowledge*

5 *Worshiping: The highway of reverence which clears earth's dust from our eyes*

6 *Helping and Enjoying Friends: The source of happiness*

7 *Loving: The main sacrament of life*

8 *Dreaming: The soul's hitch to the stars*

9 *Laughing: The song which eases life's load*

10 *Planning: The secret of making time for the first nine things*

Source: _____     Who Likes It: _____

Source: _____     Who Likes It: _____

Source: _____     Who Likes It: _____

# The Beverage Bucket

*It's a poor sheep*
*that can not carry*
*its own wool.*
PENNSYLVANIA GERMAN SAYING

*Jesus said,*
*"But the water I give them*
*becomes a perpetual spring*
*within. . . ."*
JOHN 4:14

# Cold Beverages

## Pep Cocktail

1 glass tomato juice
1 Tbsp. lecithin
granules
1 tsp. or more brewer's
yeast
1 tsp. desiccated liver
powder

Combine ingredients
in blender if possible.
Take before each
meal.
*Eunice Grover*

## Banana Crush

3 cups sugar
2 cups water
1 1/2 cups orange juice
1/4 cup lemon juice
2 bananas, mashed
1 46-oz. can pineapple
juice
1 small can crushed
pineapple
1 gallon raspberry
sherbet

Combine sugar and
water. Put bananas,
pineapple, and orange
juice in blender. Add
to sugar syrup. Add
remaining ingredients,
blending until
smooth. Freeze in
several containers.

When ready to serve,
thaw to slushy. Add 2
quarts ginger ale.
*Ruthann Wise*

## Lemony Iced Tea

1 large can lemonade
scant 3/4 cup instant
tea
1 1/4 cups sugar
water
ice

Mix above in 1 1/2-
gallon container.
*Marilyn Lynch*

## Iced Tea

6 lemons
6 Tbsp. tea
3 1/2 cups sugar
4 cups boiling water

Juice lemons and
add sugar to juice.
Slice or grind rinds
in a pan and sprinkle
with tea. Steep in
boiling water 15
minutes. Then strain
and add lemon juice
and sugar. Stir until
sugar is dissolved.
Use 1 part syrup to 2
parts cold water for
a delicious beverage.
Add plenty of ice.
*Eunice Grover*

## Iced Tea Syrup 1

2 qts. water
2/3 cup tea leaves
4 cups sugar

Bring water to a boil.
Add tea leaves. Cover
and steep for 15
minutes. Measure
sugar in pan. Strain
tea into sugar, stir-
ring well; cool. Cover
and store in refriger-
ator. Use 1 part syrup
to 4 or 5 parts water.
Note:
This recipe takes the
complication out of
making iced tea.
*Dorothy Roesel*

## Iced Tea Syrup 2

1 gallon boiled water
several peppermint
leaves
1 1/2 cups (4-oz. box)
tea leaves
6 cups sugar

Steep tea and pepper-
mint in boiled water
for 15 minutes. Strain
out leaves and add
sugar to liquid. Use 1
part syrup to 4 parts
water. Add lemon
juice, if desired.
*Linda Thompson*

## Fruit Punch 1

8 cups sugar
3 qts. water
4 pkgs. cherry-flavored
  drink mix
1 can pineapple juice
1 qt. ginger ale
1 Tbsp. lemon juice

Heat sugar and water;
cool. Add remaining
ingredients.
*Marilyn Gish*
*Mary Howser*

## Fruit Punch 2

12 oranges, seeded
12 lemons, seeded
2 qts. boiling water
2 oz. citric acid
1 46-oz. can pineapple
  juice
sugar (3-5 lbs.)
  or honey
  (1 1/2-2 1/2 lbs.)

Grind oranges and
lemons together. Pour
boiling water over
this mixture. Add
citric acid. Let stand
overnight; then drain
well. Add pineapple
juice. Sweeten to taste
with honey or sugar.
Can be put in small
containers and frozen
until needed.
*Eunice Grover*

## Citrus Punch

6 oranges
3 lemons
2 oz. citric acid
5 lbs. sugar
2 qts. boiling water

Grind fruits together.
Add remaining in-
gredients and stir
well. Let stand 12
hours. Strain and
store in refrigerator.
Makes 1 gallon syrup.
Dilute 3 to 1. Makes
4 to 5 gallons.
*Margaret Miller*
*Clara Meador*

## Golden Punch

1 pkg. orange-flavored
  drink mix
1 cup sugar
1 6-oz. can lemon juice
1 6-oz. can orange juice
1 large can pineapple
  juice
3 1/4 qts. water and
  crushed ice
1 qt. ginger ale
4 very ripe bananas,
  pureed in blender

Blend all together.
*Marianne Bowman*

## Slush

1 large can pineapple
  juice
2 cans frozen lemonade
1 can pure lemon juice
3 pkgs. berry-flavored
  drink mix
5 cups sugar (less if
  fruit is sweet)
5 cups or 40 oz.
  crushed berries*

Mix all together. Add
enough water to fill
8-qt. pan. Freeze in
freezer cartons or
milk cartons. When
ready to serve, crush
the frozen chunks,
and fill glasses. Pour
lemony soda over
mixture.
*Strawberries, raspberries,
or boysenberries.
*Barbara Gish*

# Hot Beverages

## Cocoa

2 tsp. cocoa
6 tsp. sugar
1/2 cup water
1 qt. milk
1 tsp. vanilla
pinch of salt
marshmallows,
  (optional)

Bring cocoa, sugar,
and water to a boil.
Immediately add re-
maining ingredients.
Note:
If recipe is doubled,
use 1 can evaporated
milk as part of milk
for extra richness.
*Karen L. Miller*

## Russian Tea Mix

1 cup orange-flavored
  drink mix
1/4 cup sugar
1/3 cup instant tea
  powder
3 Tbsp. presweetened
  lemonade mix or 1/2
  (3-oz.) pkg. mix
1/4 tsp. ground cin-
  namon
1/8 tsp. ground cloves

Combine ingredients
and store in airtight
container. When ready
to serve, add 8 cups
boiling water or use
about 1 level tsp. of
dry mixture per large
mug.
*Eunice Grover*

## Spiced Tea

4 Tbsp. tea leaves
2 cups hot water
2 cups sugar
2 whole cloves
1 1/2 cups orange juice
3/4 cup lemon juice
1 tsp. allspice
4 qts. boiling water

Steep the tea in 2 cups hot water. Simmer other ingredients 5 minutes; then add strained tea.

*Laurel Balsbaugh*

## Friendship Tea

2 cups sugar
1 3/4 cups orange-flavored drink mix
1 cup instant tea
2 tsp. cinnamon
2 tsp. ground cloves
2 3-oz. pkgs. instant lemonade mix

Mix all ingredients together. Dissolve 2 tsp. per cup in hot water or to taste.

*Shirley Denlinger*
*Suzanne Layman*

## Spiced Cider
### (For a crowd)

3 gallons apple cider
3 cups dark brown sugar
3 cans frozen lemonade
3 cans frozen orange juice
cheesecloth spice bag filled with:
1 Tbsp. whole cloves
1 Tbsp. allspice
1 1/2 Tbsp. nutmeg

Place all ingredients in kettle; bring to a boil. Simmer 20 minutes. Discard spice bag. Serve in mugs with cinnamon sticks. Recipe may be easily cut to 1/3 quantity, if desired.

*Lois Shirk*

## Wassail Bowl

3 qts. apple cider
2 3" whole cinnamon sticks
1/2 tsp. nutmeg
1/2 cup honey

1/3 cup lemon juice
2 tsp. grated lemon rind
2 large cans pineapple juice
cloves
2 oranges

Simmer all ingredients, except cloves and oranges. Meanwhile, stick cloves into 2 oranges 1/2" apart. Put in baking dish with small amount of water. Bake 30 minutes at 350°. Add to cider mixture. Oranges will float in punch bowl and add good flavor.

*Laurel Balsbaugh*

---

*HAPPINESS SHAKE*

*1 cup good thoughts*
*1 cup kind deeds*
*1 cup consideration for others*
*2 cups sacrifice*
*3 cups forgiveness*
*2 cups well beaten faults*

*Mix above ingredients. Add tears of joy, sorrow, and sympathy. Flavor with love and kind service. Saturate with prayer and faith. Pour into your daily life and shake well. Serve often with a smile. Satisfies thirsty souls.*

*Extra Recipes*

_____

_____

_____

_____

_____

_____

_____

_____

_____

Source: _____ Who Likes It: _____

_____

_____

_____

_____

_____

_____

_____

_____

Source: _____ Who Likes It: _____

_____

_____

_____

_____

_____

_____

_____

_____

Source: _____ Who Likes It: _____

# The Soup Tureen

*Better reap
two days too soon
than one day
too late.*
PENNSYLVANIA DUTCH SAYING

*And let us not get tired
of doing what is right,
for after a while
we will reap
a harvest of blessing
if we don't get discouraged
and give up.*
GALATIANS 6:9

# Chowders and Soup

## Clam Chowder

1/4 lb. bacon
1 medium onion, chopped
4 potatoes, diced
salt and pepper to taste
seasoned salt to taste
1 can Manhattan-style clam chowder
1 can minced clams
flavor enhancer to taste

Chop bacon and brown until crisp; drain on paper towel. Add onion to bacon grease and fry until golden. Drain. Now add diced potatoes to bacon grease and brown slightly. Cover with water; add seasonings and simmer until tender. Add clam chowder, minced clams, bacon, and onion. Serve.
Note:
If made ahead, add bacon and clams at last minute.
*Jan Cowan*

## Creole Gumbo

1 stewing hen
4 cups (2 lb.) ham, pre-cooked and cubed
2 cups onions, chopped
2 garlic cloves, crushed
2 tsp. gumbo filé powder*
1/2 tsp. oregano
3 drops Tabasco sauce
2 tsp. salt
1/2 tsp. basil
1/8 tsp. pepper
dash of cayenne
5 Tbsp. flour
1/4 cup bacon drippings
1 large can tomatoes
1/4 cup tomato paste

Put stewing hen and ham into a deep kettle. Add barely enough water to cover; then add onions and seasonings. Simmer, covered, for 1 hour or until chicken is tender. Remove meat from broth. Make roux** by lightly browning flour in bacon drippings. Add roux, tomatoes, and tomato paste to the broth. Cook until thick and blended. Remove chicken from bones in pieces as large as possible. Add to ham and sauce; cover and gently simmer 45 minutes longer. Stir carefully to prevent sticking. Crumble bacon and garnish. Serve over rice.

*powdered, tender leaves of sassafras used as a soup or stew thickener.
**a cooked mixture of flour and fat used as a thickening agent.
*Dorothy Gish*

## Corn Chowder 1

5 slices bacon, cooked and crumbled
3 Tbsp. bacon drippings
1 medium onion, thinly sliced
2 medium potatoes, diced
1/2 cup water
1 17-oz. can cream-style corn
2 cups milk
1 tsp. salt
dash of pepper
butter or margarine

Add bacon drippings and onion slices to saucepan; sauté until lightly browned. Add diced potatoes and water; cook over medium heat until tender. Add corn, milk, salt, and pepper; cook until heated through. Pour into warmed bowls; top with crumbled bacon and a pat of butter or margarine.
*Katherine Wolf*

## Corn Chowder 2

1 cup onion, thinly sliced
2 Tbsp. butter or margarine
1 cup potatoes, cooked and diced
1 cup canned ham, pre-cooked and diced
1 16-oz. can cream-style corn
1 can cream of mushroom soup
2 1/2 cups milk
3/4 tsp. salt
dash of pepper
butter
chopped parsley

In large saucepan, sauté onion in butter until tender, but not brown. Add potatoes, ham, corn, soup, milk, salt, and pepper; heat to boiling. Put pat of butter in bottom of each bowl; fill with chowder. Sprinkle with chopped parsley. Serves 6 to 8.
*Mabel I. Lynch*

## Chicken Cheese Chowder

1 cup carrots, shredded
1/4 cup onion, chopped
4 Tbsp. butter or margarine
1/4 cup flour
2 cups milk
1 3/4 cups (1 13 3/4-oz. can) chicken broth
1 cup chicken, cooked and diced
1 Tbsp. dry white wine
1/2 tsp. celery seed
1/2 tsp. Worcestershire sauce
1 cup (4 oz.) American cheese, shredded

In large saucepan, cook carrots and onion in butter or margarine until tender, but not brown. Blend in flour; add milk and chicken broth. Cook and stir until thickened and bubbly. Stir in chicken, wine, celery seed, and Worcestershire sauce. Heat through. Add cheese and stir until melted. Garnish with snipped chives. Serves 4 to 5.
*Lois Garber*

## Manhattan Clam Chowder

3 slices bacon, diced
1 cup celery, chopped
1 cup onion, chopped
2 7 1/2-oz. cans clams
1 16-oz. can tomatoes
2 cups potatoes, diced
1 cup carrots, diced
1 1/2 tsp. salt
1/4 tsp. thyme
dash of pepper
2 Tbsp. flour
2 Tbsp. water

Partially cook bacon; add celery and onion. Cook until tender. Drain clams, reserving liquid. Add water to liquid to make 4 cups. Add to bacon mixture. Add tomatoes, potatoes, carrots, and seasonings. Cover and simmer for 35 minutes. Blend flour with water to make paste; stir into the chowder. Cook until boiling. Add clams and heat. Serves 6 to 8.
*Bonnie Jamison*

## Meatball Chowder

2 lbs. ground beef
2 tsp. seasoned salt
1/8 tsp. pepper
2 eggs, slightly beaten
1/4 cup parsley, finely chopped
1/3 cup fine cracker crumbs
2 Tbsp. milk
3–5 Tbsp. flour
1 Tbsp. salad oil
4–6 small onions, cut in eighths
3/4 cup celery, diced
2/3 cup potatoes, diced
1/4 cup long grain rice
6 cups tomato juice
6 cups water
1 Tbsp. sugar
1 tsp. salt
2 bay leaves
1 can Mexicorn

Combine meat, seasoned salt, pepper, eggs, parsley, cracker crumbs, and milk. Mix thoroughly. Form into balls the size of walnuts. Dip in flour. Heat oil in large kettle; lightly brown meat balls on all sides. Add remaining ingredients, except corn, and bring to a boil. Cover, reduce heat, and cook at slow boil 30 minutes or until vegetables are tender. Add corn last 10 minutes of cooking.
*Katherine Wolf*

## Plantation Chowder

3 medium onions, sliced
2 green peppers, cut into small pieces
1/2 cup olive oil
3 frozen lobster tails, cut into 1" pieces (shell on)
2 pkgs. frozen shrimp, deveined
1 16-oz. pkg. frozen fish fillets
water to cover
1 cup tomatoes, cooked
3 large carrots, cubed
1 1/2 tsp. salt
1/4 tsp. pepper
3 cups rice, cooked
saffron (optional)

Sauté vegetables in oil in a large kettle. Add remaining ingredients, except rice and saffron. Cover and cook to boiling. Reduce heat and simmer 20 minutes. Meanwhile, following directions on the package, cook enough rice to make 3 cups. Add saffron for color and flavor, if desired. In individual bowls, serve fish and soup, topped with scoops of freshly cooked rice.
*Alice Mae Haney*

## Tomato Soup

3 cups tomato juice
3 tsp. sugar
1/8 tsp. baking soda
3 cups milk
3 Tbsp. flour
3 Tbsp. (or less) butter (optional)
1 1/2 tsp. salt
dash of pepper

In large pot, mix tomato juice, sugar, and baking soda. Heat just to boiling. In separate pan, combine remaining ingredients and heat. Mix a little milk with flour and add when mixture is almost boiling. Remove both pans from heat. Add tomato mixture to second pan very slowly, stirring all the time. Serve immediately.
*Naomi Bauman*

---

*FOOTPRINTS IN THE SAND*

*One night a man had a dream. He dreamed he was walking along the beach with the Lord. Across the sky flashed scenes from his life. For each scene he noticed two sets of footprints in the sand. One set belonged to him and the other to the Lord.*

*When the last scene of his life flashed before him, he looked back at the footprints in the sand. He noticed that many times along the path of his life there was only one set of footprints. He also noticed it happened at the very lowest and saddest times in his life.*

*This really bothered him and he questioned the Lord about it. "Lord, You said that once I decided to follow You, You would walk with me all the way. But I have noticed that during the most troublesome times in my life, there was only one set of footprints. I do not understand why in the times I needed you the most, You would leave me."*

*The Lord replied, "My precious, precious child. I love you and I would never leave you. During your times of trial and suffering, when you saw only one set of footprints, it was then that I carried you."*

*Anonymous*

_____
_____
_____
_____
_____
_____
_____
_____
Source: _____ Who Likes It: _____

_____
_____
_____
_____
_____
_____
_____
_____
Source: _____ Who Likes It: _____

_____
_____
_____
_____
_____
_____
_____
Source: _____ Who Likes It: _____

# The
# Sandwich
# Board

*As the man,*
*so his cattle.*
PENNSYLVANIA GERMAN SAYING

*Jesus said,*
*". . . the way to identify a tree*
*or a person*
*is by the kind*
*of fruit produced."*
MATTHEW 7:20

# Sandwiches

## Broiled Cheese and Egg Sandwich

1/2 lb. Cheddar cheese, finely grated
3 hard cooked eggs, shelled and chopped
1/2 cup mayonnaise
2 Tbsp. pimiento, chopped
1 Tbsp. celery leaves or parsley, chopped
1/2 tsp. horseradish
salt to taste
4 hamburger rolls, split in half

Combine first 7 ingredients. Spread roll halves with cheese mixture. Broil 4 or 5 inches from source of heat until golden brown. Garnish as desired. Serves 4.
*Virginia Trussel*

## Almond Sandwich Spreads

Spread 1:
1 cup roasted almonds, chopped
1 cup celery
2 cups chicken, cooked and chopped
1 tsp. salt

Spread 2:
1 cup ripe olives
1/2 cup American cheese

1/3 cup mayonnaise
1/2 cup almonds, chopped

Spread 3:
1/2 cup almonds, chopped
1 cup ham, diced
1 hard cooked egg, shelled and diced
1/2 cup mayonnaise
3/4 tsp. horseradish

Combine ingredients for each variation. Make sandwiches as usual. Refrigerate leftovers.
*Eunice Grover*

## Bacon "Cheeseburgers"
(For a crowd)

8 lbs. sharp cheese, grated
2 1/2 lbs. bacon, cooked and chopped
1 cup onion, chopped
3 cups catsup
1/2 cup vinegar
1/2 tsp. celery salt
1 tsp. cinnamon
1/2 cup sugar
1 cup mustard
butter, melted
rolls

Combine all ingredients, except butter and rolls. Brush tops and bottoms of rolls with melted butter. Put 1/4 cup of mixture on bottom, and cover with top half. Warm in 250° oven

about 15 minutes until filling is warm. May be frozen. Serves 100.
*Dorothy Gish*

## Barbecued Hamburger

2 1/2 lbs. hamburger
1 cup catsup
2 cups green pepper, chopped
2 onions, chopped
1 Tbsp. dry mustard
3 Tbsp. sugar
2 Tbsp. vinegar
1 Tbsp. salt

Cook first 4 ingredients until tender; then add remaining ingredients. Cook 1/2 hour on low heat. Serve over warm hamburger buns.
*Claudia Flory*

## Hot Beef or Pork Sandwich

3 cups beef or pork, cooked
1/2 cup barbecue sauce
salt and pepper to taste
1 tsp. Worcestershire sauce
1/2 cup catsup

Simmer all ingredients 1/2 hour. Serve on hamburger buns. Serves 6.
*Gwendolyn Overholtzer*

# 32

## Pizza Burgers

2 lbs. ground beef
1/2 cup onion, minced
1 tsp. salt
1/2 tsp. oregano
1/4 tsp. pepper
1 8-oz. can pizza sauce
6 slices Mozzarella
  cheese or Cheddar
  cheese
3 large English
  muffins, split

Lightly mix ground
beef, onion, salt,
oregano, pepper, and
1/2 cup pizza sauce.
Shape into 6 patties
4 1/2–5 inches in
diameter. Broil one
side, turn, and broil
other side to desired
degree of doneness.
Spoon remaining
pizza sauce over
patties. Top with
slices of cheese; re-
turn to broiler just
until cheese begins
to melt. Meanwhile
toast muffins. Serves
6.
*Jane Rumble*

## Sloppy Joe 1

1/2–1 lb. hamburger,
  browned
1 small can pork and
  beans
1 small onion, chopped
1 Tbsp. brown sugar
1 Tbsp. catsup
barbecue sauce to taste

Cook all ingredients
until thick and
brown. If too juicy,
add about 1 to 2
Tbsp. flour. Serve over
warm hamburger
buns.
*Shirley Davidson*

## Sloppy Joe 2

1 lb. hamburger
1/2 cup onion,
  chopped
1/2 cup celery,
  chopped
1 can mushrooms
1 can tomato soup
salt and pepper to taste

Crumble hamburger
and fry until brown.
Add onion and celery
a few minutes before
hamburger is done.
Then, add remaining
ingredients. Heat and
serve over warm
hamburger buns. Add
catsup, if desired.
*Ruth Wise*

## Hot Chicken Sandwich

2 cups chicken, cooked
  and chopped
1/2 lb. Cheddar cheese,
  shredded
2 sweet pickles,
  chopped
1/2 cup celery,
  chopped
1 Tbsp. onion
mayonnaise to moisten
buns, buttered

Combine all ingredi-
ents, blending well.
Spread on buttered
buns. Wrap in foil.
Store in refrigerator
until ready to eat.
Place in 350° oven
for 15 minutes. These
can be made ahead
and frozen.
*Barbara Basore*

## Bowman's Special

4 slices bread
1 can pork and beans
4 slices strong cheese
4 slices bacon

Toast bread lightly.
Spoon on beans. Place
one slice of cheese
with 2 halved strips
of bacon on top. Put
on cookie sheet and
broil.
*Nancy Bowman and
boys*

Source: _____ Who Likes It: _____

Source: _____ Who Likes It: _____

Source: _____ Who Likes It: _____

# RECIPES OUT OF THE MOUTHS OF BABES

*Peanut Butter and Jelly Sandwich*
2 pieces of bread.
Smooth peanut butter and jelly on each piece.
Put it together. Dad cuts it in 4 triangles or 4 squares.
Christa Zapfe, Age 5

*Lima Beans*
Use 100 beans.
Cook for 1 minute in the pot on the stove. Put them on the table.
Sarah Gaiser, Age 4

*Apples*
1 apple.
Mash 'em. Mouth eats the apple.
Aaron Green, Age 2

*Magic Cookies*
1 can bumpy milk—enough to fill the pan.
Couple pieces of coconut.
3 or 4 bags of chocolate chips. Put in the oven.
Bake for 4 or 5 minutes.
Tor deVries, Age 5

*Fish*
1 million pieces of fish.
Put it in a very hot oven. Look in the oven when it makes a noise.
When done, give it to me and my brother. Eat with a fork and ketchup.
Laura Fernald, Age 5

*Eggs with Meat*
5 eggs.
Smash them up. Cook more food. Daddy cook them in the noisy pan.
Cook for 2 minutes.
Renee Jones, Age 3

*Note:* These "original" recipes were given by children attending a nursery school in Wheaton, Illinois. Their teacher, Darlene Krebs, compiled these and other recipes into a *Special Recipes From Special Kids* cookbook in Spring, 1980.

# Salad
# Sashay

*Of words and feathers,*
*it takes many*
*to make a pound.*
GERMAN SAYING

*Sometimes mere words*
*are not enough—*
*discipline is needed.*
*For the words*
*may go unheeded.*
PROVERBS 29:19

# Fruit Salads

## Buttermilk Waldorf Mold

1 3-oz pkg. lemon
  gelatin
1 cup boiling water
1 cup buttermilk
1 apple, cored and
  chopped
1/4 cup celery
1/4 cup nuts, chopped

Dissolve gelatin in
water. Add buttermilk
and partially chill.
Add remaining in-
gredients and pour
into lightly greased
mold. Refrigerate
until firm.
*Mary Ann Fall*

## Cantaloupe Salad

2 3-oz. pkgs. lime
  gelatin
2 cups boiling water
2 cups ginger ale or
  lemony soda (in place
  of cold water)
1 cantaloupe, made
  into melon balls
3 bananas, sliced

Dissolve gelatin in
water. Add soda. Par-
tially chill. Add fruits
and pour into desired
mold or pan. Refrig-
erate until firm.

Variation:
Add any combina-
tion of pineapple,
peaches, or apricots.
*Rosemary Denlinger*

## Cantaloupe Grape Salad

2 3-oz. pkgs. orange
  gelatin
2 cups boiling water
1 6-oz. can orange juice
  concentrate
1 juice can water
2 Tbsp. lemon juice
2 cups fresh canta-
  loupe, finely diced
2 cups seedless green
  grapes, halved
small bunches grapes

Dissolve gelatin in
boiling water; stir in
orange juice, water,
and lemon juice. Let
mixture cool until
slightly thickened;
stir in cantaloupe
and seedless green
grapes. Pour mixture
into a 6-cup mold.
Refrigerate until set.
Garnish with small
bunches of grapes.
Serves 8.
*Joan Howser*

## Ambrosia Mold 1

1 3-oz. pkg. orange
  gelatin
1/3 cup sugar
1 cup boiling water
1 15-oz. can crushed
  pineapple, undrained
1 11-oz. can Mandarin
  oranges
1 cup miniature marsh-
  mallows
1/2 cup coconut
1 cup sour cream

Dissolve gelatin and
sugar in water; add
crushed pineapple.
Blend well and refrig-
erate until egg white
consistency. Add
Mandarin oranges,
marshmallows,
coconut, and sour
cream. Blend well.
Put in mold and let
set overnight.
*Marcelle Jarboe*
*Nancy Bowman*

Variation:
Omit the gelatin and
use pineapple tidbits.
*Lois Shirk*

## Ambrosia Mold 2

1 3-oz. pkg. orange
gelatin
3/4 cup boiling water
1 cup orange juice, cold
1 cup orange seg-
ments, halved
1 cup pineapple tidbits,
well-drained
1/2 cup coconut, flaked
1/2 cup dairy sour
cream

Prepare gelatin as
usual, except use
orange juice for cold
liquid. Combine with
remaining ingredi-
ents. Place in mold
and refrigerate.
*Genevieve Barber*

## Snow-Capped Cheese Mold

1 1/2 cups cottage
cheese, cream style
2 3-oz. pkgs. cream
cheese
1 Tbsp. unflavored
gelatin
1/4 cup cold water
1/4 cup boiling water
1/4 tsp. salt
1 cup seedless green
grapes
1/2 cup pecans, broken
2 Tbsp. chives,
chopped
1 cup heavy cream,
whipped
6–8 slices of canned
pineapple

Mash cheeses to-
gether until well
blended. Soften gela-
tin in cold water;
dissolve in boiling
water. Add salt; stir
gelatin mixture into
cheese mixture. Add
grapes, nuts, and
chives. Fold in
whipped cream.
Spoon into individual
molds or 1-qt. mold.
Chill 4 to 6 hours.
Unmold on pineapple
slices. Arrange on
lettuce ruffle and gar-
nish with avocado
and red ripe straw-
berries. Serves 6 to 8.
Offer *Honey Dressing*.

Honey Dressing:
1/4–2/3 cup sugar
1 tsp. dry mustard
1 tsp. paprika
1 tsp. celery seed
1/4 tsp. salt
1/3 cup vinegar
1/3 cup honey
1 Tbsp. lemon juice
1 tsp. onion, grated
1 cup salad oil

Mix together sugar,
mustard, paprika,
celery seed, and salt.
Add honey, vinegar,
lemon juice, and
onion. Pour oil into
mixture very slowly,
beating constantly
with rotary or electric
beater. Makes 2 cups.
Note:
This dressing is just
sweet and tart enough
to point up the flavor
of a lush fruit salad.
*Mable Lynch*

## Cherry Coke Salad

1 16-oz. can Bing
cherries
1 large can crushed
pineapple
1 6-oz. pkg. cherry
gelatin
2 6 1/2-oz. bottles
soda

Drain juice from fruit;
add water if necessary
to make 2 cups
liquid. Heat juice to
boiling; add gelatin
and stir until dis-
solved. Cool; add soda
and fruit. Pour into
1 1/2-qt. mold. Chill
until set. Serve with
salad dressing or
whipped cream.
Serves 8.
*Phyllis Rumble*

## Cherry Salad Supreme

1 3-oz. pkg. raspberry
gelatin
1 cup boiling water
1 21-oz. can cherry pie
filling
1 3-oz. pkg. lemon
gelatin
1 cup boiling water
1 3-oz. pkg. cream
cheese
1/3 cup mayonnaise
or salad dressing
1 cup (8 3/4-oz. can)
crushed pineapple
1/2 cup whipping
cream
1 cup tiny marsh-
mallows
2 Tbsp. nuts, chopped

Dissolve raspberry
gelatin in 1 cup
boiling water; stir in
pie filling. Turn into
9-inch square baking
dish; chill until par-
tially set. Dissolve
lemon gelatin in 1

cup boiling water. Beat together cream cheese and mayonnaise. Gradually add lemon gelatin. Stir in undrained pineapple. Whip the cream; fold into lemon mixture with marshmallows. Spread over cherry layer. Top with nuts. Chill until set.
Serves 12.
*Shirley Bauman*

## Christmas Salad

1 3-oz. pkg. raspberry gelatin
1 cup boiling water
1/2 cup cold water
1/2 cup pineapple chunks
1 can cranberry sauce
1 orange, cut in chunks
1/2 cup nuts, chopped

Dissolve gelatin in hot water; add cold water. Chill until partially set. Fold in remaining ingredients. Pour into mold.
*Ruth Yost*

## Apple-Cinnamon Salad

2 cups boiling water
1 3-oz. pkg. cherry gelatin
1 3-oz. pkg. strawberry gelatin
1 1/4 cups cinnamon red hot candy
1 1/2 cups red apples, diced
1/2 cup chopped nuts, (optional)

Dissolve gelatin and candy in boiling hot water (set dish in hot water to speed the dissolving). When gelatin is dissolved,

add cold water. Jell slightly and add remaining ingredients. Pour into 8-inch square dish or mold. Refrigerate until firm.
*Becky Layman*

## Cottage Cheese Salad

1 6-oz. pkg. lime gelatin
1 1/2 cups boiling water
1 8-oz. pkg. cream cheese
1 Tbsp. lemon juice
1 cup cottage cheese
1 cup crushed pineapple
1 cup whipped cream
1 cup miniature marshmallows

Mix gelatin and water with cream cheese. Cool until mixture begins to set. Add remaining ingredients; pour into mold and refrigerate.
*Deanna Davison*
*Nancy Bowman*

## Cranberry Salad 1

1 6-oz. pkg. cherry gelatin
1 cup hot water
1 large can crushed pineapple, drained (reserve liquid)
1 cup sugar
1 cup ground raw cranberries
1 cup celery, finely chopped
1/2 cup nuts, chopped

Mix hot water with gelatin and stir thoroughly. Add pineapple juice and cool. Pour sugar over ground cranberries; let stand while gela-

tin starts to thicken. Add cranberries, crushed pineapple, celery, and nuts. Place in mold and chill until firm.
*Ellen Reece*

## Cranberry Salad 2

1 lb. cranberries
5 large red apples
2 cups sugar
2 3-oz. pkgs. lemon gelatin
1 cup hot water
1 large can crushed pineapple
1 1/2 cups nuts, chopped

Medium grind cranberries and apples; add sugar and mix thoroughly. Let stand 1/2 hour. Drain pineapple. Dissolve gelatin in hot water. Add 3 cups pineapple juice and water (combined). Chill until partially set. Add cranberry-apple mixture and nuts. Mix thoroughly. Pour into mold. Refrigerate.
*Rachel Shoup*

## Cranberry Salad 3

2 3-oz. pkgs. red
  gelatin
1 pkg. cranberries
4 oranges
rind of 1 orange
4 apples
4 or 5 stalks celery,
  diced
3 cups sugar

Grind cranberries,
oranges, and apples.
Mix gelatin as usual
and combine with all
other ingredients.
Refrigerate.
*Sarah Lee Switzer*

## Cranberry
## Star Mold

1 3-oz. pkg. pineapple-
  grapefruit or orange
  gelatin
1 16-oz. can whole
  cranberry sauce
1 7-oz. bottle ginger ale

In saucepan, com-
bine gelatin and
cranberry sauce; heat
and stir until almost
boiling and gelatin is
dissolved. Chill slight-
ly. Carefully stir in
ginger ale. Pour into
a 5-cup star mold.
Chill until set. Un-
mold. Garnish with
greens and orange
and grapefruit
sections.
*Nancy Bowman*

## Berry Simple
## Cranberry Mold

4 cups (1 pkg.)
  cranberries
2 cups boiling water
2 cups sugar

Cook berries in water
until soft, about 5
minutes. Sieve and
add sugar. Bring to a
boil; boil about 3
minutes. Do not over-
cook. Pour into mold.
Refrigerate.
*Nellie Miller*

## Frozen
## Cranberry Salad

1 6-oz. pkg. cherry
  gelatin
1 cup hot water
1 16-oz. can whole
  cranberry sauce
2 Tbsp. lemon juice
1 8-oz. pkg. cream
  cheese
1 cup cream, whipped
1/2 cup nuts, chopped

Dissolve gelatin in
hot water; add cran-
berry sauce and
lemon juice. Let set
until thick; mix last
3 ingredients together
and add to mixture.
Put in mold and
freeze. Slice and serve
on lettuce leaf.
*Frances Kelley*

## Cranberry
## Waldorf Salad

2 cups raw cranberries,
  ground
3/4 cup sugar
3 cups miniature
  marshmallows
1 1/2 cups grapes
1/2 cup walnuts
2 cups apples,
  diced
1/4 tsp. salt

1 cup whipping
  cream

Combine first 3
ingredients,
cover, and chill
overnight. Add
fruits, nuts, and
salt to cranberry
mixture. Fold in
cream. Serves 8
to 10.
*Bethel Hinkle*

## Orange
## Gelatin Salad

1 4 1/2-oz. carton
  frozen non-dairy
  topping
1 16-oz. carton cottage
  cheese
1 10-oz. can crushed
  pineapple, drained
1 3-oz. pkg. orange
  gelatin

Mix frozen topping,
cottage cheese, and
pineapple. Sprinkle
dry orange gelatin
over mixture and
blend in. Pour into
13 x 9 x 2-inch dish.
Refrigerate for an
hour or until firm.
*Margaret Brubaker*

Variation:
Add Mandarin
oranges and walnuts.
*Arlene Boone*

## Cheesy
## Mandarin Salad

2 3-oz. pkgs. orange
  gelatin
1 cup hot water
1 large can crushed
  pineapple, drained
2 cans Mandarin
  oranges, drained
1 large and 1 small
  pkg. cream cheese
1/2 pt. whipping
  cream *or*

1 pkg. cream substitute topping
1 cup juice from oranges and pineapple

Make gelatin, using 1 cup hot water and 1 cup juice. Let it start to jell. Whip gelatin and cream cheese together. Whip the cream and add to gelatin mixture. Stir in fruits and chill.
*Eunice Peters*

## Fruit Salad and Dressing

1 can pineapple tidbits, drained (reserve juice for dressing.)
3 bananas
1/4 lb. miniature marshmallows
1/2 cup nuts, chopped
1 cup seedless grapes

Combine fruits, nuts, and marshmallows. Refrigerate. Prepare *Creamy Dressing*.

Creamy Dressing:
1 egg
1 rounded Tbsp. flour
1/2 cup sugar
pineapple juice
1 Tbsp. butter, melted
1 cup whipping cream

Beat egg and flour; add sugar. Heat juice from pineapple and cook until thick, stirring constantly. Add butter; cool. Add whipped cream, blend, and pour over fruit salad. *Can be used for any fruit salad.*
*Clara Selby*

## Tropical Lemon Salad

1 3-oz. pkg. lemon or orange gelatin
2 bananas
1 small can crushed pineapple, drained
reserved pineapple juice
marshmallows

Topping:
1/4 cup pineapple juice
1/2 cup sugar
1 Tbsp. flour
1 egg, beaten
1/2 cup whipping cream

Mix gelatin according to directions. Pour into 8-inch square pan. Chill until slightly set. Add fruit and marshmallows. When gelatin is set, combine topping ingredients, except whipping cream, in top of double boiler. Cook until thick. Cool and add whipped cream. Spread over gelatin.
*Lydia Wolf*

Variations:
Add 1 diced apple.
*Arleen Peters*

Add 1 can apricots, cut up, and omit the bananas.
*Deanna Davison*

## Creamy Lime Salad 1

1 8-oz. bag miniature marshmallows
2 cups boiling water
1 3-oz. pkg. lime gelatin
1 3-oz. pkg. cream cheese
1 small can crushed pineapple
1/2 pt. whipping cream, whipped

Melt marshmallows in 1 cup of the boiling water. Dissolve gelatin in remaining cup of boiling water. Add all but whipped cream to gelatin. Add whipped cream last. Blend together and pour into 1-qt. mold. Refrigerate until set.
*Nancy Bowman*

## Creamy Lime Salad 2

1 3-oz. pkg. lime gelatin
1 cup boiling water
1/2 lb. large marshmallows
1/2 cup cold water (part pineapple juice)
1 small can crushed pineapple, drained
1 cup whipped cream
1 3-oz. pkg. cream cheese, softened
1/2 cup mayonnaise

Dissolve gelatin in boiling water; add marshmallows and cook over low heat until dissolved. Add cold water; chill until partially set. Fold in remaining ingredients. Pour into mold or 8-inch square pan. Refrigerate until set.
*Janice Root*

## Citrusy Salad

1 6-oz. pkg. lemon or
  lime gelatin
2 cups boiling water
2 Tbsp. sugar
1 8-oz. pkg. cream
  cheese
1 1/2 cups crushed
  pineapple
2 tsp. vanilla
1 1/2 cups lemony
  soda

Dissolve gelatin in
hot water. Blend
sugar and cream
cheese; add to gelatin.
Cool. Add pineapple,
vanilla, and soda.
Pour into mold and
refrigerate until set.
*Phyllis Basore*
Variation:
Substitute 1 can of
applesauce for the
boiling water; add
marshmallows and
omit the pineapple.
*Dorothy Moore*

## Heavenly
## Pineapple Mold

1 3-oz. pkg. lemon
  gelatin
1 cup hot water
3/4 cups pineapple
  juice
1 Tbsp. lemon juice
1 1/4 cups crushed
  pineapple
1 cup sharp cheese,
  shredded
1 cup heavy cream,
  whipped

Dissolve gelatin in
hot water; add juices
and chill until almost
set. Then whip. Add
fruit, cheese, and
cream. Pour into
mold and refrigerate.
*Marilyn Lynch*

## Pineapple
## Cheese Salad

2 3-oz. pkgs. lemon
  gelatin
2 cups boiling water
2 cups cold water
6 bananas, peeled and
  sliced
2 cups miniature
  marshmallows
2 large cans crushed
  pineapple, undrained
1/2 cup sugar
3 Tbsp. cornstarch
1 cup heavy cream
1 cup Longhorn
  Cheddar cheese,
  shredded

Dissolve gelatin in
boiling water; add
cold water and chill
until syrupy. Stir in
sliced bananas and
marshmallows. Pour
into 13x9x2-inch
pan. Chill until set.
Mix sugar and corn-
starch; add to
undrained pineapple.
Cook over medium
heat, stirring con-
stantly, until thick-
ened. Cool. Whip
heavy cream and fold
into cooled pineapple
mixture along with
half the shredded
cheese. Spread mix-
ture on congealed
lemon gelatin.
Sprinkle remaining
shredded cheese over
top. Chill overnight.

Cut into squares.
*Mildred E. Miller*
*Esther Flora*
*Donna Rumble*

## Paper Cup
## Frozen Salad

2 cups commercial
  sour cream
2 Tbsp. lemon juice
1/2 cup sugar
1/8 tsp. salt
1 8-oz. can crushed
  pineapple, well
  drained
1 banana, sliced
4 drops red food color-
  ing for pink tint
1/4 cup nuts, chopped
1 16-oz. can pitted
  Bing cherries, well
  drained

Combine all in-
gredients except nuts
and cherries. Lightly
fold in nuts and
cherries. Spoon into
fluted paper muffin
cups (large size)
which have been
placed in 3" muffin
cup pans. Freeze. Re-
move from freezer 15
minutes before serv-
ing. Peel off paper.
Fills 12 large cups.
*Linda Lavy*

## All-Star
## Peach Whip

1 qt. canned or frozen
  peaches, sliced and
  well drained
reserved peach juice
1 1/2 cups miniature
  marshmallows, very
  finely cut
1/2 cup walnuts, very
  finely chopped
1/4 cup sugar
1 Tbsp. unflavored
  gelatin

1/4 cup orange juice
1 cup whipping cream
2 Tbsp. lemon juice
Reserve 10 to 12 peach slices. Dice rest of peaches. Combine with other ingredients. Soften gelatin in orange juice. Heat 1/2 cup peach juice to boiling. Remove from heat; add softened gelatin, stirring until dissolved. Stir into peach mixture and chill. Whip cream until fluffy. Add lemon juice and whip until stiff. Fold whipped cream mixture into peach mixture. Garnish top with peach slices. Chill 1 hour or until ready to serve.
*Annette Bowman*

# Red Raspberry Salad

1 3-oz. pkg. red raspberry gelatin
1 cup hot water
1 10-oz. pkg. frozen red raspberries
1/2 cup whipping cream
5 large marshmallows, diced
1 3-oz. pkg. cream cheese

Dissolve gelatin in hot water; add frozen raspberries and juice. Pour into 9x5x3-inch loaf pan. Chill until firm. Whip together remaining ingredients until stiff. Spread over gelatin. Refrigerate until serving time.
*Peggy Wise*

# Raspberry Cottage Cheese Whip

1 6-oz. pkg. raspberry gelatin
1 cup boiling water
1 pkg. frozen raspberries, thawed
1/2 cup reserved raspberry juice
1 cup creamed cottage cheese
1/2 cup mayonnaise
1/3 cup lemon juice

Dissolve gelatin in boiling water. Add reserved juice. Refrigerate until of egg white consistency. With mixer or beater, blend together cottage cheese, mayonnaise, and lemon juice until smooth. Beat in chilled gelatin mixture with spoon. Fold in raspberries. Pour into 1-qt. mold. Refrigerate overnight.
*Nancy Bowman*

# Strawberry Delight

1 small can crushed pineapple, undrained
1/2 cup sugar
1 pkg. strawberry gelatin
1 can sweetened condensed milk
1 8-oz. pkg. cream cheese, softened
chopped nuts

Heat pineapple and sugar to slow boil, dissolving sugar. Add strawberry gelatin. Stir well and cool for 3 hours in refrigerator. Chill bowl, beaters, and condensed milk. Then, beat milk and cream

cheese at low speed; gradually increase to high speed. Beat until thick. Add gelatin mixture and fold in. Fill 13 x 9 x 2-inch pan. Cover with chopped nuts and chill 3 to 4 hours.
*Rosemary Denlinger*

# Twenty-Four Hour Salad

3 egg yolks
2 Tbsp. pineapple juice
2 Tbsp. sugar
2 Tbsp. vinegar
1 Tbsp. butter
dash of salt
1 large can pineapple tidbits, drained
1 16-oz. can pitted sweet cherries
2 oranges, chopped
2 cups miniature marshmallows
1 cup whipping cream

In top of double boiler, beat egg yolks; add pineapple juice, sugar, vinegar, butter, and dash of salt. Cook custard over low heat until mixture thickens, about 12 minutes. Cool. Combine fruits and marshmallows. Pour custard over and mix gently. Whip cream and fold into mixture. Cover; chill 8 hours.
*Marilyn Balsbaugh*

# Vegetable/ Combo Salads

## Avocado Salad

1 head lettuce, chopped
2 avocados, sliced
1 cup Longhorn cheese, grated
4–5 chopped green onions (optional)

Mix all ingredients together and toss with an Italian salad dressing.
*Leah Garber*

## Blender Carrot Salad

1 3-oz. pkg. lemon gelatin
1 3-oz. pkg. orange gelatin
2 cups boiling water
1 cup cold water or juice from pineapple
2 cups pineapple, crushed and drained
3 large carrots, chopped
dash of salt
peel from 1/2 orange

Dissolve gelatin in hot water; add cold liquid. Refrigerate until it begins to jell. Blend rest of ingredients in a blender. Combine and let set.
*Deanna Davison*

## Cream Cheese-Carrot Salad

1 6-oz. pkg. orange gelatin
1/4 cup sugar
1 1/2 cups boiling water
1 8-oz. pkg. cream cheese *or* substitute
1/2 cup orange juice, preferably fresh
2 Tbsp. lemon juice, fresh *or* reconstituted
2 tsp. lemon rind
1 cup apples, chopped
1 cup carrots, grated

Combine first 3 ingredients. Beat cheese into hot mixture until smooth. Add juices and rind. Cool until syrupy; add apples and carrots. Pour into large mold or square pan. Refrigerate. *Rich, but delicious.*
*Marie Haney*
*Rosemary Denlinger*
Variation:
Use lime and lemon gelatin; substitute celery for the carrots.
*Gladys Oyler*

## Tropical Tossed Salad 1

1 head red leaf lettuce, washed and well drained
1 can pineapple tidbits
1 can Mandarin oranges
1 avocado, sliced
1 medium red onion, sliced in rings
grated Parmesan cheese
1 cup fresh, thinly sliced mushrooms, (optional)

Toss all ingredients together and dress with *Sweet Oil Dressing.*

Sweet Oil Dressing:
1 1/4 cups salad oil
1/2 cup sugar
flavor enhancer to taste
salt and pepper to taste
red wine vinegar to taste

Mix all ingredients together in a shaker. Use generous amount of dressing on salad.
*Suzanne Layman*

## Tropical Tossed Salad 2

2 small cans pineapple tidbits
2 cans Mandarin oranges
1 avocado, sliced
a few small onion rings
chopped lettuce

Dressing:
1 1/2 cups oil
1/2 cup sugar
salt to taste
red wine vinegar to taste
garlic to taste

Combine salad ingredients. Make dressing and refrigerate. Shake dressing hard and add to salad just before serving.
*Marie Haney*

## Yum Yum Salad

2 cups crushed pineapple
1 lemon, juiced
1 cup sugar
2 Tbsp. unflavored gelatin

1/2 cup cold water
1 cup American
cheese, grated
1/2 pt. whipping
cream, beaten stiff
1/2 cup mayonnaise
2 Tbsp. celery, finely
chopped
2 Tbsp. green pepper,
finely chopped

Heat pineapple with juice of lemon and sugar. Stir until sugar is dissolved. Soften gelatin in cold water for 10 minutes; add to hot pineapple mixture. Cool. When gelatin begins to set, add cheese and whipped cream. Mix well and pour into mold or loaf pan. Mix vegetables with mayonnaise and a few drops of lemon juice, if desired. Remove salad from mold, slice, and serve on lettuce leaf; top with vegetable dressing.
*Kathleen Barnhart*

Variation:
Omit peppers and celery; mix everything together before molding.
*Sylvia Wray*

## Four Bean Salad 1

1 can kidney beans,
drained
1 can Garbanzo beans,
drained
1 can green beans,
drained
1 can yellow wax
beans, drained
onion rings or
chopped onion to
taste
green pepper rings or
chopped pepper, as
desired

Marinade:
3/4 cup sugar
3/4 cup vinegar
1/4 cup vegetable oil
salt and pepper to
taste

Combine beans and vegetables. Make marinade and add to bean mixture. Marinate in refrigerator several hours.
*Ruby Bowman*

## Four Bean Salad 2

1 can Garbanzo beans,
drained
1 can yellow wax
beans, drained
1 can green beans,
drained
1 can kidney beans,
drained
1 onion, chopped
1 bell pepper, chopped
1/3 cup salad oil
1/3 cup vinegar
1/2 cup sugar
1 tsp. salt
1/2 tsp. pepper

Combine all ingredients. Refrigerate overnight.
*Ruth Long*
*Marg Gish*

## Hot Snap-Bean Salad

4 medium potatoes,
peeled and diced
boiling water
1 tsp. salt
2 lbs. fresh snap
beans, cut in 1-inch
pieces
1 Tbsp. bacon fat
1/3 cup mayonnaise
1/3 cup sour cream
2 Tbsp. lemon juice
1 tsp. salt
1/8 tsp. ground black
pepper

1/8 tsp. garlic powder
1/4 tsp. dry mustard
1/4 cup onion,
chopped
4 slices crisp bacon

Cook potatoes in 1 inch of salted boiling water in a covered saucepan for 5 minutes. Add beans and continue cooking until potatoes and beans are tender. Drain. Combine bacon fat with mayonnaise, sour cream, lemon juice, and seasonings. Heat. Pour over cooked vegetables. Add onion and toss lightly. Crumble crisp bacon over top. Serves 6.
*Mable Lynch*

## Molded Beet Salad

1 3-oz. pkg. strawberry
  gelatin
1 3-oz. pkg. raspberry
  gelatin
1 3-oz. pkg. cherry
  gelatin
3 cups boiling water
2 1/2 cups cold water
1/2 cup sweet pickle
  juice
sliced lemon, (optional)
1 small can crushed
  pineapple, well
  drained
1 can shoestring beets,
  well drained

Dissolve gelatins together in boiling water; add cold water and sweet pickle juice. May slice a lemon for tartness. Set aside until jelled. Then add pineapple and beets; pour into molds. Serve with or without topping.
Topping:
1/2 cup mayonnaise
1/2 pt. sour cream
3 Tbsp. green onion,
  chopped
Combine topping ingredients. Refrigerate until ready to serve.
*Mary Jane Jarboe*

## Beet-Cabbage Soufflé Salad

1 3-oz. pkg. lemon
  gelatin

1 cup hot water
1/4 cup cold water
1/4 cup beet juice
1/2 cup mayonnaise
salt and pepper to taste
1 cup beets, cooked
  and diced
1 cup cabbage, finely
  shredded
1 Tbsp. onion, finely
  chopped

Dissolve gelatin in hot water; add cold water, beet juice, mayonnaise, salt, and pepper. Blend with beater and pour into refrigerator tray. Quick chill to freezing, about 15 or 20 minutes or until firm 1" from edge, but with center soft. Turn into bowl and whip until fluffy. Fold in vegetables. Pour into individual molds or 1-qt. mold. Chill until firm in refrigerator for 30 to 60 minutes. Unmold and garnish with greens as desired.
Note:
Nicest served the same day, as beets bleed out into mayonnaise if held too long, although salad keeps well several days.
*Eunice Grover*

## Creamy Cabbage Slaw 1

1 head cabbage,
  shredded
2 half-pts. whipping
  cream, whipped
salt and pepper to taste
vinegar to taste
sugar to taste
Combine all ingredients and serve.
*Dorothy Root*

## Creamy Cabbage Slaw 2

6 cups or 1 medium
  cabbage, shredded
1/4 cup green onion,
  sliced
1 cup mayonnaise
2 Tbsp. sugar
2 Tbsp. vinegar
2 tsp. celery seed
1 tsp. salt

Combine cabbage and onion. Mix remaining ingredients and drizzle over cabbage.
*Anita Lynch*

## Super Cole Slaw

1 tsp. salt
1/4 tsp. pepper
1/2 tsp. dry mustard
1 tsp. celery salt
2 Tbsp. sugar
1 Tbsp. pimiento,
  chopped
3 Tbsp. oil
1/2 tsp. onion, grated
1/3 cup vinegar
3 cups cabbage,
  chopped
1 small green pepper,
  chopped

Place ingredients in large bowl in order given; chill thoroughly. Garnish with sliced olives.
*Mary Jane Jarboe*

## Seafoam Cole Slaw

1 3-oz. pkg. lime
  gelatin
3/4 tsp. salt
2 Tbsp. vinegar
1 cup hot water
3/4 cup cold water
2/3 cup mayonnaise
2 or 3 tsp. onion,
  grated
3/4 tsp. celery seed
2 cups cabbage,
  shredded

Combine all ingredients except cabbage; beat until well blended. Chill until slightly thickened; then fold in cabbage. Refrigerate until firm.
*Ruth Long*

## Frozen Cabbage Salad

1 medium head cabbage, shredded
1 Tbsp. salt
1 small bunch celery, finely cut
1 green mango, finely chopped

Sprinkle cabbage with salt. Mix well. Let stand for 1 hour; then squeeze juice out very hard. Combine with celery and mango. Add *Dressing*.
Dressing:
2 cups sugar
1 tsp. mustard seed
1 cup vinegar
1/2 cup water
1 tsp. celery seed

Bring ingredients to a hard boil and boil 1 minute. Cool before pouring over cabbage, celery, and mangos. Freeze.
Variation:
Add this salad to lime gelatin.
*Kathryn Beckner*

## Celery Root Salad

2 lbs. of celery root, cleaned and trimmed
1/2 cup mayonnaise
1 tsp. mustard
1 Tbsp. white wine vinegar
1/8 tsp. (or less) liquid hot pepper seasoning
3 Tbsp. green onion, finely chopped
2 Tbsp. parsley, chopped
1/8 tsp. sugar

Cover celery root with boiling salted water; simmer, covered, until just tender, about 40 minutes. Do not overcook. Drain and allow to cool slightly. When cool enough to handle, peel and dice into 1/2" cubes. Place in salad bowl. Blend remaining ingredients together and pour over celery. Mix to coat pieces. Chill for 1 hour or more. Serve on lettuce and garnish with quartered hard cooked eggs. Serves 4 to 6.
*Eunice Grover*

## Macaroni Salad

8 oz. small shell macaroni, cooked, drained, and cooled
3 Tbsp. clear French dressing
3 hard cooked eggs, chopped
1 cup peas, cooked, drained, and cold
1/2 cup celery, chopped
1/2 cup green onions, sliced
1/2 cup mayonnaise or salad dressing
1 Tbsp. prepared mustard
1/2 tsp. Worcestershire sauce
salt
savory salt

Pour French dressing over macaroni and set aside. Combine eggs and vegetables. Blend mayonnaise and seasonings. Pour over egg mixture. Add macaroni and toss to mix. Chill. Serves 8 to 10.
*Bonnie Long*

## Creamy Potato Salad

8 medium-sized potatoes, boiled, skinned, and cut up
1 cup sweet pickles, grated
5 hard cooked eggs, grated
1/2 tsp. salt
1/2 tsp. onion salt
1/4 tsp. garlic salt
1 tsp. celery seed
1-2 cups mayonnaise
3 Tbsp. mustard

Combine all ingredients carefully. Chill.
Note:
Use the salts to taste. For a differently textured salad, grate boiled potatoes also.
*Linda Thompson*

## Fifty-Pounder Potato Salad

50 lbs. of potatoes, cooked and diced
5 qts. mayonnaise
1 qt. prepared mustard
5 cans sliced olives
5 small jars pimientos
5 12-oz. jars pickle relish
10 onions, chopped
1 bunch celery, chopped
1 bunch parsley, chopped
5 dozen eggs, chopped
4 Tbsp. salt

Mix all ingredients and chill.
*Ruby Jamison*

## Sauerkraut Salad 1

1 large can sauerkraut, drained
1 1/2 cups sugar
1 cup green pepper, diced
1 cup celery, diced
1 medium onion, diced
1/2 cup salad oil

Toss ingredients thoroughly; refrigerate overnight. Keeps indefinitely.
Note:
Sauerkraut is traditional for some on New Year's Day.
*Emma Blickenstaff*

## Sauerkraut Salad 2

1 large can sauerkraut, well drained
1 cup celery, finely chopped
1 sweet green pepper*
1 1/4 cups sugar
1/2 cup onion, finely chopped
1/2 cup vinegar, esp. sweet pickle vinegar
1/2 cup salad oil

Combine all ingredients and marinate at least 4 hours.
*or any combination of green, red, or yellow*
*Iva Bauman*

## Swinging Spinach Salad

2 envelopes unflavored gelatin
1 10-oz. can condensed beef broth
1/4 cup water
1/2 tsp. salt
2 Tbsp. lemon juice
1 cup salad dressing or mayonnaise
1 10-oz. pkg. frozen chopped spinach, thawed
1/4 cup green onion, chopped
4 hard cooked eggs, chopped
1/2 lb. crispy cooked bacon, broken up in small pieces

Soften gelatin in beef broth. Stir over low heat until dissolved. Stir in water, salt, and lemon juice. Gradually add gelatin to salad dressing, mixing until well blended. Chill until slightly thickened and fold in remaining ingredients. Pour into 1 1/2-qt. mold or large oblong pan. Chill until firm. Unmold, if in mold; otherwise, cut in squares. Garnish with pimiento strips. Serves 12.
*Eunice Grover*

## Hot Turnip Slaw

3 pts. turnips, shredded or sliced
Dressing:
2 rounded Tbsp. sugar
3 Tbsp. vinegar
1/2 cup sweet or sour cream

Cook turnips in a small amount of salted water. Add a little butter, if desired. Make *Dressing* by heating ingredients together until hot. Pour over turnips.
Variation:
Use half-and-half and a scant Tbsp. flour to thicken a little. Substitute shredded cabbage for turnips.
*Elsie Wolf*

## Zucchini and Mushroom Salad

1 lb. zucchini squash, sliced
1 lb. medium mushrooms, sliced
1 bell pepper, chopped
1/2 cup onion, chopped
3 stalks celery, chopped
Dressing:
vinegar
oil
1 garlic clove, finely chopped

Combine vegetables. Place dressing ingredients in jar and shake well. Pour over salad. Serves 6 generously. Delicious with steak!
*Juanita Grover*

# Poultry, Seafood, and Beef Salads

## Chicken Salad

3 heads lettuce, shredded
2 pkgs. frozen peas
2 bunches green onions, chopped
3/4 qt. sweet pickles, chopped
reserved pickle juice
1/2 bunch celery, chopped
2 chickens, cooked, boned and cut into small pieces
3/4 qt. mayonnaise
dash of Worcestershire sauce
pickle juice

Combine all ingredients carefully. Refrigerate. Serves about 25.
*Janet E. Rumble*

## Molded Chicken Salad

1 envelope unflavored gelatin
2 cups chicken broth
2 cups chicken, cooked and ground
1/2 cup celery hearts, finely ground

2 hard cooked eggs, chopped
1/4 cup mayonnaise
1 Tbsp. sweet pickle, chopped
1 Tbsp. lemon juice
dash of salt

Soften gelatin in 1/2 cup cool broth for 10 minutes. Heat remaining broth and stir in gelatin until dissolved. Chill until it begins to set. Add rest of ingredients; pour into loaf pan, cover, and chill.
*Mary B. Flory*

## Polynesian Salad Supreme

1/2 cup blanched whole almonds
1 large can pineapple tidbits
1/2 cup scallions or green onions, sliced
1/2 cup celery, sliced
2 cups turkey or chicken, cooked and cubed
1/2 cup mayonnaise
1/2 tsp. soy sauce
1/4 tsp. salt
salad greens

Heat almonds 3 or 4 minutes in 350° oven; split into halves. Drain pineapple, saving 2 Tbsp. syrup. In a large bowl, toss almonds, pineapple, scallions, celery, and turkey. Mix mayonnaise, pineapple syrup, soy sauce, and salt together; add to salad. Toss lightly. Turn into salad bowl lined with salad greens. Serves 4 to 6.
*Danielle Boone*
*Betty Lou Garber*

## "Chicken or Shrimp" Pear Salad

1 large can pear halves
1 large can chunk pineapple, drained
1 1 1/2 cups chicken or shrimp
2 cups converted-type rice, cooked and cooled
1/4 cup onion, chopped
1/4 cup green pepper, chopped
1/2 cup tart French dressing
1/3 cup slivered almonds
watercress or other greens for garnish

Drain pears; chill 6 halves and dice remaining pears. Set aside. Marinate chicken or shrimp, pineapple, rice, onion, and green pepper in French dressing for 1 hour (overnight preferred). One hour before serving, gently toss together diced pears, almonds, and chicken or shrimp mixture including marinade. Season to taste. Mound salad on platter or in bowl. Garnish with pear halves and sprigs of watercress or other greens of choice. Serves 6.
*Mable Lynch*

## Tuna Salad

2 6 1/2-oz. cans tuna
3 carrots, grated
1/2 cup celery, chopped
1 medium onion,
  chopped
1/2 cup nuts,
  chopped
salad dressing or
  mayonnaise to
  moisten
1 can shoestring
  potatoes

Combine all ingredients, except potatoes. Just before serving, add potatoes.
*Anita Angle*

## Crab Salad

2 3-oz. pkgs. lemon
  gelatin
2 cups boiling water
juice of 1 lemon
dash of salt
1 cup celery, diced
6 hard cooked eggs,
  diced
1 small jar stuffed
  olives, sliced
1 pt. whipping cream,
  beaten stiff

Dissolve gelatin in boiling water; add lemon juice and salt. Chill until slightly thickened. Fold in celery, eggs, olives, and whipped cream. Chill until firm. Serve with *Crab Topping.* Makes 16 servings.

Crab Topping:
1 pt. mayonnaise,
  thinned with cream
2 cans crabmeat, flaked
1 sweet pickle, diced

Combine all topping ingredients.
*Shirley Bauman*

## Mexican Salad

1 lb. ground beef
1/2 cup onion,
  chopped
2 cups kidney beans
1/2 cup French
  dressing
1/2 cup water
1/2 tsp. salt
1 Tbsp. chili powder
4 cups lettuce,
  shredded
1/2 cup green onion,
  sliced
1 cup sharp cheese
fried crisp tortillas or
  corn chips

Brown meat; add onion and cook until tender. Stir in beans, salad dressing, water, salt, and chili powder. Simmer 15 minutes. Combine lettuce and green onion; add hot meat mixture and toss lightly. Sprinkle with cheese. Serve with crisp tortillas. Serves 6 to 8.
*Rosemary Denlinger*

🌷
# Salad Dressings

## French Dressing 1

1 cup sugar
1/2 cup vinegar
1 can tomato soup
1 cup salad oil

garlic salt
1 Tbsp. celery seed
1 Tbsp. mustard
salt and pepper

Blend well.
*Miriam Mohler*

## French Dressing 2

1 1/2 cups salad oil
1/2 tsp. pepper
1 tsp. celery salt
1 tsp. salt
1/2 tsp. onion salt
3/4 cup vinegar
1 tsp. dry mustard
1 tsp. paprika
1/2 tsp. garlic salt
3/4 cup sugar

Combine and shake well. Chill.
*Shirley Denlinger*

## French Dressing 3

2 cups salad oil
3/4 cup sugar
2 tsp. paprika
2 tsp. celery seed
1/2 cup vinegar, mixed
2 tsp. salt
2 tsp. dry mustard
2 tsp. onion, grated

Put all in double boiler; as mixture warms, beat with egg beater to blend. If too hot, mixture will not blend, so keep fire low. After blending, refrigerate. Will keep several days.
*Annie Silvers*

## French Dressing 4

1 tsp. salt
1 tsp. paprika
1 tsp. dry mustard
1/2 cup sugar
2 tsp. onion, grated
4 tsp. vinegar
1 cup salad oil
celery seed

Mix first 5 ingredients together with 1 Tbsp. vinegar. Add oil and remaining 3 Tbsp. vinegar alternately to above, beating well after each addition. Add some celery seed.
*Lois Root*

## Fruit Salad Dressing

2 eggs, beaten
3/4 cup sugar
1/3 cup lemon juice
1/2 cup pear or pineapple syrup, drained from fruit
1 cup sour cream

In saucepan, combine eggs, sugar, lemon juice, and fruit syrup. Cook over medium heat, stirring constantly until mixture thickens. Cool. Fold in sour cream and chill thoroughly before serving on fruit salad.
*Phyllis Boyd*

## Hidden Valley Dressing

1 cup mayonnaise
1 cup buttermilk
1 tsp. garlic salt
1/2 tsp. parsley flakes
1/4 tsp. flavor enhancer, (optional)
1/8 tsp. pepper

Combine ingredients. Use on salad, broccoli, or potatoes.
*Dorothy Root*
*Suzanne Overholtzer*
*Gladys Oyler*
Variation:
Add 1/2 tsp. minced dry onion.
*Esther Gish*

## Old Oak Ranch Salad Dressing

1 pt. mayonnaise
1/2 pt. catsup
4 Tbsp. Worcestershire sauce
1 tsp. paprika
4 Tbsp. vinegar
3 Tbsp. sugar
1 tsp. salt
1/2 tsp. garlic powder

Place all in a quart jar and shake to blend.
*Ruby Bowman*

## Potato or Bean Salad Dressing

1 cup mayonnaise
3/4 cup sugar
2 Tbsp. prepared mustard
1/2 cup vinegar
1 Tbsp. light cream
1 tsp. celery seed

Blend mayonnaise, sugar, and mustard; add remaining ingredients. Serve chilled.
*Connie Reece*

## Potato or Macaroni Salad Dressing

2 1/2 cups sugar
2 rounded Tbsp. flour
1 Tbsp. mustard
pinch of ginger
4 eggs, beaten
1 cup water
1 cup vinegar
1 tsp. salt
2 cups mayonnaise or salad dressing

Mix all ingredients except mayonnaise; cook in double boiler until thick. Add mayonnaise when ready to add to salad. Store in refrigerator. Yields 1 qt. of dressing, enough for 2 lbs. of macaroni.
*Mary Gish*

## Roquefort Dressing 1

6 oz. Roquefort or Blue cheese
1 pt. mayonnaise
1/2 pt. sour cream
1/2 tsp. pepper
2 Tbsp. oil
2 Tbsp. vinegar
1 tsp. garlic salt
1 tsp. onion salt
1 tsp. salt

Blend all ingredients together in blender or electric mixer. Makes 1 quart. Will keep in refrigerator up to 2 weeks.
*Leah Garber*

## Roquefort Dressing 2

1 cup evaporated milk
1/4 lb. Blue cheese
4 cloves garlic, crushed
1 tsp. dried oregano
1 tsp. celery seed
1 tsp. salt
1/4 tsp. pepper
2 cups mayonnaise
1 cup buttermilk

Heat evaporated milk to simmer; stir in cheese and seasonings. Continue to heat, stirring until cheese is melted; then cool. Blend in buttermilk and mayonnaise. Keep refrigerated. Makes 1 quart.
*Mildred Moore*

## Russian Dressing

1 clove garlic, crushed
1 small onion, finely chopped
1 cup vinegar
1 cup oil
1 cup sugar
1 can tomato soup

Combine ingredients. Shake well. Refrigerate about 3 days. Good for tossed salad or plain lettuce. Yields 1 qt. dressing.
*Marie Haney*

## Tally-Ho Salad Dressing

1 1/2 cups oil
1/2 cup vinegar
1 1/2 cups sugar
1/2 cup catsup
1 tsp. salt
1 tsp. paprika
1 tsp. dehydrated onion
1 tsp. celery seed

Beat oil and vinegar 15 minutes—a must. Add remaining ingredients and beat well.
*Suzie Beckner*
*Marie Haney*

## Ten-Dollar Salad Dressing

1 tsp. celery seed
1/2 cup sugar
1 tsp. mustard
1 tsp. paprika
1 tsp. salt
1/2 cup vinegar
2 Tbsp. onion, grated
1 cup salad oil

In blender, mix all ingredients except oil. Add oil slowly while beating. Refrigerate 24 hours before using.
*Marjorie Miller*
*Dorla Shuman*

## Thousand Island Dressing

6 hard cooked eggs, ground fine
1 big jar sweet pickles
1 pt. mayonnaise
1 small bunch green onions
1 Tbsp. sugar
salt and pepper to taste
flavor enhancer to taste
1/2 cup chili sauce or catsup*
1 pt. salad dressing

Mix very well and refrigerate.
*See recipes for both on pages 115 and 116.
*Ruby Jamison*

*Extra Recipes*

Source:                    Who Likes It:

Source:                    Who Likes It:

Source:                    Who Likes It:

## THE KITCHEN PRAYER

*Lord of all pots and pans and things, since I've not time to be*
*A saint by doing lovely things or watching late with Thee*
*Or dreaming in the dawn light or storming Heaven's gates,*
*Make me a saint by getting meals and washing off the plates.*
*Although I must have Martha's hands, I have a Mary mind.*
*And when I black the boots and shoes, Thy sandals, Lord, I find.*
*I think of how they trod the earth, when'er I scrub the floor.*
*Accept this meditation, Lord; I haven't time for more.*
*Warm all the kitchen with Thy love, and light it with Thy peace;*
*Forgive me all my worrying and make my grumbling cease.*
*Thou who didst love to give men food, in room or by the sea,*
*Accept this service that I do, for it's done as unto Thee.*

# Company's Coming Casseroles

*The boor remains a boor*
*though he sleeps*
*on a silken bolster.*
PENNSYLVANIA DUTCH SAYING

*When someone*
*becomes a Christian,*
*he becomes a*
*brand new person inside.*
*He is not the same any more.*
2 CORINTHIANS 5:17

# Beef Casseroles

## Beef and Potato Bake

1 lb. hamburger
3/4 cup canned milk
1/2 cup quick oats
1/4 cup chili sauce
1 tsp. salt
4 cups potatoes, sliced
1/4 tsp. salt
1/4 tsp. pepper

Mix first 5 ingredients. Spread sliced potatoes over pan. Sprinkle with salt and pepper. Put hamburger mixture on top. Bake at 350° for 45 minutes to 1 hour.
*Paula Beachler*

## Beef-Potato-Bean Casserole

3–6 potatoes, peeled
1 lb. hamburger
1/2 tsp. salt
dash of pepper
1 medium onion, chopped
1 15-oz. can kidney beans
1 can tomato soup

Slice potatoes in greased casserole. Crumble raw hamburger on top. Add salt, pepper, onion, and beans. Cover with undiluted soup. Bake 1 1/2 hours at 350°.
*Bonnie Long*

## Cornburger Casserole

1 1/2 lbs. hamburger
2 eggs, slightly beaten
1 8-oz. can tomato sauce
3/8 tsp. salt
dash of pepper
1 tsp. Worcestershire sauce
1/4 tsp. rubbed sage
1 12-oz. can whole kernel corn
1/2 cup cracker crumbs, medium coarse
1 egg, slightly beaten
1/4 cup green pepper, diced
1/4 cup onion, chopped
1/2 cup (2 oz.) sharp American cheese, shredded

Combine beef with next 4 ingredients. Spread half of the mixture in an 8-inch round or square baking dish. Combine remaining ingredients except cheese. Spoon over meat; cover with remaining meat mixture. Bake at 375° for 1 hour. During last 5 minutes, sprinkle cheese on top. Serves 6.
*Shirley Davison*

## Hamburger-Bean Dish

1 lb. hamburger
salt and pepper to taste
1/2 cup onion, chopped
1 medium can pork and beans
1 Tbsp. Worcestershire sauce
1/2 cup catsup
1/2 tsp. Tabasco sauce
brown sugar to taste

Sauté hamburger, onion, salt, and pepper together; drain fat. Mix with remaining ingredients. Pour into 1-qt. baking dish. Bake at 300-325° for 1 hour.
*Deanna Davison*

## Jackpot Burger Casserole

1 4-oz. pkg. noodles, uncooked
1 lb. hamburger
1 onion, chopped
1 can tomato soup
1 1/2 cans water
3/4 cup cheese, grated

Put uncooked noodles in a 2-qt. casserole. Mix together meat, onion, tomato soup, and water; spoon on top of noodles. Add grated cheese. Bake at 350° for 45 minutes.
*Susan Young*

## Hamburger-Cashew Casserole

1 5-oz. pkg. noodles
1 lb. hamburger
1 onion, chopped
2 Tbsp. butter
1/2 tsp. salt
1/2 lb. Cheddar cheese, cubed
1 can cream of mushroom soup
1/2 cup milk
2/3 cup chow mein noodles
1/2 cup cashews

Cook noodles and drain. Brown meat and onions in butter; add remaining ingredients, except chow mein noodles and cashews. Mix well and pour into a 1 1/2-qt. casserole. Bake at 325° for 20 minutes. Add chow mein noodles and cashews. Bake an extra 10 minutes. Serves 6.
*Dorothy Moore*

## Hamburger Stroganoff Bake

2 lbs. hamburger
1 clove garlic
1 tsp. salt
1 tsp. sugar
3 8-oz. cans tomato sauce
1 pkg. wide noodles, boiled and drained
6 green onions, chopped
1 carton sour cream
1 cup cheese, grated

Fry meat, garlic, salt, and sugar. Add remaining ingredients, except cheese. Pour into 2-qt. casserole dish; sprinkle with cheese. Bake at 350° for 20 minutes.
*Edna Boone*

## Hamburger-Noodle Casserole

2 lbs. hamburger
1 small onion, chopped
salt and pepper to taste
1 cup celery, chopped
1 12-oz. pkg. noodles, cooked
2 cans cream of chicken soup
1 can cream of mushroom soup
1 tsp. Italian seasoning
1-2 lbs. cheese, grated

Sauté hamburger and onion; add salt and pepper. Add remaining ingredients, reserving half the cheese. Fill a 3-qt. oblong baking dish. Sprinkle rest of cheese on top. Bake 30 minutes at 350°.
*Arleen Peters*
*Treva Aukerman*

## Maggie's Noodle Bake

1 1/2 lbs. hamburger
1 1/2 lbs. sausage
1 cup mango, chopped
1 tsp. salt
1/2 cup olives, chopped
1/2 cup peas (optional)
1 4-oz. can mushrooms
1 can tomato soup
1 cup hot water
1 envelope spaghetti sauce
2 1/2 lbs. Mozzarella cheese, grated
1 12-oz. pkg. wide noodles, cooked

Sauté meat; add mango. Drain fat. Stir in salt, olives, peas, mushrooms, and other liquids. Bring to a boil and simmer 5 minutes. Cook noodles and drain. Mix together in a 13x9x2 inch baking dish. When nearly done, sprinkle cheese on top. Bake 25 minutes at 350°. May be frozen.
*Linda Lavy*

Variation:
Use less sausage; add more onion and 1 cup of chopped celery.
*Nelda Driver*

## Flimmiddle

1 lb. hamburger, browned
1/2 pkg. egg noodles, boiled
4 onions, chopped and browned
1 green pepper, chopped and browned
1 can tomato soup
salt and pepper to taste

Mix all ingredients together. Bake in a 1-qt. casserole for 1/2 to 1 hour at 350°.
*Lois Shirk*

Variations:
Omit the tomato soup and add:
1 pkg. onion soup mix
1 1/2 cups water
1 can mushroom soup
*Iva Bauman*

Or add:
1 small can mushrooms
1 cup celery, chopped
1 tsp. salt
1/2 tsp. pepper
*Phyllis Basore*

## Minnesota Hot Dish

1 lb. hamburger
1/2 cup celery, chopped
1/2 cup green pepper or onion, chopped
1 5-oz. pkg. noodles, cooked until tender
1 can cream of chicken soup
1 can cream of mushroom soup
1 cup cheese, grated

Sauté meat, celery, and pepper. Combine with noodles. Grease 1-qt. baking dish. Alternately layer noodle mixture, soups, and cheese in dish. Sprinkle extra cheese on top. Bake for 45 minutes at 350°.
Note:
This can be prepared, frozen, and then baked when ready for use.
*Florence Ivie*
*Virginia Wolf*

## Sour Cream Noodle Bake

1 1/2 lbs. hamburger, lean
1 Tbsp. oil or fat
1 Tbsp. salt
1/4 tsp. pepper
1/4 tsp. garlic salt
1/2 cup onion, chopped
1 cup tomato sauce or puree
1 cup sour cream
1 cup cottage cheese
10- or 12-oz. pkg. medium wide noodles,

cooked and drained
1 cup sharp Cheddar cheese, grated

Brown meat in oil; add salt, pepper, garlic salt, onion, and tomato sauce. Simmer 10 minutes. Combine sour cream, cottage cheese, and noodles. Mix well. Put meat sauce and noodles in casserole in alternate layers; top with the grated cheese. Bake at 350° for 25 to 30 minutes.
Note:
Freezes well. If frozen, do not put shredded cheese topping on until reheated.
*Eva R. Landes*

## Romy's Beef and Spinach Casserole

1 1/2 lbs. hamburger
1 pkg. preboiled chopped spinach
1 can cream of mushroom soup
grated cheese

Cook hamburger; add spinach and mushroom soup. Pour into greased casserole dish. Heat in 350° oven until bubbly. Add grated cheese and return to oven. Bake until cheese melts.
*Leah Garber*

## Cheese and Pasta Bake

2 lbs. hamburger, lean
vegetable oil
2 medium onions, chopped
1 garlic clove, crushed
1 14-oz. jar spaghetti sauce

1 16-oz. can stewed tomatoes
1 3-oz. can mushrooms, sliced
8 oz. shell macaroni
1 1/2 pts. sour cream
1 1/2-lb. pkg. Provolone cheese, sliced
1 1/2-lb. pkg. Mozzarella cheese, sliced thin

Sauté meat in small amount of oil in a large frying pan; stir often. Drain excess fat. Add onions, garlic, spaghetti sauce, stewed tomatoes, and undrained mushrooms. Mix well. Simmer 20 minutes or until onions are soft. Meanwhile, cook macaroni according to package directions. Drain and rinse with cold water. Pour half the shells into a deep 2-qt. casserole. Cover with half the tomato-meat sauce. Spread half the sour cream over sauce. Top with slices of Provolone cheese. Repeat, ending with slices of Mozzarella cheese. Cover casserole. Bake at 350° for 35 to 40 minutes. Remove cover; continue baking until cheese melts and browns.
*Phyllis Rumble*

## Beef-Vegetable Casserole
(for a crowd)

3 lbs. hamburger
1 small onion, chopped or sliced
1 1/2 lbs. processed cheese
1 cup milk
2 1 1/2-lb. bags mixed vegetables, cooked and salted
2 cans mushroom soup
1 can chicken soup
cooked potatoes, mashed or sliced

Brown meat and onion together, seasoning to taste. Heat cheese and milk in double boiler. Add all remaining ingredients except potatoes to cheese mixture. Put in large casserole dish. Cover with potatoes. Bake at 350° for 20 minutes or until hot.
*Jill Bauman*

## Bologna Casserole

2 cups (3/4 lb.) bologna, diced
1 cup celery, sliced
1/4 cup olives, sliced
4 hard cooked eggs, sliced
1/4 cup onion
1 Tbsp. mustard
dash of pepper
3/4 cup mayonnaise
crushed potato chips

Mix all ingredients together; put in casserole dish. Sprinkle with crushed potato chips. Bake at 400° for 20 to 25 minutes.
*Linda Thompson*

## Beef and Spaghetti Casserole

1 lb. hamburger
1 large onion, chopped
2 cloves garlic, minced
oil
1 can dark olives, pitted
1 can mushroom stems and pieces
1 can mushroom sauce
1 can tomato sauce
1 can tomato soup
1 lb. spaghetti rings or choice of macaroni, cooked
1 lb. Tillamook cheese, grated

Sauté hamburger, onion, and garlic in oil. Add next 5 ingredients. In large casserole, alternately layer sauce, spaghetti, and cheese, ending with cheese on top. Bake at 325° for 30 minutes.
*Ruth Wise*

## Lasagna

2 lbs. hamburger
1 lb. ground pork
2 cups onion, chopped
2 cloves garlic, minced
1 large can tomatoes
2 6-oz. cans tomato sauce
5 Tbsp. parsley flakes
3 Tbsp. sugar
4 tsp. salt
2 tsp. crushed basil
1 large carton cottage cheese or ricotta
2 cups Parmesan cheese
2 tsp. crushed oregano
1 16-oz. pkg. lasagna noodles, cooked and well drained
1 1/2 lbs. Mozzarella cheese, shredded

Sauté beef, pork, onion, and garlic in a heavy pot or roaster until onion is tender. Drain fat. Add tomatoes and break up with fork. Stir in tomato sauce, 3 Tbsp. parsley flakes, sugar, 2 tsp. salt, and basil. Simmer, uncovered, 1 hour or until mixture is thick like a good spaghetti sauce. Heat oven to 350°. Blend together cottage cheese, 1 cup of Parmesan cheese, remaining 2 Tbsp. parsley flakes, 2 tsp. salt, and oregano. In large oblong pan, alternately layer noodles, sauce, Mozzarella cheese, and cottage cheese mixture, ending with thin layer of sauce. Sprinkle with remaining cup Parmesan cheese. Bake uncovered, 45 minutes.
*Jeanne Brubaker*

## Mazetti

2 lbs. hamburger
2 1/2 cups celery, chopped
2 large onions, chopped
2 cloves garlic, chopped
1 8-oz. pkg. noodles
1/2 tsp. pepper
2 10 1/2-oz. cans condensed tomato soup
1 6-oz. can mushrooms and liquid
2 tsp. salt
1/2 lb. sharp cheese, grated

Brown meat in skillet; add celery, onions, and garlic. Cover and steam. Remove from heat. Cook noodles according to package directions and drain. Add to beef mixture; mix in remaining ingredients except cheese. Spread in a 3-qt. casserole. Top with cheese. Bake uncovered until bubbly, about 1 hour at 325°. Makes 10 servings.
*Becky Layman*

## Mock Ravioli

1/2 lb. shell macaroni, cooked and drained
1 pkg. chopped frozen spinach, cooked and drained
1 medium onion, diced
2 cloves garlic
2 Tbsp. shortening
1/2–1 lb. hamburger
3/4 cup spinach water
1 6-oz. can tomato paste
1 8-oz. can tomato sauce
1/4 tsp. oregano
1/4 tsp. basil
1/2 tsp. rosemary
salt and pepper to taste
2 eggs, well beaten
1/2 cup bread crumbs
1 cup Cheddar cheese, grated
1/2 cup salad oil
1 can mushroom soup (optional)

Cook macaroni and spinach separately. Sauté onion and 1 clove garlic in melted shortening; add meat and cook until well browned. Add spinach water, tomato paste, tomato sauce, herbs, salt, and pepper. Simmer 15 to 20 minutes. Meanwhile, mix cooked spinach, eggs, bread crumbs, cheese, remaining garlic, oil, and additional salt. Place layers of macaroni, spinach mixture, and meat mixture in a 13x9x2-inch casserole. Cool. Then cover casserole and store in refrigerator 24 hours. Before heating, pour undiluted mushroom soup over top, if desired. Bake uncovered for 30 to 40 mintues at 350°. Serve hot. Yields 10 servings.
*Nina Austin*

## Green Chili Casserole

1 lb. hamburger
1/2 cup onion, chopped
1/2 tsp. salt
1/4 tsp. pepper
2 4-oz. cans green chilies, drained
1 1/2 cups (6 oz.) sharp Cheddar cheese, shredded
1 1/2 cups milk
4 eggs, beaten
1/4 cup flour
dash of hot pepper sauce

Brown meat and onion; drain off fat. Sprinkle meat mixture with salt and pepper. Cut chilies crosswise; remove seeds and place half the chilies in a flat 2-qt. baking dish; sprinkle with cheese. Top with meat mixture. Arrange remaining chilies over meat. Combine last 4 ingredients and beat until smooth. Pour over chilies. Bake at 350° for 45 to 50 minutes until knife inserted comes out clean. Cool 5 minutes before serving.
Note:
If milder flavor is desired, leave out 1/2 can chilies. This dish freezes well.
*Pauline Grover*

## Mexican Lasagna Casserole

1 1/2 lbs. hamburger, extra lean
1 small onion, chopped
1 small can black olives, chopped
1 pkg. taco seasoning mix
3 small cans tomato sauce
1/2 pt. cottage cheese, small curd
1/2 pt. sour cream
1 pkg. tortilla chips
Monterey Jack cheese, grated

Sauté meat. Add onion, olives, taco seasoning mix, and tomato sauce. Combine cottage cheese and sour cream; set aside. Crush tortilla chips to form crust in a 2-qt. casserole dish. Cover with meat mixture. Spoon over creamy mixture. Cover with grated Jack cheese. Layer meat and creamy mixture until ingredients are used up, ending with Jack cheese on top. Heat in oven 350° oven until bubbly.
*Karen Miller*

## Enchilada Pie 1

1 cup margarine
1/2 cup flour
1 can chicken broth
1 pt. tomato juice
1 small can chili sauce
2 lbs. hamburger
chopped onion
salt and pepper to taste
1 1/2 tsp. Worcestershire sauce
1 tsp. chili powder
1 pkg. tortillas
1 small can tomato sauce
1 cup olives, chopped
grated cheese

Melt margarine, adding flour, broth, tomato juice, and chili sauce; set aside. Cook hamburger and onion; drain fat. Add salt, pepper, Worcestershire sauce, and chili powder. Dip tortillas in chili tomato sauce; fill with meat, olives, and cheese. Pour canned sauce over filled tortillas in a flat 2-qt. casserole. Sprinkle with cheese. May cover with foil. Bake at 350° for 20 minutes.
*Donna Rumble*
*Jane Rumble*
*Dovella Boyd*
Variation:
Use cooked, deboned chicken in place of hamburger.
*Betty Lou Garber*

## Enchilada Pie 2

2 lbs. hamburger
3 onions, sliced
1 clove garlic
2 Tbsp. chili powder
1/4 tsp. cumin
2 Tbsp. flour
2 cups tomato sauce
2 cups water
2 Tbsp. vinegar
1 tsp. salt
1 pkg. tortillas
1/2 lb. Tillamook cheese, sliced or grated
1 cup chopped olives, (optional)

Sauté meat, onion, garlic, and spices. Add flour and all but last three ingredients. Simmer. Alternately layer tortillas, meat mixture, cheese, and olives in a flat 2-qt. baking dish. Bake 30 minutes at 350°. Makes 12 large servings.
*Mary Ann Fall*

## Enchilada Pie 3

2 lbs. hamburger
1 large onion, chopped
salt and pepper to taste
pinch of oregano
1 can enchilada sauce
2 cans tomato sauce
12 tortillas
1/2–1 lb. Cheddar cheese, grated
1 can kidney beans
1 can olives, pitted and sliced

Brown hamburger and onion; add seasonings and sauces. Layer with tortillas, cheese, beans, and meat sauce in buttered 13x9x2-inch casserole. Top with olives. Bake at 325° for 45 minutes.
*Ruby Bowman*

## Enchilada Pie 4

2 lbs. hamburger
1 medium onion,
  chopped
1/2 tsp. salt
1/4 tsp. garlic salt
1/8 tsp. pepper
1/2 tsp. oregano
dash of sugar
2 cans pork and beans
2 small cans tomato
  sauce
1 can enchilada sauce
1 pkg. tortillas
2 cups Cheddar cheese,
  shredded

Brown hamburger
and onion. Add sea-
sonings, beans, to-
mato sauce, and
enchilada sauce. Line
13x9x2-inch dish
with 1/2 tortillas; al-
ternately add meat
sauce, remaining tor-
tillas, and cheese.
Bake at 350° for 45
minutes.
Variation:
Omit beans; make
sauce, combining:
1 can enchilada sauce
1 can cream of mush-
  room soup
1 can cream of chicken
  soup
1 cup milk
*Mary Ellen Miller*

## Corn Chips Casserole

3 cups corn chips
1 large onion, chopped
1 cup American cheese,
  grated
2 cups (1 can) chili

Place 2 cups corn
chips in 2-qt. baking
dish. Add layer of
chopped onion, 1/2
cup cheese, and chili.
Top with remaining

chips and cheese.
Bake at 350° for 15
to 20 minutes. Serves
6 to 8.
*Marjorie Bauman*

## Tamale Pie 1

4 cups hot water
1 tsp. salt
1 cup cornmeal
1 lb. hamburger
1 small onion, diced
dash of salt
1 small can yellow
  hominy, drained
2 cans tomato sauce
1 can olives, sliced
1 1/2 tsp. chili powder
salt and pepper to taste

Combine water, salt,
and corn meal; bring
to a boil. Let simmer
until thickened.
Brown meat and
onion with salt; drain.
Add remaining ingre-
dients; simmer 15
minutes. Combine
cornmeal and meat
mixture; pour into 1
1/2-qt. baking dish.
Bake 1/2 hour at
350°.
*Mary Gish*

## Tamale Pie 2

2 lbs. hamburger
1 clove garlic
2 cups canned corn
2 cans olives
3 cups tomato puree
3 tsp. seasoned salt
1 tsp. flavor enhancer
1/2 tsp. pepper
1 1/2 cups cornmeal
3 cups milk
3 eggs, beaten

Brown hamburger
and garlic; add corn,
olives, all liquid from
both, and tomato
puree. Add 1 cup
milk to cornmeal;

combine with meat
mixture and season-
ings. Add eggs to
remaining 2 cups
milk; add to meat
mixture. Pour into
1 1/2-qt. baking dish.
Bake at 350° for 1
hour. Serves 12.
*Nellie Heinrich*

## Tamale Pie 3

3/4 lb. hamburger
2 Tbsp. shortening
1 can tomatoes
1 can corn
1 or 2 onions, chopped
1 tsp. chili powder
1 cup cornmeal
1 cup milk (or more)
3 eggs, beaten
1 cup olives, cut up or
  whole

Sauté hamburger in
shortening. Add vege-
tables and chili pow-
der. Slowly add
remaining ingredi-
ents. Cook 15
minutes or less. Pour
into greased 1-qt.
baking dish; bake at
350° 1 hour or until
done.
*Lydia Wolf*

## Tostada Casserole

1 lb. hamburger
2 cans chili beans
2 cans mushroom soup
1 onion, chopped
1 6-oz. pkg. corn chips
1/2 cup cheese, grated
1/2 head lettuce, chopped fine
2 or 3 tomatoes, chopped

Brown hamburger. Mix chili beans, mushroom soup, and onion with hamburger. Alternate layers of meat mixture and chips in lightly greased 1-qt. casserole. Sprinkle grated cheese on top. Bake at 350° for 30 minutes. Top with lettuce and tomatoes. Serves 6.

*Bonnie Long*

## Tortilla Pie

2 lbs. hamburger
1 onion, chopped or sliced
1 can cream of mushroom soup
1 can cream of chicken soup
1/2 can green chili sauce
1/2 can red chili sauce
6–8 corn tortillas
grated cheese

Sauté meat and onions. Mix remaining ingredients together and heat. Combine with meat and onion. Alternately layer tortillas and meat mixture in 1 1/2-qt. baking dish. Top with grated cheese. Bake at 450° about 30 minutes.

*Myrtle Bashor*
*Mary Wise*

## Chinese Hamburger Casserole

1 lb. hamburger
2 medium onions, chopped
1 cup celery, diced
1/2 cup rice, uncooked
1/4 tsp. pepper
1/4 cup soy sauce
1 1/2 cups water
1 can cream of mushroom soup
1 can cream of chicken soup
1 can Chinese vegetables
1 can Chinese noodles

Brown meat. Add all ingredients except noodles. Pour into 1 1/2-qt. casserole dish. Bake, covered, in 350° oven for 1 hour. Stir. Sprinkle Chinese noodles on top and bake, uncovered, for 30 minutes.

*Carla Miller*

## Chow Mein Bake

1 lb. hamburger
2 medium onions, chopped
1/2 cup celery, chopped or sliced
1 4-oz. can mushroom stems and pieces, undrained
1 10-oz. can cream of mushroom soup
1 soup can water
2–4 Tbsp. soy sauce to taste
1 cup raw rice, washed

Brown meat, onions, and celery. Add mushrooms with juice, mushroom soup, water, soy sauce, and rice; mix well. Bake covered in greased 1-qt. casserole at 325° for 1 1/2 hours. Serves 4.

*Mary Heinrich*

# Ham Casseroles

## Ham and Potato Casserole

2 cups ham, cooked and diced
6 medium potatoes, cooked, diced, and salted
1 4-oz. can pimientos
1 tsp. seasoned salt
2 cans cream of mushroom soup (or 1 can each cream of celery and cream of mushroom soup)
2 cups cheese, shredded

Lightly mix ham, potatoes, pimientos, and salt. Grease flat 2-qt. baking dish; add alternate layers of meat mixture, cheese, and soup. Reserve 1/4 cup cheese for top. Bake in 350° oven for 40 minutes. Add 1/4 cup cheese during last 10 minutes. Serves 6 or 8.

*Pearl Howser*

## Ham and Green Bean Casserole

2 4-oz. cans mushrooms
1 medium onion, chopped
1/4 cup butter
1/4 cup flour
3 cups half-and-half
2 cans Cheddar cheese soup
1/2 tsp. Tabasco sauce
1 12-oz. pkg. noodles
2–4 cups ham, cooked and cubed
2 Tbsp. soy sauce
2 5-oz. cans water chestnuts, sliced
3 pkgs. frozen French-style green beans, partially cooked

Sauté mushrooms and onion in butter. Thicken with flour and half-and-half. Add remaining ingredients. Makes one 3-qt. casserole and one 2-qt. casserole. Bake 1 hour at 300°. Freezes well.
*Suzanne Overholtzer*

# Pork Casseroles

## Rice and Sausage Casserole

2 lbs. bulk sausage
1 cup green pepper, chopped
3/4 cup onion, chopped
2 cups celery, chopped
5 oz. chicken noodle soup mix
4 1/2 cups boiling water
1 cup rice, uncooked
1/2 tsp. salt
1 cup blanched almonds, slivered

Brown sausage in large skillet; drain fat. Add green pepper, onion, and celery; sauté and set aside. Combine soup mix and boiling water in large saucepan; stir in rice. Cover and simmer 20 minutes or until tender. Add sausage mixture, salt, and scant cup almonds, stirring well. Pour into greased, flat 2-qt. baking dish. Sprinkle extra almonds on top. Bake at 375° or 20 minutes. Makes 10 servings.
*Sarah Lee Switzer*
*Marilyn Gish*

## Pork and Rice Casserole

1 lb. pork, cooked and cubed
1/2 cup onion, chopped
1 cup celery, chopped
2 cups rice, cooked
3 Tbsp. soy sauce
1 can cream of mushroom soup

Brown meat; add onion and celery. Cook until golden brown. Add remaining ingredients. Pour into 2-qt. casserole, cover, and bake for 1 hour at 350°.
*Mildred Davison*

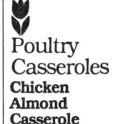

# Poultry Casseroles

## Chicken Almond Casserole

1 lb. sausage
2 cups onion, chopped
2 cups celery, chopped
2 cups brown rice
3 pkgs. chicken noodle soup
1 pkg. chopped almonds
buttered crumbs

Crumble sausage and fry in skillet. Brown onions and celery in sausage grease. Cook rice as directed on package. Cook soup in 1/2 amount of water called for on package. Mix all ingredients together, blending well. Pour into 2-qt. casserole; sprinkle top with buttered crumbs. Heat through 20 minutes in 350° oven.
Note:
Best made day before.
*Clara Meador*

## Chicken Artichoke Casserole

3 lbs. cut-up chicken
1 1/2 tsp. salt
1/2 tsp. paprika
1/4 tsp. pepper
6 Tbsp. butter
1 can whole mushrooms
2 Tbsp. flour
2/3 cup chicken consommé
3 Tbsp. sherry wine
1 15-oz. can artichoke hearts

Season chicken pieces with salt, pepper, and paprika; brown in 4 Tbsp. butter. Place in large casserole. Add remaining butter to frying pan and sauté mushrooms for 5 minutes. Sprinkle them with flour; stir in consommé and sherry. Cook 5 minutes. Arrange artichokes between the chicken pieces. Pour mushroom-sherry sauce over. Cover and bake at 375° for 1 hour.
*Lois Bauman*

## Chicken Biscuit Casserole

1 cup potatoes, diced
1/2 cup onion, sliced
1 cup carrots, diced
2 cups chicken broth
2 cups chicken, cooked, chopped, and boned
1/2 tsp. garlic salt
1/2 tsp. poultry seasoning
1/2 cup peas or mixed vegetables
biscuit dough

Combine and cook potatoes, onion, and carrots. Thicken broth as for gravy; add chicken, garlic salt, and poultry seasoning. Mix with vegetables and add peas or mixed vegetables. Pour into 1 1/2-qt. casserole dish; on top, place small biscuits cut from doughnut hole cutter. Bake 35 minutes at 350°. Serve with extra biscuits.
*Mary E. Davison*

## Chicken Broccoli Casserole 1

1 can cream of chicken soup
1/4 cup milk
1 cup medium Cheddar cheese, grated
1/4 tsp. chervil
2 pkgs. frozen broccoli *or* 3 cups fresh broccoli
2/3 pkg. noodles, cooked
2 cups chicken, cooked and cubed

Mix all ingredients together and put into greased 2-qt. baking dish. Bake at 350° for 30 minutes or a little longer. Freezes well.
*Dorothy Root*

## Chicken Broccoli Casserole 2

1 10 3/4-oz. can cream of chicken soup
1/4 cup milk
1 cup American cheese, shredded
1 Tbsp. sherry, (optional)
1 10-oz. pkg. frozen broccoli spears, cooked and drained
2 cups noodles, cooked
1 cup chicken, cooked and cubed

Heat soup, milk, 3/4 cup cheese, and sherry until cheese melts, stirring occasionally. Dice broccoli stems, saving flowerettes. In 1 1/2-qt. casserole, combine soup mixture, noodles, chicken, and broccoli stems. Top with flowerettes, pressing lightly into casserole. Sprinkle with remaining cheese. Bake at 350° for 30 minutes. Makes 3 to 4 servings.
*Barbara Gish*

Variation:
Add 1 cup mayonnaise and 1/2 tsp. lemon juice, omitting milk, sherry, and noodles. Layer broccoli, chicken, and soup mixture. Sprinkle with cheese and

buttered bread crumbs.
*Kathryn Beckner*
*Ruby Jamison*

## Chicken-Noodle Casserole

1 5-lb. hen *or* 2 fryers
12 oz. egg noodles
2 onions, chopped
1 or 2 garlic cloves, chopped
2 green peppers, chopped
1 carrot, chopped
2 or 3 stalks celery, chopped
oil or melted fat
2 cans tomato sauce
1 Tbsp. Worcestershire sauce
1 large can mushrooms
1-2 tsp. chili pepper
1 bay leaf
1 cup cheese, grated

Cook chicken until tender, saving broth. Cool, skin, and cut into large chunks. Cook noodles in chicken broth. Cook onions, garlic, peppers, carrot, and celery slowly in skillet in melted fat; do not brown. Combine all ingredients together except cheeses. Pour into 2 2-qt. baking dishes. Bake at 350° for 30 minutes or more. Sprinkle grated cheese on halfway through baking.
*Nellie Miller*

## Chinese Chicken Bake 1

1/2 cup chicken broth or milk
2 cans cream of mushroom soup

3 cups chicken, cooked and diced
1 7-oz. can tuna, drained and flaked
1/4 cup onion, chopped
1 cup celery, sliced
1 5-oz. can water chestnuts, thinly sliced
1 3-oz. can chow mein noodles
1/3 cup toasted almonds

Blend broth and soup in 2-qt. casserole. Add all ingredients except nuts. Mix well. Bake at 325° for 40 minutes. Garnish with almonds.
*Leah Miller*
*Rhonda Landes*

## Chinese Chicken Bake 2

1 1/2 cups chicken, cooked and cubed
1 cup chicken broth
1 can cream of mushroom soup
1 can chow mein noodles
1 cup celery, chopped
1/2 cup onion, chopped

Mix all ingredients together and pour into 1-qt. casserole. Bake 1 hour at 350°. Add extra noodles on top, and brown last 5 minutes.
*Kathryn Mohler*
*Ellen Reece*

## Chicken-Rice Casserole 1

2 cups rice, slightly undercooked
1 cooked chicken
1 small (1 lb.) pre-cooked ham, cubed
1 can cream of chicken soup
1 can cream of celery soup
1/2 cup onion, diced
1/2 cup green pepper, diced
1/2 cup carrots, grated
salt and pepper to taste
1/4 tsp. tarragon
1/4 tsp. summer savory
1/2 cup celery, diced
1/4 tsp. marjoram
1/4 tsp. celery salt

Put rice in bottom of 2-qt. casserole. Mix remaining ingredients and pour over rice. Bake at 300° for 20 minutes or until heated through.
*Mildred Beachler*

## Chicken-Rice Casserole 2

1 frying chicken, cut up
1 1/3 cups flour
1/4 cup butter
1 can cream of chicken soup
2 1/2 Tbsp. onion, grated
1/2 tsp. celery flakes
1 Tbsp. parsley, chopped
1 tsp. salt
dash of pepper
1 1/3 cups water
1 1/3 cups quick cooking rice
1/2 tsp. paprika
parsley

Roll chicken in flour; sauté in butter until tender. Mix soup, onion, and next 4 seasonings in saucepan. Gradually stir in water. Bring to a boil, stirring constantly. Pour rice in shallow 2-qt. casserole. Pour soup mixture into rice, reserving 1/3 cup soup mixture. Top with chicken. Pour on remaining soup mixture. Cover and bake at 375° about 30 minutes. Sprinkle with paprika; garnish with parsley. Serves 4 to 6.
*Susan Wray*
*Kathryn Jarboe*

## Chicken-Rice Casserole 3

1 1/2 cups rice, uncooked
3 1/2 cups water
1 envelope dry onion soup mix
1 can cream of mushroom soup
1 chicken, cut up and salted
mayonnaise or salad dressing

Place first 4 ingredients in flat 2-qt. dish. Brush chicken with salad dressing and place on top. Cover and bake at 375° for 1 hour or until done.
*Bonnie Long*

## Chicken-Rice Casserole 4

1 medium onion, chopped
butter
1/4 cup flour
1 6-oz. can broiled mushrooms, sliced
chicken broth
1 1/2 cups light cream
1 cup wild rice, cooked and drained
3 cups chicken, cooked and diced
1/4 cup pimiento, chopped
2 Tbsp. parsley, snipped
1 1/2 tsp. salt
1/4 tsp. pepper
1/2 cup slivered almonds

Sauté onion in butter until tender; remove from heat. Stir in flour; set aside. Drain mushrooms, reserving liquid. Add enough chicken broth to mushroom liquid to measure 1 1/2 cups. Gradually stir into flour mixture. Add light cream. Cook and stir until mixture thickens. Add rice, mushrooms, and remaining ingredients. Place in 2-qt. casserole. Sprinkle with slivered almonds. Bake at 350° for 25 to 30 minutes. Serves 8.
*Phyllis Flory*

## Chicken-Rice Casserole 5

2 or 3 cups chicken, cooked and diced
2 cups cream of chicken soup
2 tsp. onion, diced
2 cups rice, cooked
1 tsp. salt
1 1/2 cups mayonnaise
1 cup toasted almonds, diced
4 tsp. lemon juice
6 hard cooked eggs, shelled and diced
2 cups celery, diced
1 small jar pimiento
crushed corn flakes or bread crumbs

Mix all ingredients together, except corn flakes. Pour mixture into a 13x9x2-inch baking dish. Cover with corn flakes or bread crumbs. Bake about 45 minutes at 350°
*Annette Bowman*
*Esther Flora*

## Chicken Tortilla Bake

4 chicken breasts, cooked and boned
12 corn tortillas, cut in 1" strips
1 can cream of mushroom soup
1 can chili without beans
1 can cream of chicken soup
1 can green salsa sauce
1/2 lb. sharp Cheddar cheese, grated
1/2 lb. Monterey Jack cheese, grated

Place chicken in bottom of 13x9x2-inch baking dish. Top with strips of tortillas. Mix together canned ingredients (no water) and spread on top of tortillas. Sprinkle with cheese. Bake at 350° for 1 hour. Cover with foil for first 15 minutes.
*Fanny Beachler*

## Chicken Tamale Casserole

2 cups cornmeal
2 cups cold water
2 tsp. salt
6 cups boiling water
2 cups (or more) chicken, cooked and diced
1/2 lb. grated cheese for topping

Sauce:
1/2 cup butter, melted
1/2 cup plus 2 Tbsp. flour
3 cups chicken broth
1 cup onion, chopped
2 tsp. salt
1 medium can chili sauce
1/2 lb. grated cheese

Combine cornmeal, water, and salt. Then, add to boiling water. Cook 10 minutes and pour into 13x9x2-inch casserole. Arrange chicken on top. Prepare sauce by combining sauce ingredients thoroughly. Top with grated cheese and bake at 350° for 30 minutes.
*Mary Jane Root*

## Scalloped Chicken

1 5-lb. hen, cooked, boned, and cut up
1/2 cup butter or margarine
1 medium onion, chopped
1 cup celery, chopped
parsley
1 tsp. salt
dash of pepper
1 tsp. poultry seasoning
1 1/2 loaves bread, diced
chicken broth

Sauté onion, celery, and parsley in butter for 2 minutes. Add seasonings. Make a thin gravy with broth. Mix all ingredients together and pour into 13x9x2-inch baking dish. Bake at 350° for 20 minutes.
*Mary Gish*

# Seafood Casseroles

## Cashew-Tuna Hot Dish

1 3-oz. can chow mein noodles
1 can cream of mushroom soup
1 large can tuna
1/4 lb. cashew nuts
1 cup celery, diced
1/4 cup onion, minced
salt and pepper to taste
1 can Mandarin oranges

Combine 1/2 of noodles and all remaining ingredients except oranges. Mix well and place in 2-qt. casserole. Top with reserved noodles. Bake at 350° for 30 to 40 minutes. Garnish with Mandarin oranges. Serves 4 to 6.

Note:
If cashew nuts are sautéed, omit dash of salt.
*Shirley Bauman*

Variation:
Omit oranges and add 1/4 cup water.
*Fanny Beachler*

## Tuna Squash Casserole

1 cup canned tuna or salmon
2 cups summer squash, diced
2 cups milk
1/2 cup onion, diced
2 cups cracker crumbs
salt and pepper to taste
grated cheese

Combine all ingredients except cheese. Put mixture in 1-qt. baking dish and sprinkle with cheese. Bake for 45 minutes at 350° or until brown and bubbly. Serves 4 to 6.
*Mary E. Davison*

## Tuna Bake

1 large can tuna
3 Tbsp. bread crumbs
2 Tbsp. butter, melted
1 tsp. parsley, chopped
salt and pepper to taste
cayenne pepper to taste
2 eggs, well beaten

Break tuna with fork until quite fine. Mix together bread crumbs, melted butter, parsley, salt, pepper, and cayenne. Add to tuna; beat eggs and add, mixing well. Place in a but-tered mold and bake 1/2 hour at 350° or steam 3/4 hour.
*Thelma Wagoner*

## Fisherman's Rice Casserole

2 cups rice, cooked
1 1/2 cups celery, sliced
1 6-oz. can olives, sliced
2 Tbsp. green onion, sliced
1 cup mayonnaise
1 7-oz. can tuna, drained and flaked
1 4 1/2 oz. can shrimp, drained and rinsed
1/2 cup green onion-flavored almonds

Combine all ingredients but seafood and almonds; mix well. Fold in tuna and shrimp. Spoon into shallow 1 1/2-qt. casserole. Cover with almonds. Bake at 325° for 25 to 30 minutes until heated.
*Nelda Driver*

Variation:
Using 2-qt. baking dish, add:
1 can cream of celery soup
1 1/2 cups milk
1 can crab meat
2 extra cups cooked rice
*Linda Thompson*

## Hot Seafood Bake

2 cups crab meat
2 cups shrimp, shelled and deveined
2 cups celery, chopped
1/2 cup onion, chopped
1/2 cup green pepper, chopped
2 cups mayonnaise
2 tsp. Worcestershire sauce
2 Tbsp. butter, melted
5 cups corn flakes
paprika

Combine all ingredients, except paprika. Pour into 2-qt. casserole dish. Sprinkle paprika on top. Bake 1/2 hour at 350°. Serves 12.
*Margaret Jarboe*
*Lola Miller*

## Seafood Pilaf

1 medium onion, chopped
2 Tbsp. shortening
2 cups rice, cooked
2 cups (16-oz. can) tomatoes
3 stalks celery, diced
1/2 tsp. salt
1/4 tsp. paprika
1/2 bay leaf, crumbled
1/4 cup cheese, grated
1 cup shrimp or crab-meat, cooked

Sauté onion in shortening until browned; stir in rice and set aside. Combine remaining ingredients, except seafood, in saucepan. Heat until cheese melts. Fold in rice and seafood. Pour into a greased 1-qt. baking dish. Cover and bake at 325° for about 25 minutes. Serves 6.
*Alice Mae Haney*

*Extra Recipes*

_____
_____
_____
_____
_____
_____
_____
_____
_____
Source:                    Who Likes It:

_____
_____
_____
_____
_____
_____
_____
_____
_____
Source:                    Who Likes It:

_____
_____
_____
_____
_____
_____
_____
_____
Source:                    Who Likes It:

## FAVORITE QUICK SUPPER

*Measure 3 cups flour into large bowl, answer telephone, take large bowl off small son's head, and sweep up flour.*

*Measure 3 cups flour into large bowl. Measure 1/4 cup shortening, answer door bell, and wash shortening from son's hands and face.*

*Add 1/4 cup shortening to flour. Mix well and rock crying baby for 10 minutes. Answer telephone. Put son in tub and scrub well. Scrape flour and shortening mixture from floor. Add enough tears to relieve tension.*

*Open 1 can of beans and serve with remaining strength.*

# SEVEN

# Mainstay Entrees

*It is good speaking
that improves silence.*
DUTCH SAYING

*A dry crust
eaten in peace
is better than steak
every day
along with argument
and strife.*
PROVERBS 17:1

# Egg Entrees

## Breakfast Pie

10 slices bacon,
  cooked but not crisp
6 eggs
3 Tbsp. milk
1/2 tsp. salt
dash of pepper

Drain cooked bacon
on paper towels. Ar-
range bacon to cover
bottom and sides of
8-inch pie plate.
Combine eggs, milk,
salt, and pepper. Pour
into pie plate. Bake
at 375° for 30
minutes.
*Joan Cover*

## Corn Soufflé

3 eggs, separated *and*
  at room temperature
3/4 cup cornmeal
3/4 tsp. salt
1 1/4 cups milk,
  scalded
2 Tbsp. butter
1 17-oz. can cream-
  style golden corn
3/4 tsp. baking
  powder

Beat egg whites until
stiff, but not dry.
Beat egg yolks until
thick and lemon
colored. Stir corn-
meal and salt into
milk, beating hard.

Cook a few seconds
over low heat, stirring
until thick. Blend in
butter, corn, and bak-
ing powder. Fold in
yolks and then egg
whites. Pour into
greased 2-qt. baking
dish. Bake at 350–
375° about 35 min-
utes or until puffy
and golden brown
and knife inserted in
center comes out
clean. Serves 6.
*Eunice Grover*

## Easy Cheese Soufflé

4–6 slices bread
3 cups cheese, grated
1/2 tsp. Worcester-
  shire sauce
dash of pepper
2 cups milk
3 eggs, beaten
1/2 tsp. salt
1/2 tsp. thyme
1/2 tsp. dry mustard

Layer bread and
cheese in oiled 1-qt.
baking dish, starting
with bread. Beat
milk, eggs, salt, and
remaining ingre-
dients together;
pour over bread mix-
ture. Let stand for 30
minutes. Bake at
350° for 1 hour in a
pan of hot water.
*Ruth Bauman*

## Squash Fritata

1 1/2 lbs. zucchini
  squash, sliced
1/2 cup butter
2 Tbsp. oil
1/2 cup parsley,
  chopped
1 cup cheese, grated
1 small clove garlic,
  minced
1/4 loaf French bread
salt and pepper to taste
3 eggs, well beaten

Sauté sliced squash
in butter and oil
until tender. Make
dressing by soaking
bread in cold water
for 5 minutes and
then squeezing bread
until almost dry.
Combine with fried
squash. Add remain-
ing ingredients. Pour
into well buttered
pan and fry. Then,
pour eggs over mix-
ture; blend well and
brown. Serve at once.
Note:
This can be served
from the skillet or
baked in oven as a
casserole.
*Mary Jane Jarboe*

# Beef Entrees

## Chili 1

1 lb. hamburger
salt and pepper to taste
oregano to taste
celery salt to taste
onions to taste
garlic salt to taste
chili powder to taste
water to cover
2 qts. chili beans, cooked

Sauté meat until brown or no longer pink. Add remaining ingredients, except beans, and cook about 15 minutes. Then add enough water to cover. Simmer to thicken slightly. Add cooked beans.
*Ruthann Orndoff*

## Chili 2

3 lbs. hamburger
1 qt. water
6 Tbsp. chili powder
3 tsp. salt
10 cloves garlic, finely chopped
1 tsp. ground cumin
1 tsp. marjoram
1 tsp. red pepper
1 Tbsp. sugar
3 Tbsp. paprika
3 Tbsp. flour
6 Tbsp. cornmeal
1 cup water

Sear meat in large skillet or heavy pot over high heat. Stir constantly until meat turns gray, not brown. Add water, cover, and simmer for 1 1/2 to 2 hours. Then add seasonings. Cook another 30 minutes at same bubbling simmer. (Fat left on meat will rise to top after spices have been added, so skim it off.) Next, add mixture of flour, cornmeal, and water to thicken chili. Cook 5 minutes, stirring to prevent sticking; add more water if needed. Serve with red beans, diced onions, and crackers.
Note:
Decrease amounts of seasoning for a less "hot" dish.
*Maralee Oyler*

## Mexican Straw Hats

1 1/2 lbs. hamburger
1 large onion, chopped
1 can chili beans, mashed
grated cheese
corn chips
shredded lettuce
avocado
tomato

Cook meat, onion, and beans together. Put corn chips on plate; then add meat mixture, cheese, shredded lettuce, avocado, and tomato in order listed.
*Martha Gish*

## Texan Straw Hats

1 cup onion, chopped
2/3 cup celery, chopped
2/3 cup bell pepper, chopped
1 1/2 lbs. hamburger
2 tsp. salt
2 6-oz. cans tomato paste
2 cups water
3 Tbsp. cooking oil
1 tsp. chili powder
1/4 tsp. pepper
1/2 cup catsup
2 tsp. Worcestershire sauce
corn chips

In hot fat, sauté onion, celery, and bell pepper until tender, but not brown. Add remaining ingredients and simmer, uncovered, for 1 hour, stirring occasionally. Add a small amount of sugar, if desired. To serve, put corn chips in center of the plate. Top with mixture. Leave a small portion of corn chips uncovered around edge to represent the rim of a straw hat.
*Janet Rumble*

## Texan Pancake

1 1/4 cups corn muffin mix
3/4 cup milk
1 egg
2 Tbsp. salad oil
1 large clove garlic, minced
1 medium onion, coarsely chopped
1/2 lb. ground chuck
3/4 tsp. oregano
2 tsp. seasoned salt

1/2 green pepper,
  chopped
3/4 tsp. chili powder
1/3 cup tomato paste
1-lb. can tomatoes,
  drained
liquid from canned
  tomatoes
grated Parmesan
  cheese

About 50 minutes
before serving, com-
bine muffin mix,
milk, and egg; stir
until very smooth. In
skillet, place oil, garlic,
and onion. Add meat
and sauté until gray
in color. Stir in re-
maining ingredients,
except tomatoes.
Simmer, covered, 15
minutes, stirring oc-
casionally. Mean-
while, in small heated
skillet, make four
thick pancakes,
using 1/3 cup corn
muffin batter for
each pancake, and
keep warm. Add to-
matoes to meat sauce;
bring to a boil. On
serving dish, stack
pancakes with meat
sauce and generous
sprinkle of grated
Parmesan cheese.
Garnish with parsley.
Serve in wedges with
extra meat sauce.
Serves 2–4.
*Elva Benedict*

## Skillet Tamale Pie

2 lbs. hamburger
2 cans creamed corn
3 8-oz. cans tomato
  sauce
1/2 tsp. salt
1/2 tsp. onion salt
1/2 tsp. chili powder
1/4 tsp. garlic salt
3/4 cup cornmeal

Brown meat in skillet.
Add corn, tomato
sauce, seasonings,
and cornmeal; cook
for 1/2 hour. Olives
may be added before
serving.
*Edna Thompson*

## Spanish Rice

1 lb. hamburger
1/2 onion, chopped
2 1/2 cups hot water
1 cup rice
1 1/2 tsp. salt
1 tsp. chili powder
1 tsp. bacon grease
1/4 cup bell pepper,
  chopped
1 8-oz. can tomato
  sauce
1/2 tsp. garlic powder
1 Tbsp. sugar

Combine all ingre-
dients. Cook, covered,
25 to 30 minutes in
large saucepan or 10
minutes in pressure
cooker. Serves 6 to 8.
*Margaret Miller*

## Cheeseburger Pie

pastry for 9-inch pie
1 lb. hamburger
1 tsp. salt
1/2 tsp. oregano
1/4 tsp. pepper
1/2 cup dry bread
  crumbs
1 8-oz. can tomato
  sauce
1/4 cup onion,
  chopped
1/4 cup green pepper,
  chopped
1/2 cup chili sauce

Topping:
1 egg, beaten
1/4 cup milk
1/2 tsp. dry mustard
1/2 tsp. salt
1/2 tsp. Worcester-
  shire sauce
2 cups cheese, grated

Brown meat and
drain. Add salt, orega-
no, pepper, bread
crumbs, 1/2 can
tomato sauce, onion,
and green pepper.
Pour into unbaked
pie shell. Mix topping
ingredients together
and spread over meat
mixture. Bake for 30
minutes at 425°. Be-
fore serving, top with
heated mixture of
remaining 1/2 can
tomato sauce and
chili sauce.
*Bonnie Jamison*

## Pizza Pie 1

1 1/2 lbs. hamburger
2 large onions, chopped
2 15-oz. cans tomato sauce
cornstarch, (optional)
1 cup mushroom soup
1/4 cup catsup
1/4 cup sugar
1 tsp. parsley flakes
1/2 tsp. Italian seasoning
1/2 tsp. oregano
prepared pizza dough (oiled)
sliced or shredded Mozzarella cheese

Fry hamburger and onion; drain. Thicken tomato sauce with cornstarch if desired. Add remaining ingredients to sauce, omitting cheese. Add meat and onion. Pour meat sauce over dough and top with cheese. Bake at 400° for 20 minutes.
Variations:
Add cornstarch or arrowroot flour to thicken sauce. Use Cheddar in place of Mozzarella.
*Janice Root*

## Pizza Pie 2

1 1/4 cups lukewarm water
1 pkg. yeast
2 tsp. salt
2 Tbsp. sugar
2 Tbsp. oil
3 cups flour
1 can pizza sauce
sliced olives
chopped mushrooms
Mozzarella cheese
pepperoni or preferred meat

Dissolve yeast in lukewarm water; let set 5 minutes. Add salt, sugar, and oil. Add flour gradually and mix well. Let rise 20 minutes; divide dough in half. Pat dough in 2 pizza pans. Spread 1/2 can pizza sauce over each circle of dough. Layer with olives, mushrooms, cheese, and meat. Bake in 400° oven for about 20 minutes.
*Marilyn Lynch*

## Pizza Pie 3
(for a crowd)

1 lb. salami, ground
1 10-oz. pkg. sharp Cheddar cheese
1 10-oz. pkg. mild Cheddar cheese
2 4-oz. cans mushrooms, drained
2 small cans olives, chopped
1 8-oz. can tomato sauce
1 cup oil
2 Tbsp. Italian seasoning

Mix all ingredients together. Cover and keep in refrigerator. Use 35 to 40 English muffin halves. Spread about 1/4 cup on each muffin half and broil until bubbly.
*Marilyn Balsbaugh*

## Dried Beef Pie

1 cup onion, chopped
1 4-oz. pkg. dried beef, cut up
1/4 cup oil
2 Tbsp. flour
1/4 tsp. salt
1/4 tsp. pepper
2 cups carrots, thinly sliced
2 cups potatoes, thinly sliced
2 cups water
1 bouillon cube

Sauté onion and dried beef in oil; stir in flour and seasonings. Add remaining ingredients and bring to a boil. Cover and simmer 5 minutes. Pour hot mixture into 2-qt. casserole. Prepare *Pastry*.

Pastry:
1 cup flour
1/2 tsp. salt
1/3 cup shortening
2 Tbsp. water

Combine ingredients, kneading briefly. Roll out dough to fit casserole shape. Cover casserole with pastry. Bake 25 to 30 minutes at 425°.
*Naomi Bauman*

## Meat Loaf 1
Loaf:
1 lb. hamburger
1 egg, slightly beaten
1/4 tsp. pepper
1 tsp. salt
1 cup milk
2 Tbsp. butter, melted
1/2 onion, chopped
1 cup broken soda crackers
sliced potatoes, (optional)

Toppings:
bacon
cheese
tomato sauce

Combine ingredients and place in loaf pan. If desired, slice potatoes in bottom of loaf pan and place meat loaf over potatoes. Top meat loaf with bacon, cheese, or tomato sauce. Bake at 375° for 1 hour.
*Shirley Denlinger*

## Meat Loaf 2
Loaf:
1 1/2 lbs. hamburger
1 cup fine dry bread crumbs or rolled oats
1 Tbsp. onion, chopped
2 tsp. salt
1/2 tsp. pepper
3/4 cup milk
1 egg, beaten
Topping:
1/4 cup catsup
1/4 cup light corn syrup
1 Tbsp. Worcestershire sauce

Mix loaf ingredients well. Bake at 350° for 45 minutes. Mix topping ingredients and pour over loaf. Return to oven for 15 minutes.
*Arleen Boone*

## Meat Loaf 3
Loaf:
2 lbs. hamburger
2 eggs
1 8-oz. can tomato sauce
10 crackers, crushed

1 medium onion, chopped fine
salt to taste
liquid smoke
Topping:
3 Tbsp. brown sugar
1/4 tsp. nutmeg
1 tsp. dry mustard
1/4 cup catsup

Mix all ingredients together. Bake in 2-qt. baking dish for 1 hour. Mix topping ingredients. After meat loaf is done, remove from oven and drain. Add topping and return to oven for 10 to 15 minutes.
*Mary Gish*

## One-Dish Meat Loaf Dinner

1 1/2–2 lbs. hamburger
1 pkg. dried onion soup
1 tsp. garlic salt
2 eggs
1 cup bread crumbs
1/2 cup tomato sauce
1 tsp. pepper
butter
1 lb. carrots, peeled and sliced
4–5 potatoes, peeled and sliced
1/2 cup water
salt and pepper to taste
3–4 slices bacon
catsup, (optional)

Combine first 7 ingredients; if more liquid is needed, add more tomato sauce. In deep 1 1/2-qt. baking dish, put a large dot of butter; add carrots and then potatoes. Cover with water, salt, and

pepper. Put meat loaf mixture on top and mold to shape of pan. Lay bacon on top of meat and cover bacon with a little catsup, if desired. Bake covered at 400° for 1/2 hour; then uncover and bake 1 hour at 350°. Serves 8.
*Jan Cowan*

## Swiss Meat Loaf

2 lbs. hamburger
1 1/2 cups Swiss cheese, diced
2 eggs, beaten
1/2 cup onions, chopped
1/2 cup bell pepper, chopped
1/2 tsp. paprika
1 1/2 tsp. vegetable salt
1 tsp. celery salt
2 1/2 cups milk
1 cup dry bread crumbs

Mix all together in order given; then press into greased 13x9x2-inch pan. Bake uncovered at 350° for 1 1/2 hours.
*Eunice Grover*

## Savory Meat Loaf

1 4-oz. can mush-
  rooms, sliced and
  drained
1 egg
1/4 cup mushroom
  liquid
1/2 cup milk
3 cups soft bread
  crumbs
1/2 lb. pork sausage,
  browned lightly and
  drained
1 lb. hamburger, lean
1 large dill pickle,
  minced
1/2 medium onion,
  finely minced
1/2 tsp. poultry
  seasoning
1/4 tsp. salt

Grease and flour
9x5x3-inch loaf pan.
Drain mushrooms,
reserving liquid. Beat
egg in large mixing
bowl. Add mushroom
liquid, milk, and
bread crumbs. Beat
well. Add sausage to
mixture in bowl,
along with meat,
mushrooms, pickle,
onion, and season-
ings. Mix well and
bake in loaf pan.
Bake at 350° for 1
hour.
*Mary Boone*

## Lasagna à la Skillet

1 lb. hamburger
2 Tbsp. butter
1 pkg. spaghetti sauce
  mix
1/2 lb. wide noodles,
  uncooked
2 tsp. sweet basil
  leaves
1 Tbsp. parsley flakes
1 tsp. salt
1 pt. creamed cottage
  cheese, smoothed in
  blender
1 8-oz. can tomato
  sauce
1 1/4 cups water
1 16-oz. can tomatoes,
  finely chopped
1/2 lb. Mozzarella
  cheese, grated or
  sliced

Sauté meat in butter
in electric skillet (12"
size, no smaller).
Sprinkle with half
spaghetti sauce mix.
Cover with noodles.
Sprinkle rest of spa-
ghetti sauce mix,
basil, parsley, and
salt. Spoon cottage
cheese over all. Pour
tomato sauce, water,
and tomatoes with
juice on top. Bring to
a boil, cover, and
simmer 35 minutes
or until noodles are
done. Top with
cheese; let stand
about 5 minutes.
Serves 6.
*Pearl Howser*

## Macaroni à la Skillet

1 1/2 lbs. hamburger
1 onion, chopped
1 29-oz. can tomatoes
1 12-oz. can whole
  kernel corn
1 cup elbow macaroni
1 Tbsp. chili powder
2 1/2 tsp. garlic salt
1 3 1/2-oz. can olives,
  drained and
  quartered
1 cup (4-oz. pkg.)
  cheese, grated

Brown meat and
onion. Add tomatoes,
corn, and macaroni.
Cook covered 30 min-
utes or until
macaroni is tender,
stirring occasionally.
Stir in chili powder,
garlic salt, and olives;
sprinkle with cheese
and heat covered for
5 minutes. Serve
from skillet. Makes 8
to 10 servings.
*Marcele Jarboe*
*Phyllis Denlinger*
*Diane Brubaker*

## Lazy Day Spaghetti

1 lb. hamburger
1 cup onion, chopped
1 Tbsp. shortening
1 tsp. salt
1/4 tsp. pepper
1 can tomato soup
1 8-oz. pkg. spaghetti,
  cooked and drained
1 can cream of
  mushroom soup
grated Parmesan
  cheese

Sauté meat and
onion in shortening;
season with salt and
pepper. Add soup.
Cover and simmer for
20 minutes. Place
spaghetti in medium
baking dish; top with
ground beef mixture.
Sprinkle with Par-
mesan cheese. Makes
approximately 6
servings.
*Becky Layman*

## Spaghetti

2 Tbsp. garlic, crushed
2 medium onions, chopped
1/4 cup oil*
1/4 cup butter
2 lbs. hamburger
2 cups mushrooms, sliced
2 cups condensed consommé
2 cups tomato soup
2 6-oz. cans tomato paste
1 tsp. salt
1/2 tsp. pepper
1 Tbsp. Italian herbs
18 oz. spaghetti

Sauté garlic and onion in butter and oil until tender, but not brown. Add hamburger and mushrooms; continue sautéing until brown. Then add consomme, tomato soup, and paste. Add seasonings. Cover and simmer 30 minutes. Cook spaghetti in boiling salted water. Drain. Pour sauce over spaghetti. Sprinkle with grated Italian or American sharp cheese.
*Olive oil gives better flavor
*Joyce Peters*

## Tagliarini

2 lbs. hamburger
2 small onions, chopped
2 8-oz. cans whole kernel corn
2 8-oz. cans tomato sauce
1 cup water
1 Tbsp. chili powder
2 tsp. salt
1 tsp. oregano
1 16-oz. pkg. wide noodles

Sauté hamburger and onions; add next 5 ingredients and simmer 5 minutes. Add oregano and noodles. Cook until noodles are tender, stirring occasionally.
*Lydia Wolf*
*Janice Root*

## Hamburger-Zucchini Dish

1 lb. hamburger
1 clove garlic, minced
1 medium onion, chopped
1 Tbsp. oil, (optional)
1 tsp. salt
1 bay leaf
1/2 tsp. oregano
1 16-oz. can tomatoes or 4 tomatoes, peeled and chopped
1 10-oz. pkg. frozen baby lima beans, partially thawed
3 small zucchini, sliced

Brown meat with onion and garlic in a large frying pan until meat is brown and crumbly. Use oil if meat sticks to the pan. Add seasonings. Cook 5 minutes. Add tomatoes and vegetables. Cover and simmer 20 minutes. Serve over rice. Serves 4 to 6.
*Mae Gish*

## Greek Meatballs

4 slices bread
1 cup water
2 lbs. hamburger
1 small onion, grated
1/4 cup cracker meal
1 cup parsley, chopped
1 Tbsp. salt
1/4 tsp. celery seed
1/2 tsp. pepper
1/2 tsp. flavor enhancer
1/4 cup Parmesan cheese
3 eggs
1 small bottle olive oil
flour

Gravy:
1/2 the oil left
1/2 bottle catsup
2 1/2 cups water

Pour water over bread, letting moisture be absorbed. Add all ingredients except flour and olive oil. Shape into walnut-sized meatballs. Drop these into flour and roll until no moisture remains. Brown well in oil, turning only once. Keep them warm. Make *Gravy* by blending gravy ingredients together. Bring to a boil and add meatballs. Cover and simmer 30 minutes, stirring occasionally. Serve with hot rice. Serves 12 to 15.
Note:
This can be prepared ahead of time, frozen, and reheated.
*Susan Wray*

## Barbecued Meatballs

1 lb. hamburger
1 tsp. salt
1 cup bread crumbs
1/2 cup milk
1/4 cup vinegar
1 Tbsp. sugar
1/2 cup green pepper, chopped
1/2 cup catsup
1 1/2 Tbsp. Worcestershire sauce

Mix beef, salt, bread crumbs, and milk. Shape into small balls; place in baking dish. Blend remaining ingredients together. Pour over meatballs. Bake at 350° about 30 minutes.
*Annie Bowman*

## Mushroom Meatballs

1 can cream of mushroom soup
1/2 cup water
1 lb. hamburger
1/2 cup fine dry bread crumbs
2 Tbsp. onion, minced
1 Tbsp. parsley, minced
1 egg, slightly beaten
1/4 tsp. salt
1 Tbsp. oil

Blend soup and water together. Measure out 1/4 cup soup mixture and combine with remaining ingredients, except oil. Shape into meatballs about 1 1/2" in diameter. Brown in oil in large skillet. Add remaining soup mixture, cover, and cook over low heat about 15 minutes. Stir occasionally. Makes 4 servings.
*Mary Angle*

## Porcupine Meatballs 1

1 lb. hamburger
1/2 cup rice, uncooked
6 crackers, rolled into crumbs
1 egg
boiling water
1 8-oz. can tomato sauce
1 Tbsp. butter
salt and pepper to taste

Mix meat, rice, cracker crumbs, and egg together; shape into balls and drop into boiling water to cover. Cook slowly for 1 hour. Then add tomato juice and butter. Let come to a boil and serve hot.
Variation:
A can of mushroom soup may be substituted for tomato juice.
*Peggy Wise*

## Porcupine Meatballs 2

1 lb. hamburger
1 egg
1/4 tsp. powdered sage
salt and pepper to taste
1 small onion, chopped and browned in butter
pinch of oregano
1/4 cup rice, brought to a boil
1 can tomato soup
1 can water

Combine all ingredients, except soup and water; shape into balls and arrange in a shallow 1-qt. casserole. Add soup and water. Bake at 350° for 35 minutes or until done.
*Laurel Balsbaugh*

## Porcupine Meatballs 3

1 1/2 lbs. hamburger
1 tsp. baking powder
1 Tbsp. onion, minced
3/4 cup milk or water
2 Tbsp. parsley, minced, (optional)
1/2 cup rice, uncooked
2 cans tomato soup or tomatoes
salt and pepper to taste

Combine ingredients except for soup. Shape into 8 or 9 balls; pour soup over meat. Bake uncovered at 350° for 35 minutes. Then cover and bake 35 minutes longer.
*Emma Blickenstaff*

## Special Meatballs

1 1/2 lbs. hamburger, salted*
2 eggs, slightly beaten
2/3 cup Parmesan cheese, grated
1/2 tsp. thyme
oil

1 can cream of
mushroom soup
2/3 cup water
rice, cooked with
celery, onion, or
parsley

Mix meat, eggs,
cheese, and thyme.
Shape into about 30
balls. Let stand 1
hour. Brown balls
slowly in small
amount of oil or hot
fat. Remove balls;
drain off excess fat.
Add soup and water
to skillet; heat slowly
until well blended.
Return balls to skillet
and simmer, un-
covered, for 20 to 25
minutes. Mound rice
in center of platter;
arrange meat balls
around rice and drib-
ble gravy over rice.
Serve remaining
gravy as usual.
Variation:
Use chicken soup in
place of mushroom;
omit celery, onion, or
parsley in rice.
*or 1 lb. hamburger and
1/2 lb. ground pork.
*Eva R. Landes*

## Hamburger Stroganoff

1 lb. hamburger
1/2 cup onion, diced
2 Tbsp. flour
1 can cream of
mushroom *or* cream
of chicken soup
garlic salt
1/4 tsp. pepper
1/2 tsp. paprika
1 cup sour cream

Cook hamburger and
onion together; add
flour. Blend in soup
and seasonings. Just
before serving, add
sour cream. Serve
over noodles.
*Eunice Peters*

## Beef Stroganoff

2 lbs. round steak, cut
in 1/2"x2" strips
1/4 cup flour
1/2 cup onions,
chopped
6 Tbsp. butter
1 1/2 tsp. salt
1/8 tsp. pepper
1/2 cup water
1 can cream of
mushroom soup
1 can mushrooms,
drained
1 cup sour cream

Dredge steak in flour.
Brown with onions
and butter; add
seasonings and
water. Cover and sim-
mer gently until al-
most tender for 45
minutes to 1 hour.
Stir, blending in
soup and mush-
rooms. Cook gently
until beef is tender,
about 30 minutes.
At serving time, heat
mixture piping hot.
Remove from heat
and stir in sour
cream. Serve over
*Poppy Seed Noodles.*
Serves 10.

Poppy Seed Noodles:
1 12-oz. pkg. egg
noodles
1/4 cup butter
1 Tbsp. poppy seeds
1/2 cup almonds,
slivered

Cook noodles. Drain.
Brown butter in skil-
let; add poppy seeds
and almonds, mixing
well. Add noodles and
toss lightly to mix.
Serve meat mixture
over noodles.
*Shirley Bauman*

## Swiss Steak

2 lbs. Swiss or round
steak
4 Tbsp. flour
2 tsp. salt
1/4 tsp. pepper
3 Tbsp. fat or
shortening
1 can cream of
mushroom soup
1/2 cup water
1/4 tsp. garlic powder
1 4-oz. can whole
mushrooms and
liquid
1 medium onion,
sliced in rings

Cut meat in serving
size pieces. Dredge in
mixture of flour, salt,
and pepper. Heat
shortening in heavy
skillet; brown meat
well on both sides.
Mix soup, water, and
garlic powder; pour
over meat. Top with
mushrooms and
onion rings. Cover.
Simmer about 2
hours.
*Myrtle Bashor*

## Chuck Steak

2 lbs. chuck steak
2 Tbsp. oil
1 pkg. onion soup mix
1 14-oz. can tomatoes
1 tsp. oregano
2 Tbsp. wine vinegar
1/2 tsp. garlic salt
salt and pepper to taste

Slightly brown meat in oil. Cover with remaining ingredients. Simmer 1 1/2 to 2 hours or until meat is tender. Serves 6.
*Bonnie Jamison*

## Marinated Steak

2–2 1/2 lbs. round steak, cut 1-inch thick
2 garlic cloves, crushed
1/4 cup salad oil
1/4 cup light corn syrup
1 tsp. rosemary, crushed
1/2 cup wine vinegar
1/4 cup soy sauce
1/2 tsp. dry mustard
unseasoned meat tenderizer

Day before serving: In 13x9x2-inch dish, combine garlic with all ingredients, except tenderizer and steak. Pierce steak in many places with fork and place in marinade.

Cover and refrigerate, turning occasionally.

About 20 minutes before serving: Drain marinade from steak and heat in small pan. Place steak on grill and sprinkle with tenderizer. Grill 6 minutes, basting with marinade. Turn steak and grill about 6 minutes more. Cut steak into thin slices diagonally across grain. Serve leftover marinade over meat. Serves 6.
*Diane Brubaker*

## Steak and Zucchini Supper

1 lb. round steak, cut in thin strips
1 Tbsp. oil
1 10 1/2-oz. can mushroom gravy
1/2 cup water
1/2 envelope (2 Tbsp.) spaghetti sauce mix with mushrooms
3 or 4 medium zucchini, cut in 1 1/2-inch slices

Brown meat strips in oil. Add gravy, water, and spaghetti mix. Stir well. Cover and cook 20 minutes. Add zucchini and cook until tender. Serve over noodles or rice. Serves 4.
*Anita Lynch*

## Mock Sukiyaki

1 lb. round steak, thinly sliced
2 Tbsp. salad oil
1 1/2 cups celery, sliced
1 medium green pepper, sliced
1 large onion, thinly sliced
1 1/2 cups fresh or canned mushrooms, sliced
1/2 cup green onion, sliced
1 10 1/2-oz. can condensed beef broth
1 Tbsp. soy sauce
1/4 cup water
2 Tbsp. cornstarch
4 cups hot rice

Brown meat in oil; add vegetables, beef broth, and soy sauce. Cover and cook over low heat 10 minutes or until vegetables are just tender. Stir often. Combine water and cornstarch. Add to meat mixture. Stir until thickened. Serve over hot rice. Makes 4 to 6 servings.
*Naomi Barton*

## No-Brown Beef Stew

1 lb. beef stew, cubed
1 can cream of mushroom soup
2 or 3 carrots, cut in 2" chunks
1 large potato, quartered
1 medium onion, quartered
chunks of celery, (optional)

Do not brown meat. Combine all ingredients. Bake 4 1/4 to 5 hours in covered casserole at 275°. Makes beautifully browned stew.
*Lois Shirk*

## Stuffed Cabbage Rolls

2 lbs. hamburger
1 large egg
1/2 cup long grain rice, uncooked
2 tsp. salt
1/4 tsp. pepper
1/2 tsp. garlic salt
prepared cabbage leaves*
1 lb. fresh pork spareribs (or ham)
2 16-oz. cans sauerkraut, undrained
2 medium onions, peeled and sliced
1 28-oz. can tomatoes
1 cup water
1 pt. sour cream

Mix beef, unbeaten egg, rice, salt, pepper, and garlic salt. Place about 1/4 cup in center of each cabbage leaf. Fold sides together and roll up. Brown spareribs. Line bottom of large pot with 1/2 the undrained sauerkraut. Cover with onion, spareribs (or ham) and cabbage leaves. Top with remaining sauerkraut, tomatoes, and water. Cover and simmer for 3 hours. Top with sour cream and serve.

*Core head of cabbage and drop into boiling water deep enough to cover. As leaves soften, pull off and cut hard rib out. If center leaves are too small, use 2 for 1 roll.

*Dorothy Gish*

# Veal Entrees
## Veal Scallopini

3 lbs. veal steak, cut 1/4–1/3-inch thick
1/2 cup flour
1 tsp. salt
dash of pepper
2 tsp. paprika
3 Tbsp. fat
1 6-oz. can broiled mushrooms, sliced
white wine
1 8-oz. can seasoned tomato sauce
1/2 cup green pepper, chopped
1 8-oz. pkg. green noodles
Parmesan cheese

Pound meat thoroughly with meat pounder. Cut in serving pieces. Combine flour and seasonings; coat meat in mixture. Brown in hot fat. Place in 13x9x2-inch baking dish. Drain mushrooms, reserving liquid; add wine to mushroom liquid to make 1 cup. Pour liquid over meat. Bake at 350° for 30 minutes. Combine tomato sauce, green pepper, and mushrooms; pour over meat and continue baking for 15 minutes more. Meanwhile, cook noodles until tender in boiling salted water; drain. Baste meat with sauce just before serving. Sprinkle with Parmesan cheese. Serve over hot buttered noodles.

Makes 8 to 9 servings.
Variation:
Use round steak instead of veal.
*Edna Boone*

# Venison Entrees
## Venison Round Steak

4 lbs. round venison steak
flour
oil
2 cans golden mushroom soup
1 can water
1 pkg. dry onion soup mix

Pound steak; then coat with flour. Brown in oil. Add remaining ingredients and bake at 250–300° for 4 to 6 hours or until tender. Works well with beef or moose.
*Linda Thompson*

## Venison Roast

1 4-lb. venison roast
salt and pepper to taste
flour
1/2 cup onion,
  chopped or finely
  sliced
1/2 cup butter
2 cups fresh mush-
  rooms, sliced
1 can cream of mush-
  room soup
3/4 soup can water

Rub salt and pepper into roast; roll in flour and brown on both sides. Place in Dutch oven. Bake 1 hour at 350°. Sauté onions in butter and mushrooms; pour mixture over roast. Add soup and water; cover and finish roasting for 1 to 2 hours until tender.
*Marietta Pegg*

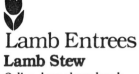

# Lamb Entrees
## Lamb Stew

2 lbs. boneless lamb
  shoulder, cut in
  2-inch cubes
2 Tbsp. fat
2 cups hot water
2 tsp. salt
1/4 tsp. pepper
1 small bay leaf
3 medium carrots, cut
  in 1-inch pieces
1 medium onion, sliced
3 medium potatoes,
  diced
1 cup frozen or fresh
  peas
flour or cornstarch
parsley

Brown meat in hot fat over medium heat in Dutch oven. Add water and seasonings. Simmer, covered, 2 hours, adding more water if needed. Add carrots, onion, and potatoes; cook for 20 minutes. Add peas. Thicken stew with flour or cornstarch and top with parsley.
*Leah Garber*

# Ham Entrees
## Creamed Ham 1

1/2 cup onions, sliced
2 cups ham, cooked
  and cubed
1/4 cup butter
4 Tbsp. flour
2 cups (1 pt.) sour
  cream
1 4-oz. can mush-
  rooms

Sauté onions and ham in butter until onion is tender, not brown. Add flour and then sour cream gradually. Stir in mushrooms. Cook over low heat several minutes until thickened. Serve over steamed rice.
Serves 4.
*Daisy Frantz*

## Creamed Ham 2

1/2 cup onions, diced
3 lbs. ham, cooked and
  cubed
4 Tbsp. butter
2 cans cream of
  chicken soup
1 cup black olives,
  sliced
1 1/2 cups pineapple,
  cubed
1 pt. sour cream

Brown onions in butter. Add remaining ingredients. Heat; serve in patty shells, or over rice or noodles.
*Dorothy Root*

## Ham Towers

1 1/2 cups baked ham,
  cubed
1 medium onion,
  chopped
2 Tbsp. butter or
  margarine
1/2 cup ripe olives,
  sliced
1 can cream of
  chicken soup
1 cup sour cream
1/2 tsp. paprika
1/3 cup slivered
  toasted almonds

Sauté ham, onion, and butter until onion is tender. Combine olives, soup, cream, and paprika. Heat through. Serve over pastry shells or Southern cornmeal rolls. Garnish with almonds.
*Edna Dutter*

## Ham-Asparagus Roll-ups

2 lbs. asparagus, canned or fresh
1/2 cup mayonnaise
1 tsp. bottled steak sauce
1 tsp. instant minced onion
8 slices processed cheese
8 slices cooked ham
8 frankfurter buns

Cook fresh asparagus, covered, in boiling salted water until tender, about 10 to 15 minutes. Drain and chill. Combine mayonnaise, steak sauce, and instant onion. Arrange cheese on ham slices. Spread with mayonnaise mixture. Top with several spears asparagus. Roll up like a jelly roll. Place in frankfurter bun and wrap in foil. Bake at 375° for 10 to 15 minutes until warm. Makes 4 to 8 servings.
Note:
These freeze well. Bake 30 minutes when ready to use.
*Mabel I. Lynch*

## Ham Chow Mein

1/4 cup butter
1 cup onions, chopped
1 tsp. salt
1/8 tsp. pepper
1 cup celery, chopped
1 cup hot water
1 can bean sprouts, drained
1–2 cups ham chunks
2 tsp. soy sauce
1 tsp. sugar
1/3 cup cold water
2 Tbsp. cornstarch
chow mein noodles

Melt butter; add onions and sauté for 5 minutes. Add salt, pepper, celery, and hot water. Cover and cook for 5 minutes. Add bean sprouts and ham. Mix thoroughly and heat to boiling point. Add flavoring and thickening ingredients. Stir lightly and cook for 5 minutes. Serve with chow mein noodles.
Variation:
Substitute shrimp for ham.
*Darleen Layman*

## Hawaiian Ham Supper

2 1/2 cups ham, slivered
1/2 cup green pepper, chopped
2 Tbsp. butter
1 large can pineapple chunks, drained
1 1/3 cups pineapple juice and water (equal parts)
2 Tbsp. vinegar
2 Tbsp. brown sugar
2 Tbsp. cornstarch
1/2 tsp. dry mustard
1/2 tsp. salt
dash of pepper
1 1/3 cups hot water
1/2 tsp. salt
1 1/3 cups fast cooking rice
2 Tbsp. scallions or green onions, chopped

Sauté ham and green pepper in butter until lightly browned. Combine pineapple juice and water with next 6 ingredients. Mix well. Add mixture to ham and cook until sauce is thickened and transparent. Add pineapple chunks. In saucepan, combine hot water with remaining ingredients. Spread ham mixture in a ring around inside of skillet. Pour rice into center of ring. Bring to a boil, cover, and simmer 5 minutes or until rice is soft and fluffy. Serves 4.
Note:
If using conventional rice, cook it separately. Spread ham mixture as directed. Pour cooked rice in center, cover, and simmer gently a few minutes. Avoid burning.
*Rachel Shoup*

# Pork Entrees

## Pork Chops and Apples

6 pork chops
oil
3 or 4 apples, cored and sliced
1/4 cup brown sugar
1/2 tsp. cinnamon
2 Tbsp. butter

Brown chops on all sides in hot fat. Place apple slices in greased baking dish. Sprinkle with sugar and cinnamon; dot with butter. Top with chops, cover, and bake at 350° for 1 1/2 hours. Makes 6 servings.
*Joy Thompson*

## Baked Pork Chops and Vegetables

4 pork chops
2 Tbsp. oil
1 cup green onion, chopped
1 1/2 tsp. salt
1/2 tsp. pepper
1/2 head cabbage, shredded
4 potatoes, sliced
1 can cream of asparagus soup
1/2 cup milk

Brown chops in oil. Toss remaining ingredients, except soup and milk, and put into casserole. Dilute soup with milk and pour over vegetables. Arrange pork chops on top.

## Ham Jambalaya

5 bacon slices, fried and drained
1 1/2 cups long grain rice, uncooked
1 medium onion, chopped
1 green pepper, chopped
1 clove garlic, minced
butter
1 16-oz. can tomatoes, undrained
1 13 3/4-oz. can chicken broth
1/2 tsp. salt
1/2 tsp. thyme
1 bay leaf
2 1/2 cups (1 lb.) ham, cooked and cut up
1/2 lb. shelled shrimp, (optional)

Crumble bacon. Sauté rice, onions, pepper, and garlic in butter until rice is browned. Add tomatoes, broth, and spices. Cover and simmer 15 minutes. Add ham and shrimp. Cook slowly 20 minutes, uncovered, or until rice is tender. Sprinkle with bacon bits.
*Lorraine Grover*
*Mable Lynch*

Cover and bake 1 hour and 15 minutes at 350°. Serves 4.
*Bonnie Jamison*

## Spicy Pork Dinner

1/4 cup flour
1 Tbsp. curry powder
1/4 tsp. pepper
2 tsp. salt
3 lbs. lean pork shoulder, cut in 1 1/2-inch cubes
2 Tbsp. margarine
3 cups chicken bouillon
1 large onion, sliced
1 lb. medium egg noodles
1 cup celery, diagonally sliced
2 medium carrots, sliced
1 6-oz. can mushrooms, broiled and sliced
1 5-oz. can water chestnuts, drained and sliced
1/2 cup seedless raisins

Combine flour, curry powder, pepper, and salt. Coat pork cubes with flour mixture; brown lightly in margarine. Stir in bouillon and half onion slices. Simmer until tender, about 60 minutes. Stir occasionally. Cook noodles as directed on package; drain. Add remaining onion slices and other ingredients to pork. Cover and cook about 15 minutes or until carrots are tender. Serve over noodles.
*Iva Jamison*

## Sweet and Sour Pork

1 1/2 lbs. lean pork
  shoulder, cut in 2x
  1/2-inch strips
fat
1/2 cup water
2 1/2 cups pineapple
  chunks
1/4 cup brown sugar
2 Tbsp. cornstarch
1/4 cup vinegar
2–3 Tbsp. soy sauce
1/2 tsp. salt
1 small green pepper,
  cut in strips
1/4 cup onion, thinly
  sliced

Brown pork in small
amount of hot fat.
Add water, cover, and
simmer (do not boil)
about 1 hour until
tender. Drain pine-
apple, reserving syrup.
Combine sugar and
cornstarch; add pine-
apple syrup, vinegar,
soy sauce, and salt.
Add to pork; cook
and stir until gravy
thickens. Add pine-
apple, green pepper,
and onion. Cook 2 or
3 minutes. Serve over
hot fluffy rice and
pass extra soy sauce.
Serves 7.
*Esther Huffman*

## Barbecued Spareribs 1

Spareribs, cut into
  serving-size pieces
1–1 1/2 cups tomato
  sauce or puree
1 3-oz. can tomato
  paste
1/4 cup chili sauce
1/4 cup vinegar
1/4 cup Worcestershire
  sauce
1 Tbsp. sugar
1 Tbsp. butter
1 medium onion,
  chopped
1/8 tsp. mustard
1/2 tsp. salt and pepper
  (combined)
1/2 tsp. chili powder
1 can mushrooms or
  mushroom soup,
  (optional)
1/2 tsp. Tabasco sauce,
  (optional)
1/2 tsp. oregano,
  (optional)

Brown spareribs in
baking pan at 400°
for 15 to 20 minutes.
In saucepan, mix re-
maining ingredients.
Simmer 20 minutes.
Pour over spareribs.
Bake 1 hour or
longer, basting fre-
quently with sauce.
*Carla Miller*

## Barbecued Spareribs 2
(oven-baked)

5–6 lbs. ribs, rolled in
  flour
1 cup catsup
1 cup tomato sauce
1/2 cup vinegar
2 Tbsp. lemon juice
1/2 cup wine
1 cup water
2 cloves garlic, crushed
2 Tbsp. Worcestershire
  sauce
1 cup brown sugar
1 bay leaf
1/2 tsp. salt
dash of pepper

Place ribs in roaster.
Mix remaining in-
gredients together
and pour over ribs.
Bake at 325° for 2 to
3 hours. Ladle off fat.
Serve with cooked
rice.
*Cora Eller*

## Barbecued Spareribs 3

3–4 lbs. spareribs
1 lemon, thinly sliced
1 large onion, thinly
  sliced

Basting Sauce:
1 cup catsup
1/3 cup Worcestershire
  sauce
1 tsp. chili powder
1 tsp. salt
2 dashes of Tabasco
  sauce
1 1/2 cups water

Salt ribs; place in
shallow roasting pan,
meaty side up. Roast
at 450° about 30
minutes. Drain fat.
Top meat with un-
peeled lemon slices
and onion slices.
Make Basting Sauce:
Combine ingredients
and bring to a boil.
Pour over ribs. Lower
temperature to 350°;
bake until well done,
about 2 hours. Baste
ribs with sauce oc-
casionally. If sauce
gets too thick, add
more water.
Note:
This is also good on
pork chops, steak,
and chicken.
*Phyllis Denlinger*

## Hawaiian Spareribs

2 lbs. spareribs, country-style preferred
2 Tbsp. fat
2 Tbsp. brown sugar
1 Tbsp. cornstarch
1/4 tsp. salt
1/4 cup vinegar
1/4 cup cold water
1/2 cup pineapple juice *or* crushed pineapple
1/2 cup onion, chopped
1/3 cup green pepper, chopped

Cut spareribs into serving pieces. Simmer in boiling salted water about 2 hours or until tender. (Use 1 1/2 tsp. salt per quart of water.) Remove from water and drain well. Brown meat in fat. Combine sugar, cornstarch, salt, vinegar, water, and pineapple juice. Add to ribs and cook, stirring until sauce is transparent. Add onion and green pepper; cook about 5 minutes or until sauce is almost absorbed. Serves 2 to 4.
*Lois Shirk*

## Sweet and Sour Spareribs

lean spareribs or pork chops
salt and pepper to taste
Sauce:
1 cup brown sugar
1 Tbsp. prepared mustard
1/4 cup vinegar
1 cup pineapple juice

Season and roast spareribs in 350° oven for 1 hour. Drain and remove to a second pan. Cook for 3/4 hour, basting with sauce. Make Sauce: Boil first 3 ingredients for 10 minutes; then add pineapple juice. Serve with pieces of fresh pineapple.
*Laurel Balsbaugh*

## Pig Maw (Dutch Goose)

1 pig stomach
1 1/2 lbs. sausage
10 large potatoes, peeled and chopped
3 onions, chopped
1 1/2 Tbsp. salt
1 tsp. pepper

Soak pig stomach in salt water 2 hours. Mix sausage, potatoes, onions, salt, and pepper. Stuff into pig stomach and sew opening shut with needle and thread. Bake in covered casserole at 350° for 3 hours.
*Betty Eller*

# Poultry Entrees

## Chicken Loaf

1 cup spaghetti, broken
1 cup chicken, cooked and diced
1 cup dry bread crumbs
1 cup cheese, grated
3 eggs, slightly beaten
1 1/2 cups warm milk
1/4 cup butter
1/4 cup green pepper, chopped
2 Tbsp. pimiento
1 tsp. salt
1 can cream of mushroom soup

Cook spaghetti in boiling salted water. Drain, rinse with hot water, and drain again. Add remaining ingredients. Bake in greased loaf pan at 325° for 1 hour. Heat soup for sauce.
*Dorothy Gish*

## Pressed Chicken

3–4 lb. fryer, whole or cut up
salt and pepper to taste

Boil chicken until tender over slow heat with enough water to barely cover. Reserve broth. Remove meat from bone and grind through food chopper. Put chicken in mold or dish. Add salt and pepper to hot broth to taste; pour over chicken. Refrigerate to jell. Slice cold for serving.
*Elsie Wolf*

## Baked Chicken 1

2/3 cup sherry wine
2/3 cup water
2 cans cream of
  mushroom soup
24 pieces of chicken
salt and pepper to taste
paprika
dried parsley
rosemary

Mix wine, water, and
soup together; set
aside. Place chicken
in pan with skin side
down. Salt and
pepper lightly.
Sprinkle with paprika
until red; then with
parsley and rosemary.
Turn pieces over, and
season the same way.
Cover with sauce and
baste occasionally.
Bake at 350° for
1 1/2 hours.
*Mary Angle*

## Baked Chicken 2

3 frying chickens,
  cut up
salt and pepper to taste
2 cups tomato juice
oregano or dried
  onion, (optional)
mushrooms, (optional)

Place chicken pieces
in 2 large baking
dishes. Salt and
pepper to taste. Add
tomato juice. Sprinkle
oregano or dried
onion and mush-
rooms over chicken,
if desired. Bake,
covered, at 325° for
1 1/2 hours. Uncover
for last 20 minutes.
*Ethel Rumble*

## Baked Chicken Breasts

6 chicken breasts,
  split
1/4 cup flour
1 1/2 tsp. salt
1/4 tsp. pepper
1/4 cup butter or
  margarine
1 can cream of
  mushroom soup,
  undiluted
1/2 cup water
1/2 cup sour cream
1/2 cup dry white
  wine, (optional)

Dredge chicken in
flour seasoned with
salt and pepper;
brown on all sides in
butter. Place pieces in
13x9x2-inch baking
dish. Mix soup and
water; blend in sour
cream and wine. Pour
mixture over chicken
and cover with foil.
Bake at 375° for 1
hour.
*Frances Kelley*

## Chicken Aloha

1 cup celery, sliced
1 green pepper, cut in
  strips
2 Tbsp. cooking oil
1 1/2 cans cream of
  chicken soup
1 cup (1 can) pine-
  apple tidbits, drained
1/4 cup water
2 Tbsp. soy sauce
2 cups chicken,
  cooked and cubed
1/4 cup slivered
  almonds

In saucepan, cook
celery and green
pepper in hot oil
until tender crisp.
Stir in soup, pine-
apple, water, and soy
sauce. Add chicken;
cook, stirring occa-
sionally, until hot.
Serve over hot cooked
rice. Sprinkle
almonds over each
serving. Serves 6.
*Marianne Bowman
Gwendolyn
Overholtzer*

## Chicken Continental

1/2 cup onions,
  chopped
1 1/2 cups carrots,
  diced
1 cup celery, chopped
1/2 cup margarine or
  butter
4 cups chicken broth
1 cup white rice,
  uncooked
1 1/2 tsp. salt
1/4 tsp. pepper
4 cups chicken,
  cooked and boned

Sauté onions, carrots,
and celery in mar-
garine until tender;
add broth, rice, salt,
and pepper. Cook
slowly 20 to 30
minutes or until rice
is done. Add chicken;
heat until hot.
Serves 8.
*Connie Reece*

## Chicken Diablo

1/4 cup butter, melted
1/2 cup honey
1/4 cup mustard
1 tsp. salt
1 tsp. curry
  powder
1 whole chicken, cut
  up

Combine ingredients,
except chicken. Place
chicken in large bak-
ing dish. Pour sauce
on top. Bake 1 1/2
hours at 300°, turn-
ing often.
*Suzanne Overholtzer
Nina Austin*

## Chicken in White Wine

1/4 cup salad oil
1/2 lb. small onions,
  peeled
1 clove garlic, finely
  chopped
1 3-lb. fryer chicken,
  cut up
2 Tbsp. flour
1 cup dry white wine
1 tsp. salt
1/2 tsp. pepper
1 tsp. thyme
2 Tbsp. parsley,
  chopped
1 3-oz. can mush-
  rooms, sliced and
  drained

Heat salad oil in
heavy skillet. Sauté
onion and garlic
until golden; remove
and set aside. Add
chicken and sauté.
Remove pan from
heat; remove chicken.
Drain all but 2 Tbsp.
fat from pan. Stir in
flour until smooth.
Gradually stir in
wine; add chicken
and all remaining
ingredients. Simmer,
covered, for 30 min-
utes. Serve on warm
platter. Garnish with
extra parsley. Makes
4 servings.
*Linda Lavy*

## Golden Orange Chicken

1 3–4 lb. fryer, cut up
1 egg
1/4 cup orange juice
1 cup bread crumbs
1 tsp. salt
1 Tbsp. orange peel,
  grated
1/2 cup butter

Dry chicken pieces.
Beat egg and juice
slightly. Combine
bread crumbs, salt,
and peel. Dip chicken
pieces first in juice;
then roll in crumbs.
Lay pieces on rack to
dry at least 1/2 hour
(longer is better). Melt
butter in baking pan.
Roll chicken in
butter to coat well.
Bake, skin side down,
30 minutes; then
turn pieces over and
bake 30 to 45
minutes more or
until well done and
brown. If browning
too fast, cover with
foil.
*Daisy Frantz*

## Honeyed Chicken

1 3-lb. fryer, cut up
1 egg yolk
2 Tbsp. butter, melted
2 Tbsp. soy sauce
2 Tbsp. lemon juice
1/2 cup honey
salt and pepper to taste
paprika to taste

Place chicken in shal-
low pan. Mix remain-
ing ingredients and
pour over chicken.
Bake at 325° for 1
hour or until done.
Turn several times
while baking.
*Eunice Peters*

## Chicken 'N Dressing 1

1 chicken, cut up
1 stalk celery, cut up
1 Tbsp. salt
3 peppercorns
Dressing:
1 1/2 cups bread cubes
1/2 tsp. sage
1/8 tsp. pepper
1/2 tsp. salt
1/3 cup butter
1/2 cup onion, minced
1 cup celery, chopped

Simmer chicken,
celery, onion, salt,
and peppercorns in
enough water to
cover until chicken is
tender. Bone chicken
and cut in large
chunks. Arrange in
2-qt. casserole dish.
Prepare *Dressing*.
Combine bread
cubes, sage, pepper,
and salt. Brown but-
ter, onion, and celery;
add to bread mixture.
Spread over chicken.
Prepare *Gravy*.

Gravy:
1/2 cup butter
3/4 cup flour
1 1/2 tsp. salt
1/8 tsp. pepper
4 cups broth
4 egg yolks, beaten

Melt butter in heavy skillet; add flour, seasonings, and broth. Stir until smooth and thick. Mix eggs with a little hot gravy; pour into remaining gravy and cook over medium heat about 3 minutes. Pour over bread cubes. Bake at 375° for 35 minutes. Serves 12.
*Susan Wray*

## Chicken N Dressing 2

1 8-oz. pkg. herb-seasoned stuffing
3 cups chicken, cooked and cubed
1/2 cup butter
1/2 cup flour
1/4 tsp. salt
dash of pepper
4 cups chicken broth
6 eggs, slightly beaten

Prepare stuffing according to package for dry stuffing. Spread in 13x9x2-inch baking dish. Top with layer of chicken. In large saucepan, melt butter. Blend in flour and seasonings. Add cool broth and cook, stirring, until sauce is thickened. Stir small amount of sauce into eggs, and add to sauce. Pour over chicken. Bake at 325° for 40 to 45 minutes. Let stand 5 minutes to set. Cut in squares and serve with *Pimiento Sauce.*

Pimiento Sauce:
1 10 1/2-oz. can cream of mushroom soup
1/4 cup milk
1 cup sour cream
1/4 cup pimientos, chopped

Heat ingredients together.
*Phyllis Flory*

## Parmesan Fried Chicken

2 chickens, cut up and salted
1 cup flour
2 tsp. salt
1/4 tsp. pepper
2 tsp. paprika
2 eggs, slightly beaten
3 Tbsp. milk
1 1/3 cups Parmesan cheese, grated
2/3 cup bread crumbs
2 Tbsp. butter or margarine
2 Tbsp. shortening
1/4 cup butter or margarine, melted

Coat chicken with mixture of flour, salt, pepper, and paprika. Combine eggs and milk. Dip chicken into egg mixture; then roll in mixture of cheese and bread crumbs. In oven, melt butter and shortening in pan. Place chicken in pan. Drizzle with melted butter. Bake 1 hour at 400°.
*Mary D. Miller*

# Game Birds
## Cornish Hens

2 Cornish hens
salt and pepper
garlic salt
2 Tbsp. slivered almonds
2 Tbsp. onion, chopped
3 Tbsp. butter
1 cup water
1/3 cup rice
1 3-oz. can mushrooms
1 5-oz. can water chestnuts
1/2 cup celery, chopped
melted butter

Season Cornish hens inside and out with salt, pepper, and garlic salt. Cook almonds, onion, and butter together. Add water and rice. Cook until rice is fluffy. Stir in mushrooms, water chestnuts, and celery. Stuff hens with rice mixture. brush with melted butter and place in shallow roaster. Add a little water and cover. Bake at 400° for 3 minutes; then lower heat to 350° and bake 1 hour longer or until drumstick twists in socket.
*Phyllis Boyd*

# Seafood Entrees

## Banquet Fish Pie

2 eggs, beaten
1/2 cup milk
1 Tbsp. butter, melted
1/4 cup onion, chopped
2 Tbsp. parsley, minced
3/4 tsp. basil
1/4 tsp. salt
2 cups salmon (1 lb. can) *or* 2 6 1/2-oz. cans tuna
1 stick of pkg. pastry mix *or* pastry crust for 8-inch pie

Combine all ingredients, except fish and crust. Remove skin and bones from salmon and break salmon or tuna into chunks. Stir fish into egg mixture. Pour into well-greased 8" pie plate. Prepare stick of packaged pastry mix according to directions or make your own. Roll dough 1/2-inch thick and cut an 8-inch circle. Then cut circle into 6 wedges and place on top of pie. Bake at 425° for about 25 minutes. Garnish with parsley and lemon wedges. Serve immediately. Pass chilled *Cucumber Sauce* or *Tartar Sauce* to spoon on top of hot wedges. Serves 6.

Cucumber Sauce:
Scoop out seeds from 1 medium sized cucumber (unpeeled). Grate to yield about 1 cup. Drain. Combine with:
1 Tbsp. onion, grated
2 tsp. vinegar
1/2 cup sour cream
dash of pepper
1/4 cup mayonnaise
1 Tbsp. parsley, minced
salt to taste

Blend well and chill. Makes 1 1/2 cups.

Tartar Sauce:
Combine all ingredients thoroughly and chill.
1 cup mayonnaise
1 Tbsp. dill pickle, minced
1 tsp. pimiento, chopped
1 tsp. onion, grated
1 tsp. parsley, minced
dash of Tabasco sauce
*Eunice Grover*

## Salmon Loaf 1

1 16-oz. can salmon
3 cups fine bread crumbs
1 1/2 Tbsp. parsley, chopped
1 Tbsp. lemon juice
1 1/4 tsp. salt
1/2 tsp. celery salt
dash of cayenne pepper
2 Tbsp. onion, grated
3 Tbsp. butter
2 eggs, well beaten
3/4 cup salmon liquid plus milk

Drain and flake salmon, reserving liquid. Mix all ingredients. Shape into a loaf and place in loaf pan. Bake at 350° for 45 minutes or until loaf is firm in center.
*Ruth Bauman*

## Salmon Loaf 2

2 16-oz. cans salmon
1/4 cup onion, finely minced
1/4 cup parsley, chopped
1/4 cup lemon juice
1/2 tsp. salt
1/2 tsp. pepper
1/2 tsp. thyme
2 cups cracker crumbs
1/2 cup milk
4 eggs, beaten
1/4 cup butter, melted

Drain salmon, reserving liquid, and flake in bowl. Add onion, parsley, lemon juice, seasonings, and crumbs, mixing well. Add salmon liquid plus enough milk to make 1 cup; blend in eggs and butter. Mix lightly. Put into 2-qt. loaf pan. Bake at 350° for 1 hour. Serves 8. Pass *Shrimp Sauce.*

Shrimp Sauce:
1/4 cup milk
1 can shrimp soup

Add milk to soup and stir until smooth. Spoon over hot loaf.
*Joan Cardin*

## Salmon Patties

1 can salmon
1 cup cracker crumbs
1 Tbsp. butter, melted
salt and pepper to taste
1 egg, beaten
1/2 cup milk

Combine all ingredients thoroughly. Make patties and fry until well browned on both sides.

*Jeanette Scrivner*

## Versatile Croquettes

3 Tbsp. butter
4 Tbsp. flour
1 cup milk
2 cups meat, cooked and ground*
1 Tbsp. onion, chopped
1 tsp. salt
1/8 tsp. garlic salt
2 eggs, beaten
1 cup corn flake crumbs

Make white sauce of butter, flour, and milk. Add meat and seasonings. Cool thoroughly. Then shape into balls 2 inches in diameter. Dip in beaten eggs; then roll in crumbs. Fry in deep fat 3 to 5 minutes until golden brown. Serve with hot gravy.

*salmon, tuna, pork, beef, or chicken

*Joan Swearingen*

---

*DINNER RECIPE*

*Blend together: One carefully thought-out ahead menu, one genuinely friendly hostess, and one handful of congenial guests.*

*Stir in: Several children trained in good manners and one husband trained in helpfulness.*

*Add: An unhurried, unruffled appearance, flavored with a smile.*

*Mix in: A "So-Glad-To-Have-You" attitude.*

*Sweeten with: Plenty of pleasant conversation.*

*Serve in: A relaxed atmosphere.*

*Results: A warm feeling in the stomach and a warm glow in the heart.*

*Extra Recipes*

Source: _____ Who Likes It: _____

Source: _____ Who Likes It: _____

Source: _____ Who Likes It: _____

*Extra Recipes*

Source: _____ Who Likes It: _____

Source: _____ Who Likes It: _____

Source: _____ Who Likes It: _____

Source: _____   Who Likes It: _____

Source: _____   Who Likes It: _____

Source: _____   Who Likes It: _____

# Vegetable and Cereal Side Dishes

*One must carve*
*one's life*
*out of the wood*
*one has.*
GERMAN PROVERB

*However,*
*Christ has given each of us*
*special abilities—*
*whatever he wants us to have*
*out of his rich storehouse*
*of gifts.*
EPHESIANS 4:7

# Vegetable Side Dishes

## Artichokes

artichokes
4 stalks celery
4 carrots
salt and pepper
paprika
vinegar
oil
garlic

Cover artichokes, celery, and carrots with water. Add other ingredients according to taste. Simmer all day.
*Marilyn Lynch*

## Baked Beans 1

4 slices bacon, cooked and drained
2 Tbsp. bacon drippings
1/2 cup onion, chopped
4 cups (2 16-oz. cans) pork and beans
2 Tbsp. brown sugar
1 tsp. Worcestershire sauce
1 tsp. prepared mustard

Crumble bacon. Sauté onion in reserved drippings until tender, but not brown. Add onion and crumbled bacon into remaining ingredients, mixing well. Pour into 1 1/2-qt. casserole. Bake uncovered at 350° for about 2 hours. Serves 6.
*Dorothy Moore*

## Baked Beans 2

2 16-oz. cans pork and beans
1 cup brown sugar
1 cup catsup
1/2 cup bacon or ham, diced
1 tsp. prepared mustard
1 tsp. liquid smoke
1 whole onion

Put all ingredients in bean pot and bake at 325° several hours.

## Chili Beans

4 cups (2 lbs.) pink beans
boiling water
3 cloves garlic
1 large onion, chopped
3/4 lb. bacon, chopped
1 small can tomato sauce
1 Tbsp. salt
3–4 Tbsp. chili powder
1/2 tsp. cumin

Wash beans thoroughly, removing any imperfect ones. Cover with boiling water, and let stand until the water cools enough to allow lifting the beans out with bare hands. Put into large heavy kettle. Cover with hot water; immediately add other ingredients. Cook slowly 3 hours or more until a rich sauce has formed. Stir as little as possible to avoid mashing beans. Serves 18 or 20.
*Ruth Yost*

## Carrot Ring

2 Tbsp. butter
2 Tbsp. flour
1/2 cup milk
1/2 tsp. salt
2 cups carrots, mashed
4 eggs, separated
1/4 bell pepper, chopped
green onions, chopped

Make a white sauce from butter, flour, and milk; add salt. Beat egg yolks slightly. Add carrots. Beat egg whites and add to carrots, along with green onions and bell pepper. Pour in buttered pan set in pan of water. Bake at 350° for 1 hour.
Note:
This can be baked in a ring mold to look more attractive.
*Gladys Oyler*

## Carrot Pennies

2 lbs. carrots, sliced
1 small onion, sliced
1 small green pepper,
  cut in small strips
Dressing:
1 can tomato soup
1 tsp. Worcestershire
  sauce
1/2 cup salad oil
1 cup sugar
3/4 cup cider vinegar
1 tsp. prepared
  mustard

Boil carrots in salted water until slightly tender. Cool and place in bowl. Mix all dressing ingredients together. Pour dressing over carrots, onions, and peppers. Marinate overnight.
*Ruthanne Wise*

## Corn Custard

1 32-oz. can creamed
  corn
1 cup sugar
1 cup milk
1 egg, beaten
salt and pepper to taste
1 cup cracker crumbs
butter

Combine all ingredients except crumbs and butter; pour in large baking dish. Sprinkle crumbs over top and dot with butter. Bake at 325° until brown.
*Barbara Rumble*

## Corn Spoon

1 1/4 cups milk,
  scalded
2/3 cup cornmeal
3/4 tsp. salt
1 Tbsp. sugar
2 Tbsp. butter
2 cups crushed corn
3 eggs, separated
3/4 tsp. baking
  powder

Stir cornmeal into scalded milk, and cook 3 minutes or until thick like mush. Add salt, sugar, butter, corn, egg yolks, and baking powder. Beat egg whites stiff and fold in. Pour into greased 2-qt. baking dish. Bake at 375° about 35 minutes or until puffy and golden brown. Serves 5 or 6.
*Edith Fox*

## Eggplant Lasagna

1 23 7/8-oz. pkg.
  complete lasagna
  dinner
1 small eggplant,
  thinly sliced
oil
1/2 lb. Mozzarella
  cheese, grated

Cook pasta as package directs and drain. Meanwhile, brown eggplant in 1/2 inch of oil and drain. Spread 2 Tbsp. packaged tomato sauce in bottom of shallow 1 1/2-qt. casserole. Top with 3 lasagna noodles, several slices of eggplant, slices of packaged cheese, 2 Tbsp. sauce; layer 3 noodles across. Repeat until all ingredients are used, ending with remaining sauce and grated cheese. Serves 4.
*Leah Garber*

## Eggplant Casserole 1

2 fresh eggplants
salt
flour
2–3 eggs, well beaten
spaghetti sauce
Parmesan cheese

Slice eggplant into medium thin slices and salt lightly. Let set until juice rises. Pat eggplant dry, dip in flour, and then in beaten eggs. Fry in oil until both sides are lightly browned. Place on paper toweling to absorb grease. In 13x9x2-inch pan, layer eggplant, spaghetti sauce, and Parmesan cheese. Bake at 350° until bubbly.
*Janice Jarboe*

## Eggplant Casserole 2

2 1/2 cups eggplant,
  peeled and cubed
18 soda crackers,
  crumbled
1/2 cup sharp cheese,
  shredded
1/4 cup celery,
  chopped
2 Tbsp. pimiento,
  chopped
1 Tbsp. butter, melted
1/2 tsp. salt
pepper to taste
1 cup cream or
  evaporated milk

Cook eggplant in salted water 10 minutes. Drain. Combine with remaining ingredients and turn into 1-qt. casserole. Bake at 350° for 45 minutes. Serves 6.
*Lois Shirk*

## Green Bean Casserole 1

3 16-oz. cans green beans
3/4 cup milk
1 can cream of mushroom soup
1/8 tsp. pepper
1 3 1/2-oz. can French-fried onions

Drain beans. Combine milk, soup, and pepper; pour over beans. Add 1/2 can onions and pour into 1 1/2-qt. casserole. Bake at 350° for 20 minutes. Garnish with remaining onions; bake 5 minutes longer.
*Virginia Wolf*

## Green Bean Casserole 2

3 10 1/2-oz. cans cream of mushroom soup
1/2 cup milk
1 Tbsp. soy sauce
1/4 tsp. pepper
9 cups French-style beans, cooked, *or* 6 9-oz. pkg. frozen, *or* 6 1-lb. cans, drained
3 3 1/2 oz. cans French-fried onions

Combine soup, milk, soy sauce, and pepper; stir until smooth. Mix in beans and 1 1/2 cans onions.

Spoon into 2 small or 1 large casserole. Bake at 350° for 30 minutes or until bubbling. Top with remaining onions. Bake 5 minutes more. Makes 20 servings, 1/2 cup each.
*Marjorie Bauman*

## Green Corn Tamale Bake

8 or 9 ears of corn
2 tsp. salt
3 Tbsp. butter or margarine, melted
1–1 1/2 cups cornmeal
sharp Cheddar cheese, cut in thin strips
1 4-oz. can green chilies, drained and rinsed

Shuck corn, reserving husks, and cut from cobs. Grind corn, using fine blade, or process in blender until mushy to make 3 cups. Add salt, butter, and enough cornmeal to make a thick mixture. Remove seeds and veins from chilies and cut into strips. Rinse and drain corn husks; then spread flat. Line bottom and sides of greased casserole with husks. Place thin layer of corn mush into dish to hold husks in place. Top with alternate layers of cheese, chilies, and mush. Top with remaining mush, spreading to edges. Fold husks over top, cover with foil, and bake 1 hour

at 350°. Serve hot with barbecued chicken or steaks. Makes 6 servings.
*Kathleen Barnhart*

## Marinated Mushrooms

1 lb. fresh mushrooms, medium sized
3 green onions, thinly sliced
2/3 cup salad oil
4 Tbsp. lemon juice or vinegar
1 tsp. Worcestershire sauce
1/2 tsp. salt
1/8 tsp. pepper
1/2 tsp. dry mustard

Rinse mushrooms and dry. Slice about 1/4-inch thick. In a jar, combine remaining ingredients. Shake very well; then pour over sliced mushrooms. Mix gently. Cover and refrigerate at least 4 hours, shaking or stirring occasionally. Note: Use for salads or alongside meats.
*Daisy Frantz*

## Mushrooms in Sour Cream

1/2 cup onions, minced
1 lb. mushrooms, sliced
1/4 cup butter
1 Tbsp. flour
1/2 cup beef broth
salt and pepper to taste
1/2 tsp. crushed dill seed, *or*
dill weed to taste
1 cup thick sour cream

Sauté onions and sliced mushrooms in butter. When lightly browned, add flour, broth, salt, pepper, and dill. Simmer; then add the sour cream. Heat and serve over toast or scrambled eggs or as a vegetable with roast beef. Serves 4.
*Annie Silvers*

## French-Fried Onions

6 Bermuda onions, cut in 1/4-inch slices
1 cup flour
1/2 tsp. salt
1 tsp. sugar
1/2 cup milk
1 egg, well beaten
1 Tbsp. fat, melted

Cover onion slices with cold water for 1/2 hour. Dry and separate into rings.

Sift dry ingredients. Combine milk and egg; add to dry mixture. Add fat. Dip onion slices in batter and fry at $385°$ until golden.
*Joan Cover*

## Oven Vegetables

6 cups green beans, cooked
1 cup cheese, grated
1 can cream of mushroom soup
2/3 cup canned milk
1 3 1/2-oz. can French-fried onion rings

Place green beans in 2-qt. casserole; sprinkle with grated cheese. Blend mushroom soup with milk and pour over beans and cheese. Bake at $350°$ about 20 minutes. Remove from oven and top with onion rings; bake 8 to 10 minutes longer or until golden brown. Makes 8 or 9 servings.
Variation: Substitute asparagus, peas, or broccoli for beans.
*Wilma Filbrun*

## Cheesy Potatoes 1

2 Tbsp. butter
2 Tbsp. flour
1/4 tsp. salt
dash of pepper
1 cup milk
1 cup (4 oz.) sharp processed American cheese, shredded
1 Tbsp. pimiento, chopped
1 16-oz. pkg. frozen French-fried potatoes

Melt butter over low heat; blend in flour, salt, and pepper. Add milk all at once. Cook quickly, stirring constantly, until thickened and bubbling. Add half the shredded cheese; stir until cheese melts. Add pimiento. Place potatoes in flat 1 1/2-qt. baking dish. Top with cheese sauce. Sprinkle with remaining cheese. Bake, covered, at $350°$ for 15 minutes. Uncover and bake 25 minutes. Serves 4.
*Leah Garber*

## Cheesy Potatoes 2

1/2 cup milk
3 eggs, beaten
1/2 tsp. salt
1/8 tsp. pepper
1 cup sharp cheese, grated
2 Tbsp. butter
1/2 small onion, chopped
3 medium potatoes, grated

Combine all ingredients. Pour into greased 1 1/2-qt. baking dish and bake 35 to 40 minutes at $375°$.
Serves 6.
*Anita Lynch*

## Cheesy Potatoes 3

12 medium potatoes, boiled and skinned
6 Tbsp. butter
2 cups cheese, grated
1 cup milk
1 tsp. salt
2 eggs, beaten

Mash potatoes; add other ingredients,

folding in eggs. Pour into greased 13x9x2-inch pan. Bake at 350° for 30 to 45 minutes. Serves 10.
*Claudia Flory*

## Gourmet Potatoes 1

6 medium potatoes, boiled in skins
2 cups Cheddar cheese, shredded
1/4 cup butter
1 1/2 cups sour cream
1/3 cup green onion, chopped
1 tsp. salt
1/4 tsp. pepper
2 Tbsp. butter
paprika

Cool potatoes. Peel and shred coarsely. In a saucepan over low heat, combine cheese and butter; stir occasionally until cheese is almost melted. Remove from heat and blend in sour cream, onion, salt, and pepper. Fold in potatoes and turn into a greased 2-qt. casserole. Dot with butter and sprinkle with paprika. Bake uncovered at 350° for 30 minutes or until heated through.
*Esther Flora*
*Katherine Wolf*

## Gourmet Potatoes 2

1 qt. potatoes, mashed
1 large carton sour cream
milk
garlic salt to taste
1 8-oz. pkg. cream cheese

chunk of butter
salt and pepper to taste
grated Longhorn cheese

Combine all ingredients, except cheese, and pour into 13x9x2-inch baking dish. Sprinkle cheese on top. Bake 1/2 hour at 350°. Can be frozen.
*Martha Gish*

## Scalloped Potatoes 1

5 cups raw potatoes, peeled
3 Tbsp. butter
1 cup boiling water
1 14 1/2-oz. can evaporated milk
3/4 tsp. salt

Cut potatoes in 1/2-inch cubes. Melt butter in 10-inch skillet. Add potatoes and sauté 3 or 4 minutes. Stir once or twice. Add boiling water and milk. Cook 20 to 30 minutes over low heat. Season as needed.
*Janet Rumble*

## Scalloped Potatoes 2

1 can cream of mushroom *or* cream of celery soup
1 can evaporated milk
4 cups raw potatoes, peeled and thinly sliced
3 Tbsp. butter or margarine
1 Tbsp. onion, minced
salt and pepper to taste

Mix soup and evaporated milk together. Put half the sliced potatoes in buttered 1 1/2-qt. baking dish. Dot with butter; season with onions, salt, and pepper. Pour soup and milk mixture over potatoes. Layer last half of potatoes. Repeat seasoning process. Cover and bake at 350° for 45 minutes. Uncover and continue baking 30 minutes or until potatoes are tender.
*Nancy Bowman*

## Scalloped Potatoes 3

1 can cream of mush-
  room soup *or* cream
  of chicken soup
1/2–3/4 cup milk
dash of pepper
dash of paprika
4 cups raw potatoes,
  sliced
1 small onion,
  thinly sliced
1 Tbsp. butter

Combine soup, milk,
pepper, and paprika.
Layer potatoes,
onions, and soup
mixture in baking
dish, ending with
soup mixture. Dot
with butter. Bake,
covered, at 375° for
1 1/2 hours. Uncover,
sprinkle with cheese,
and bake 15 minutes
longer. Doubled
recipe fills a 13x9x2-
inch casserole.
*Nelda Driver*

## Scalloped Potatoes 4

1/2 cup butter or
  margarine
1 cup flour
6 Tbsp. salt
1 tsp. onion salt
1 tsp. pepper
3–4 qts. milk, heated
16 qts. potatoes,
  peeled and sliced
water

1 lb. processed cheese
  *or* Tillamook, if
  preferred
1 small can diced
  pimiento, (optional)

Make a thin white
sauce by melting
butter and adding
flour, salt, onion salt,
and pepper; stir until
smooth. Then slowly
add heated milk, stir-
ring constantly until
thickened. Add cheese
and stir until melted.
Bring potatoes and
water to a boil in
large pot; drain. Alter-
nately layer potatoes
and white sauce in
roaster. Sprinkle
pimiento over pota-
toes. Cover and bake
at 350° for 1 hour or
until potatoes are
tender. To keep pota-
toes hot for serving,
set control at 150°
Serves 75.
Note:
Use of an electric
roaster is recom-
mended.
*Mary Heinrich*

## Spinach Loaf

2 1/2 lbs. fresh
  spinach *or*
  2 12-oz. pkgs. frozen
  spinach
3 Tbsp. butter
1 Tbsp. onion,
  chopped
3 Tbsp. flour
1/2 cup milk
1/2 cup cream
3 eggs, separated
1/2 tsp. paprika
1 tsp. salt
1/2 tsp. nutmeg
3 hard-boiled eggs,
  peeled

Cook spinach in
water until stems are
tender. Chop fine.
Melt butter in skillet.
Add onion and cook
until soft and yellow.
Blend in flour. Stir in
milk and cream
slowly. Beat egg yolks.
When sauce is bub-
bling, add chopped
spinach; reduce heat
and stir in beaten
yolks. Cook, stirring 1
minute to thicken.
Season spinach with
seasonings. Beat egg
whites stiff and fold
lightly into spinach.
Pour into greased
9x5x2 1/2-inch pan.
Slice hard-boiled eggs
and push into center.
Set in pan of water
and bake at 325° for
40 minutes.
*Anna Miller*

## Squash Casserole 1

1 lb. yellow squash
1 lb. zucchini squash
1 medium onion,
  grated
2 Tbsp. oil
2 Tbsp. parsley flakes
salt and pepper to taste
1/4 tsp. or less oregano
3 eggs, beaten
1 cup cracker crumbs
1 cup Cheddar cheese,
  grated

Cook squash and
onion together. Add
remaining ingre-
dients. Pour in a
1 1/2-qt. baking dish
and bake at 350° for
3/4 hour or until
done.
*Marilyn Lynch*

## Squash Casserole 2

4 cups squash, cooked and mashed
1 onion, chopped
1/2 pepper, ground
oil
1/2 cup parsley, chopped
4 eggs, beaten
2/3 cup oil
1 cup hamburger, (optional)
1 cup cracker crumbs
dash of cayenne pepper
grated cheese

Sauté onion and pepper in oil. Combine all ingredients. Pour into 1 1/2-qt. baking dish. Bake 1 hour at 325°. Cover with grated cheese last 10 minutes.
Note:
If including hamburger, use only 1/2 cup oil.
*Mary Heinrich*

## Squash Casserole 3

1 1/2 qts. squash, cooked
8 slices white bread, cubed
4 eggs, beaten
1 cup milk
1 tsp. onion flakes
3/4 lb. Longhorn cheese, grated
salt and pepper to taste
grated processed cheese

Mix all ingredients together and place in 1 1/2-qt. baking dish. Bake 1 hour at 325°. Top with cheese before removing from oven. One and one-half recipes fill a 13x9x2-inch casserole.
*Suzanne Layman*

## Scalloped Squash

3 lbs. squash, parcooked and drained
2 eggs, beaten
16 crackers, crumbled
1 1/2 cups cheese, grated
1/3 cup bacon bits, (optional)

Slice and season squash. Place in a 13x9x2-inch baking dish. Mix together remaining ingredients and pour over squash. Top with extra cheese. Bake at 350° for 30 minutes.
*Ann Crawmer*

## Squash Combo

1/4 cup butter or margarine
zucchini squash
yellow summer squash
1 large onion, sliced
1 large tomato, peeled and cubed
salt and garlic powder to taste, (optional)

Put butter in bottom of skillet. Slice squash into skillet. Add onion, tomato, and optional seasonings. Steam slowly, stirring occasionally, until tender. A little water may be added to speed cooking.
Note:
Adjust amounts of squash according to preference.
*Wilma Filbrun*

## Sweet Potatoes 1

2 1/2 lbs. sweet potatoes or yams
2 grapefruits, peeled
2 Tbsp. butter, melted
1 egg, slightly beaten
3/4 tsp. salt
5 Tbsp. brown sugar
1/8 tsp. ground allspice

Cook potatoes until tender; peel. Put into bowl and beat until smooth. Section grapefruit; save 2 Tbsp. juice. Grate peel to yield 2 teaspoons. Add peel, juice, 3 Tbsp. of brown sugar, and remaining ingredients to the potatoes. Beat until thoroughly blended. Put into buttered 1 1/2-qt. baking dish; sprinkle remaining 2 Tbsp. sugar over top. Bake at 350° for 30 minutes.
*Martha Reece*

## Sweet Potatoes 2

sweet potatoes or yams
1 cup sugar
1 cup brown sugar
4 Tbsp. cornstarch
2 cups pineapple juice
1/2 cup butter
salt to taste

Cook potatoes in salt water; cook, skin, and slice crosswise. Put into 13x9x2-inch baking dish. Mix remaining ingredients in saucepan and boil together. Pour over potatoes. Bake at 375° for 30 minutes.
Serves 12.
*Martha Blom*
*Gladys Oyler*

## Zucchini Casserole 1

5 medium-sized zucchini, cut into 1/2-inch pieces
1/4 cup sour cream
1 Tbsp. butter
1 Tbsp. cheese, grated
salt
dash of paprika
1 egg, beaten
1 Tbsp. onion or chives, finely chopped
bread or corn flake crumbs
shredded cheese

Simmer zucchini 6 to 8 minutes; drain thoroughly. Place in 1 1/2-qt. casserole.

Combine sour cream, butter, cheese, salt, and paprika; stir over low heat until cheese melts. Stir egg and onion into sour cream mixture. Pour over zucchini. Top with crumbs; dot with butter and sprinkle shredded cheese over all. Brown in 350° oven until topping is well browned.
*Flossie Rumble*

## Zucchini Casserole 2

6 medium zucchini, quartered lengthwise
salt to taste
garlic salt to taste
pinch of oregano
coarse pepper to taste
3 ripe tomatoes
2 onions, peeled and sliced
sliced cheese
bacon slices, cooked and drained

Place zucchini in shallow 13x9x2-inch baking dish. Sprinkle with seasonings. Slice tomatoes and place over squash. Season tomatoes as for zucchini. Layer onions and season same as before. Place a layer of cheese slices over onion and top with a layer of bacon. Bake, uncovered, at 350° for 45 minutes.
*Nancy Bowman*

## Zucchini Casserole 3

2 lbs. zucchini
1/2 tsp. salt
1 medium onion, chopped
1 clove garlic, minced
1 Tbsp. butter
3 slices fresh bread, cut up
2 tsp. fresh parsley, minced
1 cup Cheddar cheese, grated
4 eggs, beaten
1/2 tsp. Worcestershire sauce
dash of Tabasco sauce
1 tsp. salt
1/2 tsp. paprika
1/2 tsp. pepper

Cook squash in small amount of water and salt until tender. Drain and mash. Cook onions and garlic in butter. Now combine *all* ingredients. Pour into 1 1/2-qt. baking dish and set in pan of water while baking. Bake at 350° for 30 minutes or until set. Serves 8.
*Martha Blom*

## Stuffed Zucchini

6 medium-sized zucchini, washed
3 cups soft bread crumbs
1/2 cup Parmesan cheese, grated
1 small onion, minced
3 Tbsp. parsley, minced
1 tsp. salt
1 tsp. pepper
2 eggs, beaten
2 Tbsp. butter

Cut ends off zucchini, but do not pare. Cook in boiling salt water

5 minutes. Halve lengthwise; remove pulp with spoon. Combine with all ingredients except butter. Fill squash shells and dot with butter; sprinkle with more cheese. Bake at 350 °for 25 to 30 minutes. Serves 6.
Note:
Can be frozen prior to baking. Allow extra time in oven.
*Clara Selby*

# Rice
# Side Dishes

## Cheese-Almond Rice

1 can mushrooms, sliced
2 tsp. onions, chopped
1/3 cup almonds, chopped or sliced
1 cup (1/4 lb.) Cheddar cheese, shredded
1 1/4 cups long grain rice, uncooked
1/8 tsp. pepper
3 1/2 cups beef bouillon and water
4 tsp. soy sauce
salt to taste
parsley, (optional)
pimiento, (optional)
Combine mushrooms, onions, almonds, cheese, rice, and pepper. Put into greased 2-qt. casserole. Heat bouillon to simmering point; add soy sauce and pour over ingredients in casserole. Cover and bake at 375° for 45 minutes to 1

hour, until liquid is absorbed. Add parsley and pimiento after baking, if desired. Makes 6 to 8 servings.
*Phyllis Denlinger*

## Fried Rice 1

4 cups rice, cooked and cold
3 Tbsp. oil
1 Tbsp. soy sauce
1 cup mushrooms, sliced
2 Tbsp. green onion, minced
1 tsp. ground ginger
2 eggs
slivered almonds, (optional)

Lightly brown rice in oil. Stir constantly. Add remaining ingredients, except eggs and almonds; cook 3 minutes. Then break in eggs and keep stirring until eggs are set. Slivered almonds may be added. Serve plain or garnished with chopped green onion and diced cold ham or chicken.
*Maralee Oyler*

## Fried Rice 2

2 Tbsp. oil
1 cup white rice, uncooked
1 envelope onion soup mix
2 1/2 cups water
1 Tbsp. soy sauce
2 eggs, beaten
Sauté rice in oil until golden. Add soup mix, water, and soy sauce. Simmer 20 minutes. Make a hole in center and quickly stir in eggs until set. Serves 4 to 6.
*Anita Lynch*

## Rice Vermicelli

1/2 cup vermicelli, crumbled
2 Tbsp. butter
2 cups water
1/2 tsp. salt
1 cup rice

Melt butter in top half of double boiler placed directly over flame. Add crumbled vermicelli and brown lightly in melted butter. Then add water and salt; bring to a boil. Slowly add rice. When water returns to boil, cover and place over lower half of double boiler filled with boiling water. Cook 25 minutes. Serves 4 to 5.
Note:
This dish may be cooked ahead of time and reheated before serving since rice will not become gummy.
*Mary Lou King*

## Pilaf

1/4 cup butter
3/4 cup onion, chopped
1 cup celery, chopped
1 cup converted raw rice
1 envelope chicken and noodle soup
1/4 tsp. pepper
1/2 tsp. sage
1 tsp. salt
2-2 1/2 cups water

Sauté butter, onion, celery, and rice until brown. Stir in remaining ingredients, cover, and simmer about 15 minutes. Remove from heat and let stand for 10 minutes.

Note:
Reheat with extra seasoning for another meal.

*Marie Haney*
*Ruth Wise*

## Rice and Vegetable Bake

3 cups fluffy cooked rice (1 cup uncooked)
1 10-oz. pkg. frozen chopped broccoli, *or* spinach, thawed
1 egg
2 tsp. instant minced onion
1 Tbsp. Worcestershire sauce
1 1/4 tsp. salt
1 1/2 cups milk
2 Tbsp. butter or margarine, melted
1/2 cup Cheddar cheese, grated
paprika

Heat and drain green vegetable; combine with rice. Mix egg, onion, Worcestershire sauce, salt, and milk. Stir into rice-vegetable mixture. Pour into a greased 2-qt. casserole. Top with melted butter and cheese. Sprinkle with paprika. Bake at 325° for 30–40 minutes. Serve with meat and salad. Serves 6.

*Dorla Shuman*

---

*LIFE'S RECIPE*

*1 cup good thoughts*
*1 cup kind deeds*
*1 cup consideration for others*
*2 cups sacrifice for others*
*3 cups forgiveness*
*2 cups well-beaten faults*

*Mix all ingredients thoroughly. Add tears of joy, sorrow, and sympathy for others. Fold in 4 cups of prayer and faith to lighten the other ingredients and to raise the texture to great heights of Christian living. After pouring all this into your daily life, bake well with a smile. Lasts forever.*

Source: _____ Who Likes It: _____

Source: _____ Who Likes It: _____

Source: _____ Who Likes It: _____

_____

_____

_____

_____

_____

_____

_____

_____

_____

Source: _____     Who Likes It: _____

_____

_____

_____

_____

_____

_____

_____

_____

_____

Source: _____     Who Likes It: _____

_____

_____

_____

_____

_____

_____

_____

_____

Source: _____     Who Likes It: _____

# Top
# of the
# Sauces

*Put your hand*
*in your conscience*
*and see if*
*it does not come out*
*as black as pitch.*
PENNSYLVANIA DUTCH SAYING

*If we confess our sins,*
*he is faithful and just*
*and will forgive us our sins*
*and purify us*
*from all unrighteousness.*
I JOHN 1:9 (NIV)

# Entree Sauces:

## Barbecue Sauce 1

1 cup catsup
1 cup tomato paste
1/4 cup vinegar
3 Tbsp. Worcestershire sauce
1 cup water
1 tsp. liquid smoke
juice of 2 lemons
1 1/2 tsp. garlic powder
1/2 tsp. chili powder
1/4 tsp. allspice
1 1/2 tsp. black pepper
1/4 cup sugar

Mix all ingredients together with egg beater. Let stand several hours before using. Will thicken a little as it sets. Brush or pour over meat.
*Jan Wolf*

## Barbecue Sauce 2

1/4 cup butter
1/2 cup hot water
1/3 cup lemon juice
1 tsp. salt
1/2 tsp. pepper
1 medium onion, chopped
1 Tbsp. Worcestershire sauce
1 cup tomato puree or catsup
1 Tbsp. paprika
1 tsp. sugar

Mix all ingredients in pan and heat to boiling. Remove from heat. Yields enough to baste 2 chickens.
*Phyllis Denlinger*

## Barbecue Sauce 3

1 medium onion, chopped
1 Tbsp. bacon fat
1 tsp. salt
1/2 tsp. pepper
2 Tbsp. brown sugar
2 Tbsp. flour
2 Tbsp. prepared mustard
1 cup catsup
1/2 tsp. cloves
2 Tbsp. Worcestershire sauce
1/2 cup sugar
1/2 cup vinegar
1/2 cup water

Sauté onion in bacon fat until tender. Add remaining ingredients and simmer 20 minutes. Makes 2 cups. Delicious on steaks, ribs, or chicken.
*Connie Reece*

## Barbecue Sauce 4

2 Tbsp. butter
2 onions, chopped
1/2 cup catsup
3/4 cup water
1/4 cup vinegar
1/8 tsp. pepper
1/8 tsp. paprika
1 tsp. mustard

1 tsp. brown sugar

Brown onion in butter. Add remaining ingredients. Simmer 1/2 hour.
Variation:
Pour over hot dogs in small casserole dish and bake at 350° for 20 to 25 minutes. *Or* use as a dipping sauce for cut-up hot dogs pierced with toothpicks.
*Nancy Bowman*

## Catsup

4 qts. tomatoes
1/2 cup mixed spices
3 Tbsp. salt
1 tsp. red pepper
1 cup onions, chopped
2 cups vinegar
2 cups sugar

Peel tomatoes, cut up, and cook 10 minutes. Cool and put through food mill; discard seeds. Tie spices in a cheesecloth bag. Add spice bag, salt, pepper, and onion to tomato pulp. Boil until thick; then add vinegar and sugar. Boil until water does not separate. Seal in hot sterilized pint jars.
Note:
Tomatoes are actually *fruits* and were once called "Love Apples."
*Edith Fox*

## Chili Sauce

15 lbs. tomatoes, peeled and drained
3 cups bell peppers, chopped
5 onions, peeled and chopped
4 1/2 cups sugar
3 pts. vinegar
1/2 cup salt
3 tsp. cloves
3 tsp. cinnamon
2 tsp. nutmeg
2 tsp. allspice
1 Tbsp. chili powder
6 chili peppers

Combine all ingredients together, keeping spices together in cheesecloth bag. Boil for 3 hours, stirring often. Pour into hot sterilized pint jars and seal.
*Wilma Filbrun*

## Cranberry Applesauce

2 large cans applesauce
1 can jellied cranberry sauce
1 cup sugar
1 tsp. red coloring

Combine ingredients. Heat enough to dissolve sugar and melt cranberry sauce. Use egg beater to blend slightly. Serve with pork or poultry.
*Myrtle Landes*

## Italian Spaghetti Sauce

1/2 cup butter
3 Tbsp. garlic, chopped fine
1 medium onion, chopped fine
1 lb. hamburger
2 cups mushrooms, sliced
2 cans condensed consommé
2 cans tomato sauce
2 cans tomato soup
1 Tbsp. Italian seasoning

Sauté garlic and onions in butter until tender, but not brown. Add ground beef and mushrooms and sauté until meat is brown. Then add consommé, tomato sauce, tomato soup, and seasoning. Cover and simmer 30 minutes to blend flavors.
*Janice Root*
*Nancy Layman*

## Pizza Sauce

3 cans tomato puree
1 hunk of Cheddar cheese (about 1/2–3/4 cup)
dash of black pepper
dash of vinegar
1 tsp. salt
1 tsp. oregano
1 tsp. sugar

Combine and cook down. Use immediately or freeze.
*Janice Root*

## Sweet 'N Sour Sauce

1 tsp. salt
1/8 tsp. pepper
1 large onion, sliced
2 Tbsp. soy sauce

1/2 cup water
1/4 cup vinegar
1/2 cup brown sugar
meat of choice

Combine all ingredients. Put meat and sauce into pressure cooker for 1/2 hour to 45 minutes.
Note:
Sauce is very tasty on short ribs.
*Joyce Miller*

# Dessert Sauces

## Butterscotch Sauce

2 cups brown sugar
1/2 cup light corn syrup
1/2 cup water
evaporated milk

Bring sugar, syrup, and water to a boil; cook for about 10 minutes until thick. Let cool 10 to 15 minutes. Thin to desired consistency with evaporated milk. Makes 1 pint.
*Juanita Grover*

## Caramel Sauce

1 cup brown sugar
3 Tbsp. margarine
1/4 cup cream
2 Tbsp. light corn syrup
nuts, chopped

Boil ingredients for 3 minutes and pour over ice cream or cake.
*Margaret Root*

### Chocolate Sauce 1

2 cups sugar
1/2 cup light corn
  syrup
3 Tbsp. cocoa
1/2 cup water
evaporated milk

Bring ingredients, except milk, to a boil and cook for about 10 minutes until thick. Let cool 10 to 15 minutes. Thin to desired consistency with evaporated milk. Makes 1 pint.
*Juanita Grover*

### Chocolate Sauce 2

1 cup boiling water
4 Tbsp. cocoa
2 Tbsp. butter
1 1/2 cups sugar
1 tsp. vanilla

Bring water to a boil; then add cocoa. Add butter to melt; then add sugar. Boil for 5 to 10 minutes until smooth and thick. Then add vanilla. Makes 1 pint.
*Janice Root*

### Chocolate Sauce 3

1/3 cup cocoa
1 cup sugar
1 cup hot water
1 Tbsp. cornstarch
pinch of salt
1 tsp. vanilla
1 Tbsp. butter

Blend all ingredients in saucepan; cook 8 minutes.
*Dorothy Moore*

*THE SAUCE OF LIFE*

*1 cup friendship*
*1 cup thoughtfulness*
*1 cup faith*
*1 cup hope*
*1 cup charity*

*Mix the above in a tremendous bowl of loyalty. Then add:*

*1 Tbsp. of gaiety that sings*
*1 Tbsp. of ability to laugh at little things*

*Slowly blend in tears of heartfelt sympathy. Pour over a good-natured soul and serve warm.*
*Anonymous*

# Out of the Crock Condiments

*Everyman must*
*carry his own hide*
*to the tanner.*
PENNSYLVANIA GERMAN SAYING

*And so we keep on*
*praying for you*
*that our God*
*will make you*
*the kind of children*
*he wants to have . . .*
*rewarding your faith*
*with his power.*
2 THESSALONIANS 1:11

# Fruits in a Jar

## Apple Butter 1

9 gallons snits
(dried apples)
6 gallons water
1/2 gallon vinegar
20 lbs. sugar
1 gallon light corn
syrup

Grind apples. Place apples and water in kettle; heat to boiling and immediately add vinegar, sugar, and corn syrup. Boil about 3 hours or until mixture adheres well to spoon. Pour into hot, sterilized jars and seal at once. Makes 6 gallons.
*Alice Mae Haney*

## Apple Butter 2

8 cups applesauce
5 cups sugar
1/2 cup vinegar
1/2 cup red hot
candies

Combine ingredients and cook in large pan for 20 minutes or until red hots dissolve. Add cinnamon for flavor. Cool and refrigerate.
*Jane Rumble*

## Canned Thompson Grapes

Pick off Thompson grapes, wash, and pack them in jars. Fill with water and seal. Process 20 minutes. Good for salads.
*Verna Kinzie*

## Grape Butter

1 lb. Concord grapes, washed
1 lb. sugar

Crush Concord grapes. Add sugar; bring to a hard boil and cook for 30 minutes. Put through sieve to remove seeds; seal in hot, sterilized jars.
*Jane Layman*

## Flowering Plum Jelly-Jam

4 cups juice and pulp from red leaf flowering plums*
6 1/2 cups sugar
1/2 bottle fruit pectin

Measure plum juice and pulp into a large saucepan. Add sugar and mix well. Bring to a boil and stir in pectin. Bring to a full rolling boil and boil 1 minute, stirring constantly. Remove from heat; skim and pour into glasses. Yields about 10 glasses of jam.
*Cook about 4 pounds of plums in 1 cup water until tender. Put all through a colander to remove pits and skin.
*Edith L. Deeter*

## Strawberry Preserves

2 cups strawberries, washed and hulled
boiling water
4 cups sugar

Pour boiling water over prepared berries; cool 1 minute. Drain off. Put 2 cups sugar over berries; stir to mix and boil 3 minutes. Add remaining 2 cups sugar and boil 3 minutes. Pour into hot, sterilized jars. Seal at once.
*Eunice Grover*

## Pectin Syrup
(for freezing fruit)
3 1/3 cups water
1 pkg. powdered
 pectin
1 1/4 cups sugar

Mix water and pectin in pan. Bring to a boil and boil hard 1 minute, stirring constantly. Remove from heat and add sugar. Stir until sugar is dissolved. Cover and chill.
To use:
Slice fresh ripe fruit, such as strawberries, apricots, or peaches, into freezer containers, leaving about 3/4" from top. Cover fruit with cold syrup. Put on lid and freeze.
Note:
Fruit frozen by this method keeps well. The color is still bright and clear after a year's storage. It's easy on the sugar, too.
*Clara Belle Barton*

# Canned and Pickled Vegetables
## Chili Beans
red beans
1 tsp. salt
2 tsp. sugar
2 tsp. chili powder
1/2 tsp. garlic powder

Use 1 cup red beans per quart jar. Place beans into jars and fill with water. Soak overnight. Next morning, add other ingredients, per quart. Seal. Cook in hot water bath for 3 hours.
*Margaret Miller*

## Quick Pickled Beets
4 cans beets
2 cups sugar
2 cups water or beet
 juice
2 cups vinegar
1 tsp. allspice
1 tsp. cinnamon
1 tsp. cloves

Mix all ingredients, except beets, in saucepan; boil until sugar dissolves. Pour over beets and let stand 1/2 hour in refrigerator.
*Ivalyn Gish*
*Phyllis Denlinger*

## Bread and Butter Pickles 1
1 gallon cucumbers, sliced
4 large onions, chopped
1/2 cup salt

Syrup:
5 cups sugar
1 1/2 tsp. turmeric
1/2 tsp. ground cloves
2 Tbsp. mustard seed
1 tsp. celery seed
5 cups vinegar

Mix vegetables and salt; let stand 3 hours. Drain vegetables. Combine syrup ingredients; pour over vegetables. Let set 1/2 hour; drain, reserving syrup. Scald syrup; add vegetables. Heat through, but not to boiling. Pour into sterilized jars. Seal at once.
*Joan Cover*

## Bread and Butter Pickles 2
5 qts. cucumbers, sliced paper thin
2 large white onions, sliced
2 green peppers, ground or chopped
1/2 cup ice cream salt

Syrup:
6 cups sugar
1 Tbsp. turmeric powder
1 Tbsp. white mustard seed
1 tsp. celery salt
5 cups white vinegar

Mix vegetables and salt; let stand 3 hours, stirring occasionally. Drain and rinse well. Combine syrup ingredients; heat until scalding hot. Stir to dissolve sugar. Add vegetables; mix well. Heat through, but do not boil. Process in pint jars.
*Joan Benedict*

## Bread and Butter Pickles 3

2 gallons cucumbers, sliced
1 cup salt
2 qts. onions, sliced
cauliflower flowerets
carrot sticks, 1 1/2-inches long
celery 1 1/2-inches long
Optionals:
red and green peppers
1 jar small whole onions
1 can yellow wax beans, drained and rinsed
1 can kidney beans, drained and rinsed
1 can yellow corn, drained and rinsed
1 can garbanzo beans, drained and rinsed
Syrup:
3 pts. vinegar
6 cups sugar
1 tsp. turmeric powder
1 tsp. whole cloves
4 tsp. whole mustard seed
3 tsp. celery seed

Combine cucumbers and salt; let stand overnight. Drain and rinse; add sliced onions. Bring syrup ingredients to a boil. Add cucumbers and onions; cook several minutes. Drain, reserving syrup. Cook cauliflower, carrots, and celery in separate pans until crisp tender; drain and keep in ice water until ready to use. Place cucumbers, onions, cauliflower, carrots, and celery, along with any optional vegetables, in large baking dish. Bring syrup to a boil and pour over vegetables. Place in 350° oven and heat mixture to boiling point. Spoon vegetables and syrup into hot sterilized jars. Seal at once.
*Ethel Rumble*

## Dill Pickles 1

cucumbers
1/4 tsp. alum
2 cloves garlic
2–3 clusters fresh dill
Brine:
1 1/4 cups vinegar
2 1/2 cups water
1/4 cup pickling salt
1 cluster fresh dill

Wash cucumbers and pack into sterilized jars. Add alum, garlic, and dill as listed per quart jar. Combine brine ingredients and bring to a boil. Pour into packed jars; let stand overnight. Drain brine and reheat it to boiling. Pour into packed jars and seal. Let stand several weeks before opening.
Note:
Add one grape leaf in the bottom of each jar, if desired.
*Diane Brubaker*

## Dill Pickles 2

cucumbers
1–2 cloves garlic
1 tsp. pickling spice*
dill weed (head and stem)
Brine:
1 cup pickling salt
2 qts. vinegar
2 qts. water
1 tsp. powdered alum

123

Pack sterilized jars with cucumbers, garlic, spice, and dill. Combine brine ingredients and bring to a boil. Pour into packed jars. Place hot lids on jars and seal. Cure 2–4 weeks before eating.
*red pepper may be removed.
*Dovella Boyd*

## Lime Pickles

2 gallons water
2 1/2 cups lime
7 lbs. cucumbers, sliced
Syrup:
6 cups (3 pts.) vinegar
8 cups (4 lbs.) sugar
2 Tbsp. salt
2 Tbsp. celery seed
1 Tbsp. mustard seed
1/3 box cinnamon sticks
1 tsp. green food coloring

Blend water and lime together. Pour over cucumbers; let stand 24 hours. Drain cucumbers and rinse. Cover them with cold water or ice water and soak 12 hours. Mix syrup and bring to a boil. Add cucumbers. Boil slowly 30 to 40 minutes. Seal in quart or pint jars.
*Kathryn Jarboe*

## Old-Fashioned Pickles

4 qts. cucumbers,
  sliced 1/2 inch or less
4 cups vinegar
3 Tbsp. salt
1 Tbsp. mustard seed
1/4 cup sugar
Syrup:
3 1/2 cups vinegar
5 3/4 cups sugar
2 1/4 Tbsp. celery seed
1 Tbsp. whole allspice

Put cucumbers, vinegar, salt, mustard seed, and sugar in pan. Boil about 10 minutes in covered pan. Stir occasionally. Drain and pack pickles in hot sterilized jars. Combine syrup ingredients; boil and pour over pickles. Seal. Makes 4-5 quarts.
*Louise Root*

## Sweet Chunk Pickles

1 gallon cucumbers,
  cut in 1-inch chunks
1/2 cup salt
boiling water
3 cups sugar
3 cups vinegar
1 cup water
1 tsp. dry mustard
1 tsp. mustard seed
1 tsp. celery seed
1/2 tsp. turmeric
1 tsp. allspice

Combine cucumbers and salt; cover with boiling water. Let stand overnight and drain. Combine sugar, vinegar, water, and spices. Bring to a boil and add pickles. Reheat to boiling point; then pack into sterilized jars and seal. Makes 4 quarts.
*Martha Cover*

## Pickled Okra

small okra pods,
  washed
1 pod hot red pepper
1 garlic clove
1 Tbsp. mustard seed
1/2 tsp. powdered
  alum
3 cups white vinegar
1 cup water
6 Tbsp. salt

Pack okra pods into sterilized pint jars. Add next 4 ingredients. Combine vinegar, water, and salt to make a brine. Boil and pour over okra. Seal. Let set 4 to 6 weeks before opening. Jars may not seal, but okra will still keep.
*Suzie Beckner*

## Pickled Olives

green olives
7 Tbsp. lye
water
13 Tbsp. salt

Make lye solution using 4 Tbsp. lye to 1 gallon of water. Pour over olives; let stand 24 hours. Stir often; drain and rinse. Make second solution using 2 Tbsp. lye to 1 gallon of water; let stand 48 hours. Stir often; drain and rinse. Then make third solution using 1 Tbsp. lye to 1 gallon water; let stand 24 hours. Drain and rinse. Now make salt solution using 1 Tbsp. salt to 1 gallon of water; let stand 24 hours. Stir often; drain and rinse. Make second salt solution using 3 Tbsp. salt to 1 gallon of water; let stand 24 hours. Stir often; drain and rinse. Then make third salt solution using 4 Tbsp. salt to 1 gallon of water; let stand 24 hours. Stir often. Drain. Finally, make fourth salt solution using 5 Tbsp. salt to 1 gallon water, adjusting amount of salt to make olives tasty. Keep refrigerated.
*Ethel Rumble*

## Stuffed Peppers

8 green bell peppers
2 cups salt
1 gallon water
Pickling Solution:
2 cups water
8 cups vinegar
1 Tbsp. celery seed
1 cup sugar
1 Tbsp. whole mustard seed
1 Tbsp. salt

Pepper Stuffing:
1 medium cabbage,
  grated or shredded
2 Tbsp. celery seed

Cut tops off peppers, keeping them whole, and clean out the insides. Place peppers and tops in large crock or stone jar; cover with brine made of salt and water. Be sure peppers are completely covered. Allow to stand 4 days; then pour off brine and wash in cold water. Next, soak peppers overnight in alum water (1 1/2 Tbsp. alum to 1 gallon water) to make them crisp.

Make *Pickling Solution:* Heat ingredients to a scald. Cool. Combine cabbage and celery seed. Stuff peppers and place in crock or stone jar; they must be *stacked,* not packed. Pour cooled pickling solution over peppers, covering them completely. Put waxed paper and lid on crock. Peppers will be ready to use in 24 hours and will keep indefinitely in a cool place.
*Mary Heinrich*

## Pickled Vegetables 1

1 gallon water
1/2 gallon vinegar
1/2 cup salt
1/2 cup sugar

Boil water, vinegar, salt, and sugar. Cool and pour over choice of washed and sliced vegetables:

green tomatoes
carrots
cauliflower
cucumbers
celery
onions
bell peppers

Add spices, dill, and garlic. Three-fourths of this recipe makes 2 gallons of vegetables. Refrigerate.
*Esther Gish*

## Pickled Vegetables 2

6 large green tomatoes
12 large green sweet peppers
6 large red sweet peppers
6 medium onions
3 cups celery
3 cups cauliflower
boiling water
5 cups sugar
5 cups vinegar
1/3 cup salt
2 Tbsp. white mustard seed

Cut all vegetables into bite-sized pieces. Cover with boiling water for 30 minutes in tightly covered container. Pour into a colander and drain well. Put vegetables in sterilized jars; drain any excess liquid. Heat sugar, vinegar, salt, and mustard seed to boiling. Pour boiling mixture into filled jars and seal.
*Kathryn Mohler*

# Relishes
COOKED

## Corn Relish

12 ears corn, cut into kernels
1 head cabbage, cut fine

2 red peppers
2 yellow peppers
2 green peppers
1 stalk celery
1 tsp. celery seed
2 oz. ground mustard seed
2 cups sugar
3 pts. vinegar

Boil corn 5 minutes. Chop vegetables fine. Combine all ingredients and boil 20 minutes. Refrigerate covered.
*Myrtle Landes*

## Late Summer Relish

1 qt. green tomatoes, chopped
1 qt. (about 7) sweet red peppers, chopped
1 qt. mild onions, chopped
hot green peppers, (optional)
1 qt. cabbage, chopped or shredded
1 qt. vinegar
4 cups sugar
1/2 cup salt

Grind vegetables. Combine all ingredients and boil gently until tender, about 1 hour. Seal in hot sterilized jars. Makes about 8 pints.
*Mildred Moore*

## Pepper Relish 1

12 green peppers
12 red peppers
12 medium onions
1 1/2 pts. vinegar
3 cups sugar
3 Tbsp. salt

Grind vegetables and pour boiling water over. Let stand 15 minutes. Drain well. Combine syrup ingredients in saucepan. Add vegetables. Boil a few minutes; pour into hot sterilized jars and seal. Makes 6 or 7 pints.
*Lillie Dunlop*

## Pepper Relish 2

24 bell peppers, green or red*
12 onions
boiling water
1 rounded Tbsp. mixed pickling spice
1 qt. mild vinegar
2 cups sugar
3 Tbsp. salt

Seed peppers, peel onions, and put both through coarse food grinder. Cover with boiling water and drain. Cover with cold water, heat to boiling, and drain. Place spices in cheesecloth bag, and combine with vinegar, sugar, and salt. Add to vegetables and cook 5 to 7 minutes. Adjust sugar and salt as desired. Seal mixture in hot sterilized pint or quart jars. Makes 6 or 7 pints.
Note:
Remove tiny red peppers from spice mix for a milder taste.
Alternate Method:
Use blender and fill to about 2/3 with vegetables. Cover with water and process to coarseness desired.
*or any combination of the two
*Mary Heinrich*

## Zucchini Relish

2 qts. zucchini, coarsely grated
4 large onions, finely ground
2 large bell peppers, finely chopped*
1 medium head cabbage, coarsely grated
1/4 cup salt
water
2 1/4 cups sugar
1/4 tsp. whole cloves
1 tsp. turmeric
1 tsp. dry mustard
2 1/2 cups vinegar
1 tsp. celery seed
1 tsp. mustard seed

Combine vegetables in large bowl; sprinkle with salt. Add enough water to cover; let stand 4 hours or overnight. Boil remaining ingredients until sugar dissolves. Pour over drained mixture. Bring syrup to a scald; remove mixture and place in sterilized jars. Bring syrup to a boil and pour into filled jars. Seal at once.
*red and green for color
*Martha Cover*

# Relishes
UNCOOKED

## Apple Relish

2 large (3 small) red apples, cored and cubed
1 large dill pickle, chopped
1 medium onion, finely chopped
1/3 cup sugar
1/4 cup cider vinegar

Combine apples, pickle, and onion. Combine sugar and vinegar, mixing until sugar dissolves. Toss with chopped mixture. Chill at least 1 hour before serving. Good with pork roast.
Note:
Adjust degree of sweetness to taste.
*Joan Swearingen*

## Chili Relish

2 gallons tomatoes, peeled and chopped
6 green peppers, chopped fine
10 medium onions, chopped fine
1 or 2 cups celery, cut fine
1 1/2 cups salt
3 1/2 lbs. light brown sugar
3 pts. vinegar
1/2 cup mustard seed
4 sticks cinnamon, crushed

Combine prepared vegetables in large bowl and refrigerate. Twelve hours later, add salt and mix well. Place in cheesecloth and let drain 12 hours in sink. Dissolve remaining ingredients, and combine with vegetables. Store in the refrigerator. Keeps for a year.
*Gladys Beachler*

## Fresh Tomato Relish

1 cup (2 medium) tomatoes, coarsely chopped
1/2 cup onion, chopped
1/2 cup green pepper, chopped
2 Tbsp. vinegar
1 tsp. sugar
1/2 tsp. salt
1/2 tsp. celery seed
dash of pepper

Combine tomatoes, onion, and green pepper. Stir together vinegar, sugar, salt, celery seed, and pepper. Stir into tomato mixture; chill thoroughly. Drain well before serving. Makes 2 cups.
Note:
Great with roast pork, beef, or chicken.
*Virginia Trussel*

---

*PRESERVED CHILDREN*

*1/2 dozen children*
*2 or 3 small dogs*
*1 large grassy field*
*colorful flowers*
*a pinch of brook*
*small pebbles*
*a deep blue sky*
*a hot sun*

*Mix children and dogs together. Put them in the field, stirring constantly. Sprinkle the field with flowers. Sprinkle brook over pebbles. Spread over all a cloudless blue sky. Bake in hot sun. When thoroughly browned, remove and let cool in a nicely rounded bathtub.*

# Extra Recipes

_____
_____
_____
_____
_____
_____
_____
_____

Source: _____  Who Likes It: _____

_____
_____
_____
_____
_____
_____
_____
_____

Source: _____  Who Likes It: _____

_____
_____
_____
_____
_____
_____
_____
_____

Source: _____  Who Likes It: _____

# Bread Raisings and Other Slices of Life

*Many a man
lives by the sweat
of his frau.*
ANONYMOUS

*Man does not live
by bread alone,
but on every word
that comes from
the mouth of God.*
MATTHEW 4:4 (NIV)

# Yeast Breads

## Best-Ever White Bread

2 cups milk
2 Tbsp. sugar
2 tsp. salt
1 Tbsp. shortening
1 pkg. yeast
1/4 cup warm water
6–6 1/2 cups flour, sifted

Scald milk. Stir in sugar, salt, and shortening. Cool to lukewarm. Sprinkle yeast in warm water; stir to dissolve. Add yeast and 3 cups flour to milk mixture. Beat with spoon until batter is smooth and sheets off spoon. *Or* beat with electric mixer at medium speed until smooth, about 2 minutes, scraping bowl occasionally. Add enough remaining flour, a little at a time, first by spoon and then by hand, to make dough that leaves the sides of the bowl. Turn dough over to grease top. Cover and let rise in warm place until doubled, about 1 1/2 hours. Punch down, cover, and let rise again until almost doubled, about 45 minutes. Turn onto board and shape into ball. Divide in half. Shape in 2 greased 9x5x3-inch loaf pans. Cover and let rise until doubled, about 1 hour. Bake at 400° for 35 minutes or until tops are golden brown. Cool on racks. Double recipe for 4 loaves.
*Donna Switzer*

## Braided Bread

2 cups milk
1/4 cup sugar
1 Tbsp. salt
1/3 cup shortening
2 pkgs. dry yeast
1/4 cup warm water
3 eggs
7–7 1/2 cups flour
melted butter

Heat milk to boiling point. Pour into mixing bowl; add sugar, salt, and shortening. Cool to lukewarm. Soften yeast in warm water; add to milk mixture. Add 3 cups flour and beat well. Add eggs and beat thoroughly. Stir in remaining flour. When dough begins to leave sides of pan, turn out on floured board and knead until smooth and satiny. Place in greased bowl and cover. Let rise in warm place until doubled.

When doubled, divide into 3 parts; divide each third into 3 portions. Roll each portion into a rope about 14" long on a greased cookie sheet; make an "x" with 2 of the ropes in center of the sheet. Place the third rope across top braid from center to ends on both sides. Seal and tuck ends under. Brush with melted butter. Let rise until doubled. Place in loaf pans or make buns. Brush with egg whites, if desired. Bake at 350° for 35 to 40 minutes.
*Verna Kinzie*

# 132
BREAD
RAISINGS
AND OTHER
SLICES
OF LIFE

## Braided Sesame Seed Bread

1/2 cup warm water
2 pkgs. dry yeast
1 3/4 cups warm water
3 Tbsp. sugar
1 Tbsp. salt
2 Tbsp. shortening, softened
7 cups flour
1 egg, beaten
sesame seeds

Combine water and yeast in mixing bowl. Add remaining ingredients, stirring to dissolve. Knead a few minutes. Let rise 1 hour. Punch down and let rise again. Divide in 1/2; then divide each 1/2 into 3 portions. Make long pieces and braid into a loaf. Place on long cookie sheet. Brush dough with beaten egg for glaze, and sprinkle sesame seeds on while dough is damp with egg. Let rise. Bake 20 to 25 minutes or until done at 350°. Makes two loaves.
*Marietta Pegg*

## Honey Bread

3 1/2 cups milk
1/3 cup honey
1/3 cup peanut oil
2 Tbsp. salt
4 pkgs. dry yeast
1 cup warm water
4 cups whole wheat flour
4 1/2 cups white flour

Scald milk and cool. Add honey, oil, and salt. Soak dry yeast in warm water and add to milk mixture. Add 4 cups of warmed whole wheat flour* and stir into yeast mixture. Let set 45 minutes; then mix in white flour. Add a little white flour to bottom of pan and knead well. Let stand 10 to 15 minutes and knead again. Let rise about 1 hour and put into loaf pans. Let rise until doubled in size. Bake 15 minutes at 350°, then 25 minutes at reduced heat.
Note:
Use more whole wheat or all white flour.
*Heat flour in 200° oven for 5 minutes, stirring. Let cool until just slightly warm.
*Kathryn Jarboe*

## Cottage Onion Loaf

2 pkgs. dry yeast
1 cup warm water
1 cup creamed cottage cheese, well drained
2 Tbsp. butter or margarine
2 eggs, well beaten
1/2 cup onion, finely chopped
2 Tbsp. sugar
2 Tbsp. dill seed
1 Tbsp. salt
2 tsp. baking soda
1 cup wheat germ
3 1/2 cups flour*

Soften yeast in warm water. Heat cottage cheese and butter until lukewarm. Combine cheese mixture, eggs, onion, sugar, dill seed, salt, and baking soda. Mix well. Stir in softened yeast. Add wheat germ and flour gradually to make stiff dough. Beat well. Cover and let rise in warm place until doubled in size. Stir down. Knead on lightly floured board about 1 minute. Pat evenly into well greased loaf pan. Bake at 350° until well done and nicely browned, 50 to 60 minutes, depending on size of pan.
*May use all flour and no wheat germ.
*Pearl Howser*

## Dilly Bread

1 pkg. dry yeast
1/4 cup warm water
1 cup creamed cottage cheese, heated to lukewarm
1 Tbsp. butter or margarine
2 tsp. dill seed
1 egg, unbeaten
1 tsp. salt
1/4 tsp. baking soda
2 Tbsp. sugar
1 Tbsp. instant onion flakes
2 1/4–2 1/2 cups flour

Soften yeast in water. Combine all remaining ingredients except flour. Add flour to form a stiff dough, beating well after each addition. Cover and let rise in warm place until light and doubled in size, 50 to 60 minutes. Stir down dough; turn into well-greased 8-inch round pan, 1 1/2-qt. casserole, or 1 loaf pan. Let rise 30 to 40 minutes. Bake at 350° for 40 to 45 minutes until golden brown. Brush with soft butter and sprinkle with salt.

*Ethel Rumble*
*Joan Cover*
*Eva Landes*

## French Bread

1 1/4 cups warm water
1 pkg. yeast
1 1/2 tsp. salt
1 Tbsp. shortening
1 Tbsp. sugar
3 1/2 cups flour
egg white, (optional)
sesame or poppy
  seeds, (optional)

Dissolve yeast in warm water; then add remaining ingredients. Knead a few times, then cover, and let rise 40 minutes. Work down and shape into loaf on cookie sheet. Let rise 30 minutes. Slash after it has risen a little. Brushing with egg white and sprinkling with sesame or poppy seed are optional. Bake at 375°

for 25 minutes. Turn off oven and let set 10 minutes in oven.
*Fanny Beachler*
*Joan Howser*

## Whole Wheat Bread 1

1 pkg. dry yeast
1 cup lukewarm water
1 tsp. sugar
3 cups milk, scalded
4 tsp. salt
1/2 cup brown sugar
5 cups white flour
5 cups whole wheat
  flour
1/4 cup shortening,
  melted

Soften yeast in lukewarm water with sugar. Stir to blend. Combine hot milk, salt, and brown sugar. Cool to lukewarm and add to yeast. Add 2 cups white flour and 2 cups whole wheat flour. Beat thoroughly. Stir in shortening. Add remaining white flour; stir in rest of whole wheat flour. Knead on floured board until smooth. Let rise until doubled in bulk. Bake at 400° for 10 minutes; then at 375° until done.
*Freda Beachler*

## Whole Wheat Bread 2

1 Tbsp. yeast
2 3/4 cups warm
  water*
1/2 cup brown sugar
1 Tbsp. salt
1/4 cup salad oil
3 cups whole wheat
  flour
4–6 cups white flour

Dissolve yeast in 1/4 cup warm water; set aside. In mixing bowl, put remaining warm water, sugar, salt, and oil. Add wheat flour, 1 cup of white flour, and yeast mixture. Mix thoroughly; then add more white flour, a cup at a time (about 3 to 5 cups) to make dough easy to handle. Turn dough onto lightly floured board and knead until smooth and elastic, 8 to 10 minutes. Place in greased bowl; grease top also. Cover and let rise in warm place until doubled in bulk, about 1 hour. Punch down and let set 10 minutes. Shape into 2 loaves and put into greased bread pans. Cover and let rise until doubled. Bake 35 minutes at 375°.
*Water should feel warm on the inside of your wrist.

*Lorraine Grover*

# 134
BREAD
RAISINGS
AND OTHER
SLICES
OF LIFE

## Whole Wheat Bread 3

2 cups milk, scalded
6 Tbsp. shortening
1 Tbsp. salt
3/4 cup brown sugar
1 egg, beaten
1 cake yeast
1/2 cup warm water
2 cups whole wheat
  flour
4 cups white flour

Let scalded milk cool slightly; add shortening, salt, and brown sugar. Stir until well blended. When lukewarm, add egg, yeast (dissolved in warm water), whole wheat flour, and white flour. Stir until all flour has been moistened. Let rest for 5 minutes. Knead bread for 10 minutes on well floured board; let rise until doubled in bulk. Punch down. Let rise again; then form into 2 loaves. Let rise again 20-30 minutes. Bake at 375° for 50 to 60 minutes.
*Lillie Dunlop*

## Whole Wheat Bread 4

1 3/4 cups milk,
  scalded
2 tsp. salt
1/3 cup olive oil
1/2 cup water
1/3 cup honey
2 eggs
2 pkgs. yeast
5 cups whole wheat
  flour
2 cups white flour

Let scalded milk cool slightly. Add salt, oil, honey, water, eggs, and yeast. Mix well. Sift flours and add to mixture (enough to make dough consistency of cake). Let set for 15 minutes. Sift and add more flour until too thick to stir with spoon. Knead for 10 to 20 minutes. Let rise until doubled, 45 minutes. Divide into 2 pieces and shape into loaves. Place in buttered loaf pans. Cover and let rise until doubled. Place in oven and set oven at 350°. Do not preheat for better rising. Bake for 1 hour.
*Barbara Fall*

## Cinnamon Bread

2 pkgs. yeast
1 cup warm water
1 Tbsp. honey
1 cup milk, scalded
1/3 cup butter
1/2 cup sugar
1 tsp. salt
1 cup potatoes,
  mashed
3 eggs, slightly beaten
about 8 cups flour,
  sifted
1 tsp. baking powder
1/3 cup butter
1 1/2 cups brown
  sugar
1 tsp. cinnamon

Mix yeast, water, and honey together. Cool scalded milk to lukewarm. Add butter, sugar, and salt to milk. Add yeast mixture; then add potatoes, eggs, flour, and baking powder. Let dough rise until doubled. Divide into thirds; roll out in oblong shape. Spread with butter. Cut into 2-inch thick slices; then flatten each slice to 1-inch thickness. Place upright in greased loaf pans. Bake 40 to 50 minutes at 350°.
*Denise Metzger*

## Potato Bread

1 cake yeast
1/2 cup lukewarm
  water
1/2 cup shortening
1/2 cup sugar
2 eggs
1 cup milk, scalded
1 tsp. salt
1 cup potatoes,
  mashed
2 cups graham flour
white flour

Dissolve yeast in water. Combine other ingredients except flour. When potato mixture cools, add yeast mixture. Add graham flour and enough white flour to knead well. Let rise until doubled in size. Form into loaves or rolls and bake at 375° for 15 minutes or until done.
*Mary E. Davison*

## Pizza Dough

1 cup lukewarm water
1 pkg. yeast
1 tsp. salt
1/2 cup plus 1 Tbsp. oil
2 tsp. sugar
flour
cornmeal

Combine ingredients, except flour and 1 Tbsp. oil; mix well. Add flour to form dough. Add 1 Tbsp. salad oil on top. Let set 45 minutes. Let rise until 3 times its size. Knead down and let rise 3 times its size again. Roll out in pan sprinkled with cornmeal.
Note:
Frozen bread works well for dough. Just let it thaw and spread on pan. After fixing dough, grease with salad oil before putting sauce on.
*Janice Root*

# Yeast Dinner Rolls

## Southern Cornmeal Rolls

1 cup cornmeal
1 1/2 cups boiling water
1/2 cup milk
1/2 cup butter or margarine
4 1/4–5 cups flour
1/4 cup sugar
2 tsp. salt
2 pkgs. active dry yeast
1 egg

In large mixing bowl, combine cornmeal and boiling water; stir until thoroughly mixed. Add milk and butter. Stir until butter is softened. Add 2 cups flour, sugar, salt, dry yeast, and egg. Blend at lowest speed until moistened; beat 3 minutes at medium speed. By hand, stir in remaining flour to form stiff dough. Knead on well floured surface until smooth and no longer sticky, about 3 minutes. Place in greased bowl, turning to grease top. Cover and let rise in warm place until light and doubled in size, about 30 minutes. Bake at 400° for 15 to 18 minutes until golden brown.
*Edna Dutter*

## Light Rolls

2 cakes yeast
2 cups warm water
1 cup sugar
1/4 cup shortening
1 1/2 tsp. salt
1 egg, beaten
6 cups white flour
1 cup whole wheat flour
1 cup coarse wheat flour

# 135

Mix first 6 ingredients together, using only 1/2 cup sugar. Set aside 10 minutes. Add remaining ingredients and let rise 1 hour or more until light. Then put in muffin pan and let rise until light. Bake 30 minutes at 350°.
*Ida Garber*

## Quick Rolls

3 Tbsp. sugar
1 tsp. salt
1/2 tsp. baking soda
1/2 cup shortening
1 1/2 cups buttermilk, lukewarm
2 pkgs. yeast, dissolved in 1/4 cup warm water
4 1/2 cups flour

Mix sugar, salt, baking soda, and shortening. Add buttermilk and dissolved yeast. Add flour gradually. Knead until smooth. Let stand 10 minutes. Shape into rolls and let rise. Bake 25 to 30 minutes at 350°.
*Eva R. Landes*

# 136
BREAD
RAISINGS
AND OTHER
SLICES
OF LIFE

## Quick Croissants

1 pkg. yeast
1 cup warm water
3/4 cup evaporated
   milk
1 1/2 tsp. salt
1/3 cup sugar
1 egg
5 cups flour, unsifted
1/4 cup butter or
   margarine, melted
   and cooled
1 cup firm butter or
   margarine, at refrig-
   erator temperature
1 egg, beaten with 1
   Tbsp. water

In a bowl, let yeast soften in water. Add milk, salt, sugar, egg, and 1 cup of the flour. Beat to make a smooth batter and blend in melted butter; set aside. In a large bowl, cut firm butter into remaining 4 cups flour until butter particles are the size of dried kidney beans. Pour yeast batter over top and carefully turn the mixture over with spatula to blend just until all flour is moistened. Cover with clear plastic and refrigerate until well chilled, at least 4 hours or up to 4 days. Remove dough to a floured board;

press into a compact ball. Knead about 6 turns to release air bubbles. Divide dough into 4 equal parts. Shape 1 part at a time, leaving remaining dough in refrigerator. To shape croissants, roll 1 part of the dough on a floured board into a circle 17 inches in diameter. Using a sharp knife, cut the circle into 8 equal pie-shaped wedges. For each croissant, loosely roll wedges toward the point. Shape each roll into a crescent and place on an ungreased bak-ing sheet with the point down. Allow at least 1 1/2 inches of space around each croissant. Cover light-ly and let rise at room temperature in a draft-free place. When almost doubled after about 2 hours, brush with egg and water mixture. Bake at 325° for about 35 minutes. Makes 32.
*Betty King*

## No-Knead Rolls

1 cup boiling water
1/4 cup shortening
1 1/4 tsp. salt
2 Tbsp. sugar
1 cake yeast, dissolved
   in 1/4 cup lukewarm
   water
1 egg, beaten
flour to make stiff
   dough

Add boiling water to shortening, salt, and sugar. When luke-warm, add yeast and egg. Mix well. Add enough flour to make a stiff dough, and beat well. Place in greased bowl and chill 2 to 24 hours. Pinch off dough and fill muffin pans 1/2 full. Top with melted butter and let rise 2 hours. Bake 15 min-utes or until golden brown at 375°.
*Ethel Rumble*

## Overnight Refrigerator Rolls

2 pkgs. dry yeast
2 1/2 cups warm
   water
3/4 cup soft shorten-
   ing or oil
2 eggs, well beaten
3/4 cup sugar
8–8 1/2 cups flour
2 1/2 tsp. salt

Soften yeast in warm water. Add shorten-ing, eggs, sugar, 4 cups flour, and salt. Stir and beat until smooth. Stir in remaining flour to make soft dough. Cover tightly and put in refrigerator. Divide in 3 portions and turn onto floured board. Shape as de-sired. Place on cookie sheet; bake 20–35 minutes, depending on size, at 350°.
Note:
This may be used for dinner rolls, coffee cakes, tea rings, cinnamon rolls, or raised doughnuts.
*Annie Bowman*

## Refrigerator Rolls

1 cup milk
1 pkg. dry yeast
1 cup lukewarm water
1 egg, beaten
1 tsp. salt
1/2 cup sugar
4 Tbsp. shortening, melted
6 cups flour

Heat milk to lukewarm. Dissolve yeast in warm water. Combine and add egg, salt, sugar, and shortening. Mix well. Add half of flour and beat until smooth. Gradually add rest of flour and knead until smooth. Put dough in greased bowl. Let dough double in size; punch down. Turn over, cover, and place in refrigerator until ready to use for hamburger buns, plain rolls, or cinnamon rolls. Bake 20–25 minutes at 350°.

*Iva Jamison*
*Mary Jane Root*

## Butter Rolls

1 Tbsp. sugar
1 pkg. yeast
1/4 cup warm water
3 eggs, beaten
1/2 cup sugar
1 tsp. salt
1/2 cup shortening or butter, melted and cooled
1 cup lukewarm water
5 cups flour

Dissolve sugar and yeast in 1/4 cup water. Add remaining ingredients. Let rise until doubled (or let rise in refrigerator overnight). Divide in 2 parts and roll out. Spread with butter and cut in pie-shaped wedges. Roll up, starting at wide end. Let rise and bake at 350°-400° for 10 to 15 minutes.
*Carolyn Miller*

## Variation Dough

2 pkgs. yeast, dissolved in 1 cup warm water
1/2 cup shortening
1/2 cup sugar
1 Tbsp. salt
3 1/2 cups milk, scalded and cooled
12 cups flour or enough for stiff dough

Combine flour, sugar, and salt. Cut in shortening. Add yeast and milk, mixing well. Knead until smooth. Let rise and knead down once; then shape into dinner rolls. Bake rolls until light brown at 350° for 15 to 20 minutes. Cool; serve or freeze. Thaw, if frozen, and heat in warm oven.
*Deanna Davison*

# Yeast Treats

## Cinnamon Rolls

1 1/2 cups milk, scalded
2 pkgs. yeast
1/2 cup warm water
1/2 cup sugar
1 1/2 tsp. salt
2 eggs
1/2 cup shortening
6 1/2-7 1/2 cups flour
4 Tbsp. butter, melted
1 cup sugar
4 tsp. cinnamon

Cool scalded milk to lukewarm. Dissolve yeast in warm water; add sugar, salt, eggs, shortening, and milk. Then add 3 cups flour and beat until smooth. Add enough flour to handle dough. Let rise until doubled. Then knead to get air bubbles out. Let rise and roll out dough to make rolls. Add butter, sugar, and cinnamon. Roll tightly and cut into 1 to 1 1/2-inch rolls. Place in baking pans to rise. Shortly before rolls are to be baked, make *Topping*:

Topping:
1/2 cup butter
1 cup brown sugar
3 Tbsp. corn syrup
1/2-1 cup walnut meats

Heat until well blended and pour over rolls. Bake at 350° for about 20 to 25 minutes or until light brown.
*Susan Young*

## Cinnamon Horns

1 pkg. dry yeast
1/4 cup warm water
2 cups flour, sifted
1/2 cup butter
1 Tbsp. shortening
dash of salt
2 eggs, beaten
1/4 cup sugar
2 tsp. cinnamon
nuts
raisins

Combine yeast and water, stirring until dissolved; set aside. Mix flour, butter, shortening, and salt as for a piecrust. Add eggs and yeast mixture; mix well. Refrigerate at least 2 hours. Divide dough into 3 parts. Roll each part out into a circle on waxed paper covered with the sugar and cinnamon. Spread with nuts and raisins. Cut into 8 pie wedges and roll, starting from wide end up to point. Place on greased cookie sheets and let rise 1 hour. Bake at 400° for 15 to 20 minutes.
*Joyce Peters*

## Rich Rolls

1 cup milk
1/2 cup butter or shortening
1/2 cup sugar
1 1/2 tsp. salt
2 pkgs. yeast
1/2 cup warm water
5 cups (or more) flour
2 eggs, well beaten

Bring milk to a boil; add shortening, sugar, and salt. Cool to lukewarm. Sprinkle yeast over warm water. After 5 minutes or so, stir and mix with warm milk, beaten eggs, and about 1/2 of the flour. Mix well with mixer. Work in flour to a soft dough. Turn out on floured board and knead about 10 minutes or until smooth and satiny. Place in greased bowl; grease top of dough. Cover with cloth and let rise until doubled in bulk. Work down and let rise again. The more you let the dough rise and work it down, the better it is. Shape as desired and let rise until doubled in bulk. Bake at 375° for about 15 to 20 minutes.
Variation:
Mix in 1 tsp. cinnamon and nuts, if desired.
*Annie Bowman*

## Caramel Pecan Rolls

1 pkg. active dry yeast
1 cup warm water
1/4 cup sugar
1 tsp. salt
2 Tbsp. margarine, softened
1 egg
3 1/4–3 1/2 cups flour
1/3 cup margarine, melted
1/2 cup brown sugar, packed
1 Tbsp. corn syrup
2/3 cup pecan halves
1/2 cup sugar
2 tsp. cinnamon

In mixing bowl, dissolve yeast in warm water (105° to 115°). Stir in sugar, salt, 2 Tbsp. margarine, egg, and 2 cups of flour. Beat until smooth. With spoon or hand, work in enough remaining flour until dough is easy to handle. Place greased side up in greased bowl; cover tightly. Refrigerate overnight or up to 4 to 5 days. Combine melted margarine, brown sugar, corn syrup, and pecan halves. Pour into greased oblong pan. Combine 1/2 cup sugar and cinnamon. On floured board, roll dough into 15x9-inch oblong. Spread with melted margarine and sprinkle with sugar-cinnamon mixture. Roll up tightly, beginning at wide side. Seal edge well. Cut into 1-inch slices and place in prepared pan. Cover and let rise in warm place, 85° until doubled, about 1 1/2 hours. Heat oven to 375°. Bake 25 to 30

minutes. Immediately remove from oven and invert on large plate.
*Mildred E. Miller*

## Honey Nut Crescents

1 box hot roll mix or bread dough
6 Tbsp. butter, melted
1 cup sugar
3 tsp. cinnamon

Prepare hot roll mix or bread dough and when dough has doubled in bulk, divide in half. Roll each in an 8-inch circle. Spread with butter, sugar, and cinnamon. Cut each circle in 8 pie-shaped pieces. Roll from outside in and place point side down in greased pan. Cover and let rise 1 hour. Brush with melted butter and bake at 350°. After 10 minutes of baking, remove and spread with *Honey-Nut Topping.* Bake 10 minutes longer.

Honey Nut Topping:
1/4 cup honey
1/3 cup sugar
1/4 cup nuts, chopped
3 Tbsp. butter
1/8 tsp. cinnamon

Combine all in saucepan; bring to boiling point only. Remove and let cool slightly.
*Mary Gish*

## Jam Triangles

1 pkg. yeast
1/4 cup warm water
3 cups flour
1 Tbsp. sugar
1 tsp. grated lemon rind
1/2 tsp. salt
1 cup butter
1/3 cup milk
jam, 1 or more of your choice

Dissolve yeast in the warm water; set aside. Combine flour, sugar, lemon rind, and salt. Cut in butter until mixture is crumbly. Add yeast and milk; mix well. Cover and let rise until doubled. Turn onto floured board. Roll 1/4-inch thick into an 18x12-inch rectangle. Cut into 3-inch squares. Spoon a heaping tsp. of jam in the center of each square. Fold each square over, corner to corner, to form a triangle. Press edges together firmly. Place on baking sheet. Bake at 375° until lightly brown, 18 to 20 minutes. Sprinkle with powdered sugar while warm. Makes 2 dozen. Serves 15 to 18.
*Susan Wray*

## Crispy Cookie Coffee Cake

1 pkg. dry yeast
1/4 cup warm water
4 cups flour
1 tsp. salt
1/4 cup sugar
1 cup margarine
2 eggs, beaten

1 cup warm milk
Filling:
1 cup sugar
1 tsp. cinnamon

Dissolve yeast in warm water; set aside. In a large bowl, combine flour, salt, and 1/4 cup sugar. Cut in margarine. Combine yeast mixture, eggs, and milk; add slowly to flour mixture. Cover and refrigerate 2 hours or overnight. Divide dough in half and roll each piece out to 18x12-inch rectangle.

Combine *Filling* ingredients; sprinkle half on each rectangle of dough. Roll and cut into 1-inch pieces. Place on greased cookie sheet and mash lightly with palm of hand. Bake at 350° for 12 to 15 minutes. Make *Quick Icing.*

Quick Icing:
Moisten powdered sugar with lemon or orange juice to spreading consistency. Spread lightly on warm "cookie cakes."
*Blanche Moore*

# 140
BREAD
RAISINGS
AND OTHER
SLICES
OF LIFE

## Quick 'N Chewy Crescent Bars

1 8-oz. can refrigerated quick crescent dinner rolls
1 14-oz. can sweetened condensed milk
1 pkg. coconut-almond frosting mix
1/4 cup butter or margarine, melted

Unroll crescent dough; place rectangles in ungreased 15x10x1-inch jelly roll pan. Gently press dough to cover bottom of pan. Seal perforations. Pour condensed milk evenly over dough. Sprinkle with frosting mix. Drizzle with butter. Bake at 400° for 12 to 15 minutes until golden brown. Cool. Cut into bars. Makes 3 to 4 dozen bars.
*Marilyn Gish*
*Myrtle Basher*

## Yeast Tea-Rings

2 pkgs. dry yeast
3/4 cup sugar
8–8 1/2 cups flour
2 1/2 tsp. salt
2 eggs, well beaten
2 1/2 cups warm water
3/4 cup oil or butter

Mix all dry ingredients. Beat eggs, water, and oil; mix well with dry ingredients. Stir all together. Form into desired shape; let rise. For 3 tea rings, add filling and bake at 350° for 15 to 20 minutes. For 30 rolls, bake at 350° for 12 minutes.
Filling:
1/3 cup butter
2/3 cup brown sugar
1 Tbsp. corn syrup
chopped nuts
Cook butter, sugar, and syrup over low heat until sugar dissolves. Spread over 1/3 of above dough and sprinkle with nuts. Form into ring and bake at 350° for 20 minutes or until lightly browned.
*Cora Eller*
*Mary Ann Fall*

## Frosted Pineapple Squares

Filling:
1/2 cup sugar
3 Tbsp. cornstarch
1/4 tsp. salt
1 egg yolk, slightly beaten
1 1-lb. 14-oz. can crushed pineapple
Batter:
3 3/4–4 1/2 cups flour, unsifted
1 pkg. dry yeast
1 tsp. sugar
1/2 cup milk
1/2 cup water
1 cup margarine
4 egg yolks, room temperature
powdered sugar

Mix sugar, cornstarch, and salt together in saucepan. Stir in slightly beaten egg yolk and undrained pineapple. Cook over medium heat, stirring constantly, until mixture boils. Set aside to cool. In a large bowl, thoroughly mix 1 1/3 cups flour, 1 tsp. sugar, and undissolved yeast. Combine milk, water, and margarine in saucepan. Heat over low heat until liquids are warm (margarine does not need to melt). Gradually add to dry ingredients and beat 2 minutes at medium speed of electric mixer, scraping bowl occasionally. Add egg yolks and 1/2 cup flour, or enough flour to make a thick batter. Beat at high speed 2 minutes, scraping bowl occasionally. Stir in enough additional flour to make a soft, moist dough. Divide dough in half. Roll out 1/2 of the dough on floured board to fit the bottom of ungreased 15x10x1-inch jelly roll pan. Spread with cooled pineapple filling. Roll remaining dough large enough to cover filling. Seal edges together. Snip surface of dough with scissors to let steam escape. Cover; let rise in warm place, free from draft,

until doubled in bulk, about 1 hour. Bake at 375° about 35 to 40 minutes or until done. Let cake cool in pan. Frost while warm. Cut into squares and serve.
*Janice Root*

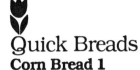

# Quick Breads

## Corn Bread 1

1 cup cornmeal
1 tsp. salt
1 cup flour
1/2 cup wheat germ
3/4 tsp. baking soda
1 tsp. baking powder
2 eggs, beaten
1 1/2 cups buttermilk
2 Tbsp. brown sugar
1/4 cup shortening or bacon drippings

Mix first 6 ingredients in bowl. Add eggs to buttermilk and sugar; combine with dry mixture. Add shortening. Bake in well-greased 8-inch square pan at 425° for 30 to 35 minutes.
*Gladys Oyler*

## Corn Bread 2

1 egg
1 1/2 cups buttermilk
1 tsp. baking soda
1 1/2 cups flour
1/2 cup cornmeal
1 scant Tbsp. sugar
1 tsp. salt
3 level tsp. baking powder
1/4 cup shortening

Mix all together and bake in long baking dish at 350° for 25 minutes or until golden brown.
*Edna Denlinger*

## Spanish Corn Bread

1 cup butter
1/2 cup sugar
4 eggs
1 can green chili peppers, chopped
1 large can cream-style corn
1/2 cup Jack cheese, grated
1/2 cup Tillamook cheese
1 cup flour
1 cup cornmeal
4 tsp. baking powder
4 tsp. salt

Combine all ingredients. Bake in long baking dish at 350° for 45 minutes or until golden brown.
Note:
If doubling recipe, do not double amount of chili peppers for those who prefer less pepper.
*Eunice Grover*

## Communion Bread Mix

3/4 cup milk
3 cups flour
1/2 cup butter
pinch of salt

Combine ingredients and place in long baking dish. Bake 20 minutes at 375°. Brush extra milk over top.
*Ruthann Orndoff*

## Apricot Nut Bread

1 1/3 cups dried apricots, cut in small pieces
1 3/4 cups sugar
3 Tbsp. soft butter or margarine
2 eggs, beaten
1/3 cup water
3/4 cup fresh or frozen orange juice
3 cups flour
3 tsp. baking powder
1/2 tsp. baking soda
1/2 tsp. salt
3/4 cup nuts, chopped

Soak apricots in warm water for at least 2 hours. Drain well. Mix sugar, butter, eggs, water, and orange juice together well. Sift dry ingredients and add to first mixture, mixing thoroughly. Fold in cut-up apricots and chopped nuts. Pour batter into large, greased loaf pan. Bake at 350° for 55 minutes or until well done.
Note:
You may use three 1-lb. size coffee cans, having sides greased and bottoms lined with waxed paper.
*Clara Belle Barton*

142
BREAD
RAISINGS
AND OTHER
SLICES
OF LIFE

## Banana Nut Bread

1/2 cup shortening, very soft
1 cup sugar
2 eggs
3 bananas, very ripe and crushed
2 cups flour
1 tsp. baking soda
pinch of salt
chopped walnuts

Mix shortening, sugar, eggs, and bananas. Then add flour, baking soda, and salt. Add nuts last. Bake at 350° for 1 hour in large loaf pan or 2 small ones.
Note:
Use shortening only.
*Leah Garber*

## Blueberry Nut Bread

2 eggs
1 cup sugar
1 cup milk
3 Tbsp. salad oil
3 cups flour
1 tsp. salt
4 tsp. baking powder
1 cup fresh or canned blueberries
1/2 cup nuts, broken

Beat eggs; gradually add sugar. Add milk and oil. Sift flour with salt and baking powder; add to liquid mixture. Stir only until blended. Care- fully fold in blue- berries and nuts. Pour into large, well- greased loaf pan. Bake at 350° for 50 to 60 minutes.
*Irene Edgecomb*

## Carrot Bread

1 cup sugar
3/4 cup salad oil
2 eggs
1 1/2 cups flour
1 tsp. baking soda
1 tsp. cinnamon
1/2 tsp. nutmeg
1/2 tsp. salt
1 1/2 cups carrots, grated
1/2 cup nuts, chopped

Cream together sugar, oil, and eggs. Sift dry ingredients together and add to creamed mixture. Stir carrots into bat- ter. Fold in chopped nuts. Pour into loaf pan or tube pan for a doubled recipe. Bake loaf pan for 25–35 minutes and tube pan for about 60 minutes at 350°.
*Nancy Bowman*

## Cranberry Bread

2 cups flour
1 1/2 tsp. baking powder
1/2 tsp. baking soda
1/2 tsp. salt
1 cup sugar
juice and grated rind of 1 large orange
2 Tbsp. salad oil
3/4 cup boiling water (minus 2 Tbsp.)
1 egg, beaten
1 cup walnuts, chopped
1 cup raw cranberries, chopped

Sift first 5 ingredi- ents together. Put salad oil in a cup and fill up to 3/4 full with boiling water. Add oil and water mixture to flour mixture. Add remaining ingre- dients. Mix and bake about 1 hour at 375° in loaf pan.
*Eunice Grover*

## Nut Bread

1 egg, beaten
1 cup sugar
2 cups milk
3 cups flour
3 tsp. baking powder
1/4 tsp. salt
1 cup nuts, chopped and covered with flour

Combine egg and sugar; beat well. Combine dry ingre- dients. Add milk and dry ingredients alter- nately. Add nuts. Put into greased loaf pan. Bake for 1 hour at 350°.
*Ethel Rumble*

## Orange Slice Nut Bread

1 cup candied orange slices, finely chopped
1 Tbsp. sugar
1/4 cup butter
1/2 cup sugar
1 egg
1/2 cup banana, mashed
2 1/2 cups flour, sifted
2 tsp. baking powder
1/2 tsp. baking soda
1/2 tsp. salt
1/2 cup nuts, chopped
1 cup milk

Sprinkle sugar over chopped orange slices to prevent sticking. Cream butter and sugar; add egg and banana. Mix well. Sift dry ingredients together. Add nuts and orange slices. Add alternately with milk to creamed mixture. Pour into large greased and floured loaf pan. Bake at 350° for 65 minutes or until done.
*Fern Boyd*

## Pumpkin Bread 1

1 1/2 cups sugar
1 1/2 cups pumpkin
3 eggs
1 1/8 cups salad oil
2 1/4 cups flour
1 1/2 tsp. baking powder
1 1/2 tsp. baking soda
1 1/2 tsp. salt
1 1/2 tsp. vanilla
1 1/2 tsp. cinnamon

Mix first 4 ingredients. Combine with remaining ingredients. Pour into greased loaf pan and bake for approximately 1 hour in 350° oven.
Note:
This burns easily.
*Ethel Rumble*

## Pumpkin Bread 2

3 cups flour
2 cups sugar
1 tsp. baking soda
1 tsp. salt
3 tsp. cinnamon
2 cups pumpkin
1 1/4 cups oil
1 cup nuts, chopped

Mix dry ingredients together. Add remaining ingredients, mixing well. Bake in 2 pans at 350° for 1 hour and 15 minutes.
*Marjorie Bauman*

## Pumpkin Bread 3

3 1/2 cups flour, sifted
2 tsp. baking soda
1 1/2 tsp. salt
1 tsp. cinnamon
1 tsp. nutmeg
3 cups sugar
1 cup nuts, chopped
4 eggs, slightly beaten
1 1/2 cups canned pumpkin
1 cup salad oil
2/3 cup water

Mix and sift dry ingredients; add nuts and mix. Combine eggs with moist ingredients. Pour all at once into dry ingredients and blend lightly. Bake in 2 greased loaf pans for 1 hour at 350°.
Note:
Three small loaf pans may also be used.
*Carolyn Fisher*
*Joy Thompson*
*Shirley Denlinger*

## John's Favorite

bread slices, cut in 4 strips
sweetened condensed milk
coconut or chopped nuts

Dip bread strips in sweetened condensed milk and roll in either coconut or chopped nuts. Toast in oven until brown.
*Orpha Barton*

# 143

# Biscuits
## Angel Biscuits

5 cups flour
3/4 cup shortening
1 tsp. baking soda
1 tsp. baking powder
1 tsp. salt
3 Tbsp. sugar
2 cups buttermilk
1 cake yeast
1/2 cup lukewarm water

Sift dry ingredients together. Cut in shortening thoroughly. Add buttermilk and yeast dissolved in water. Mix with spoon until all flour is moistened. Cover bowl and store up to 2 weeks in refrigerator until needed. Roll out 1/2- to 3/4-inch thick on floured board. Cut biscuits. Bake at 400° for 12 minutes.
*Wilma Filbrun*

# 144
BREAD
RAISINGS
AND OTHER
SLICES
OF LIFE

## Stir and Roll Biscuits

2 cups flour
3 tsp. baking powder
1 tsp. salt
1/3 cup vegetable oil
2/3 cup milk

Preheat oven to 475°. Sift together flour, baking powder, and salt. Pour oil and milk into a measuring cup, but don't stir. Then pour at once into flour mixture. Stir with a fork until mixture cleans sides of bowl and rounds up into a ball. Smooth by kneading dough 10 times, without additional flour. Roll out 1/2-inch thick. Cut biscuits. Bake 10 to 12 minutes.
*Fern Boyd*

## Rich Biscuits

2 cups flour
2 Tbsp. sugar
4 tsp. baking powder
1/2 tsp. salt
1/2 tsp. cream of
  tartar
1/2 cup or less
  shortening
1 egg
2/3 cup milk

Mix dry ingredients together. Cut in shortening. Add egg and milk. Roll to 1/2-inch thickness. Cut biscuits.
*Lois Root*

## Butter Dips

1/3 cup butter
2 1/4 cups flour
1 Tbsp. sugar
1/4 tsp. garlic salt
3 1/2 tsp. baking
  powder
1 1/2 tsp. salt
1 cup milk

Melt butter in 8-inch square pan. Measure dry ingredients in bowl; add milk and stir until dough clings together. Turn out on floured board and knead a few times. Roll into rectangle 1/2-inch thick. Cut in half lengthwise, then in 1-inch strips. Dip each strip in melted shortening on both sides. Bake at 425° for 15 to 20 minutes. Makes 28–30.
Note:
Part bacon drippings may be used for extra flavor instead of all butter.
*Joan Swearingen*

# Muffins

## Bran Muffins

3 cups bran cereal
1 tsp. baking powder
1 cup boiling water
1/2 cup shortening
1 cup sugar
2 eggs
1 pt. buttermilk
2 1/2 cups flour
2 1/2 tsp. baking soda
1/2 Tbsp. salt

Mix 1 cup cereal with baking powder and water; set aside. Cream together shortening, sugar, and eggs. Add remaining ingredients, including 2 cups bran cereal. Then combine with bran-and-water mixture, stirring once lightly. Pour into greased muffin pan. Bake at 350° for 15 to 20 minutes. Makes approximately 24 muffins.
Variation:
If doubling recipe, add an extra 1/8 cup shortening.
Note:
If tightly covered and refrigerated, batter will keep 6 weeks.
*Ann Crowmer*
*Ivalyn Gish*
*Nancy Layman*
*Rhonda Landes*

## Date-Oatmeal Muffins

1 cup flour
1/4 cup sugar
3 tsp. baking powder
1/2 tsp. salt
1 cup quick rolled
  oats
1/2 cup dates,
  chopped
3 Tbsp. oil
1 egg, beaten
3/4 cup milk
orange glaze, (optional)

Sift first 4 ingredients. Stir in oats and dates. Beat oil, milk, and egg together; add to flour mixture. Stir until just moistened. Fill muffin tins 2/3 full. Bake 15 minutes at 425°. If desired, drizzle with orange glaze made of powdered sugar and orange juice.
*Chloie King*

### Doughnut Muffins

1/3 cup oil
1 cup sugar
1 egg, beaten
1 1/2 cups flour
1 1/2 tsp. baking powder
1/2 tsp. salt
1/2 tsp. nutmeg
1/2 cup milk
Topping:
1/4 cup butter, melted
1/2 cup sugar
1 tsp. cinnamon

Cream oil and sugar in mixing bowl. Add remaining ingredients and pour into greased muffin tins. Bake 20 to 25 minutes at 350°. Let cool 10 minutes. Remove from pans. Roll in melted butter and then in cinnamon-sugar. Makes 12 large size muffins or 18 small size muffins.
*Doris Boyd
Anna Brubaker
Darleen Layman
Marilyn Balsbaugh*

# Pancakes and Waffles

## Buttermilk Pancakes

1 cup flour
1 tsp. baking soda
2 eggs
1/4 tsp. salt
1 tsp. baking powder
1–1 1/4 cups buttermilk

Combine all and pour on slightly greased griddle. Serves 2 to 3 people.
*Phyllis Basore
Emma Blickenstaff
Mary Wise*

### Pancake Syrup

1 pkg. brown sugar
1 cup water
2 Tbsp. butter
1 tsp. maple flavoring

Cook sugar and water for 7 minutes. Remove from heat and stir in butter and flavoring. Makes 2 cups.
*Edna Thompson*

### Oatmeal Pancakes

2 eggs, beaten
2 cups buttermilk
1 1/2 cups oatmeal
1/2 cup flour
1 tsp. sugar
1 tsp. baking soda
1 tsp. salt

Mix eggs, buttermilk, and oatmeal. Add dry ingredients. Pour on lightly greased griddle. Serves 4.
*Phyllis Denlinger*

### Pure Buckwheat Cakes

1 cup buttermilk
1 egg
1/4 tsp. baking soda
1/2 tsp. salt
1 Tbsp. soya or other vegetable oil
1 Tbsp. blackstrap molasses
1/4 cup whole wheat flour
1 Tbsp. soy flour
3/4 cup pure buckwheat flour
1 tsp. sesame Tahini, (optional)

Mix all ingredients together. Pour on greased griddle.
*Edith L. Deeter*

### Pancake Mix

12 cups flour, sifted
2 Tbsp. salt
3/4 cup baking powder
3/4 cup sugar
4 cups dried milk

Combine ingredients. When ready to use, for each 1 1/2 cups pancake mix, add:
1 egg, beaten
1 cup water
1 Tbsp. oil or melted shortening

Mix well and fry on hot griddle.
*Kathryn Mohler*

# 146
BREAD
RAISINGS
AND OTHER
SLICES
OF LIFE

## Buttermilk Waffles

2 eggs, well beaten
2 cups buttermilk
1 tsp. baking soda
2 cups flour
2 tsp. baking powder
1/2 tsp. salt
6 Tbsp. shortening or margarine, melted

Combine eggs, buttermilk, and baking soda; then add dry ingredients and last, melted margarine. Bake waffles as usual. Serves 4.
*Edna Thompson*

## Plain Waffles

2 cups flour
4 tsp. baking powder
1 tsp. salt
2 eggs, separated
1 cup milk
1/4 cup shortening *or* oil

Combine ingredients, except egg whites; mix well. Beat egg whites and fold in last. Bake in hot waffle iron.
*Edith Fox*

## Date-Nut Waffles

2 cups flour
1/2 tsp. baking soda
3 tsp. baking powder
1/4 tsp. salt
1/4 cup sugar
1 tsp. nutmeg
1 cup dates, finely cut
1/2 cup walnuts, finely chopped
3 eggs, separated
1 3/4 cups buttermilk
1/2 cup butter, melted

Combine first 8 ingredients. Beat egg yolks with buttermilk and butter. Add liquid at once to dry ingredients. Beat until smooth. Beat egg whites until stiff; fold into batter. Bake on hot waffle iron. Yields 8 to 10 4-inch waffles.
*Esther Flora*

# Deep-Fried Treats

## Hush Puppies

1/2 cup flour, sifted
2 tsp. baking powder
1/2 tsp. salt
1 Tbsp. sugar
1 1/2 cups white corn meal
1 egg, beaten
3/4 cup milk
1 onion, finely chopped

Measure and sift dry ingredients together. Combine egg, milk, and onion; pour into flour mixture. Stir only enough to moisten dry ingredients. Drop from teaspoon into hot, deep fat. Fry until golden brown, turning oc-casionally. Drain on paper towels. Serve hot with fried fish.
*Mary Heinrich*

## Calas

1 1/2 cups cooked rice, very soft
1/2 pkg. yeast, active dry or compressed
1/2 cup warm water
3 eggs, beaten
1 1/4 cups flour, sifted
1/4 cup sugar
1/2 tsp. salt
1/4 tsp. nutmeg

Mash rice grains and cool to lukewarm. Soften yeast in warm water and stir in lukewarm rice. Mix well. Cover and let rise overnight. The next morning, add eggs, flour, sugar, salt, and nutmeg. Beat until smooth. Let stand in a warm place for 30 minutes. Drop by tablespoons into deep hot fat, 360°, and fry until golden brown, about 3 minutes. Serve sprinkled with powdered sugar or sugar mixed with cinnamon. Makes 2 dozen. These are excellent served with fruit or maple syrup.
*Alice Mae Haney*

## Apple Fritters

1 cup flour
1 1/2 tsp. baking powder
1/2 tsp. salt
2 Tbsp. sugar
1 egg, beaten
1/2 cup plus 1 Tbsp. milk.

1 1/2 cups (2 large) apples, pared and chopped

Sift dry ingredients together. Combine beaten egg and milk. Pour into dry ingredients. Stir until batter is smooth. Add apples to batter and blend together. Drop by spoonfuls into deep hot fat, 370°–375°. Fry until golden brown on all sides. Drain on paper towels and roll in powdered sugar. Serve hot. Makes 12 to 15 fritters.

*Lois Shirk*

## Raised Doughnuts

1 cup warm water
2 pkgs. yeast
1 cup milk
1/2 cup sugar
1/2 cup oil
2 eggs
1 cup potatoes, mashed
1 Tbsp. salt
7–7 1/2 cups flour

Dissolve yeast in warm water. Add milk, sugar, oil, eggs, potatoes, salt, and part of the flour, blending together. Add remaining flour and knead until smooth. Let rise until doubled. Roll out and cut into doughnuts. Let rise 30 to 40 minutes. Fry in hot fat. Drain on paper toweling. Cool and spread with *Glaze*.

*Glaze:*
1/2 cup brown sugar
1/4 cup margarine
1/2 tsp. milk
1 box powdered sugar
water

Boil margarine and sugar together for 2 minutes. Add milk and boil again. Add powdered sugar and a little water. Beat until smooth.

*Bonnie Jamison*

## Orange Drop Doughnuts

2 eggs
1/2 cup sugar
2 Tbsp. shortening
2 cups flour
2 tsp. baking powder
1/4 tsp. salt
1/2 cup orange juice
2 Tbsp. grated orange rind

Beat eggs, sugar, and shortening together. Sift together dry ingredients. Slowly stir in orange juice and rind. Drop by teaspoonfuls into hot fat. Fry until golden and then glaze or sugar, if desired.

*Deanna Davison*

---

*SIMPLE RHYME*
Back of the loaf is the snowy flour,
And back of the flour is the mill;
And back of the mill are the wheat and the shower,
And the sun, and the Father's Will.

*Extra Recipes*

Source:                    Who Likes It:

Source:                    Who Likes It:

Source:                    Who Likes It:

# From the Pie Safe

*Bird never flew so high
that it had not
to come down to earth.*
PENNSYLVANIA DUTCH SAYING

*If we live
in the Spirit,
let us also walk
in the Spirit.*
GALATIANS 5:25 (KJV)

# Pie Crusts

## Almond Pie Crust

2 cups ground almonds
3 Tbsp. sugar
4 Tbsp. butter, softened

Put all ingredients in mixing bowl and mix well with fork. Press into 9-inch pie pan. Use unbaked; otherwise, bake about 8 minutes in 425° oven; watch closely to avoid burning. Cool. Fill with favorite filling. Chocolate chip filling is very tasty.
Variation:
Use 1 cup graham cracker crumbs and 1 cup almond meal *or* 1 cup crushed cereal and 1 cup almond meal, in addition to sugar and butter.
*Pearl Howser*

## Pie Crust 1

4 cups flour
1/2 cup cold water
2 tsp. salt
1 1/3 cups shortening

Take out 2/3 cup flour and mix with cold water to form paste. To remaining flour, add shortening. Blend until size of small peas. Add flour paste. Mix well. Divide into 4 balls and roll 1/8-inch thick.
*Lois Root*
*Doris Moore*

## Pie Crust 2

5 cups flour
2 cups shortening
1 tsp. salt
1 egg
1 Tbsp. vinegar
cold water

Mix flour, shortening, and salt into crumbs. Put egg and vinegar into a cup. Mix together and fill cup with cold water. Add slowly to crumbs and mix again. Makes 5 pie shells.
*Rachel Shoup*
Variation:
Add 1/2 tsp. baking powder and 4 tsp. sugar.
*Clara Selby*

## Pie Crust 3

3 cups flour
1 1/2 tsp. salt
1 1/4 cups shortening
1 whole egg
1 Tbsp. vinegar
5 Tbsp. cold water

Mix flour and salt; then cut in shortening. Stir remaining ingredients into flour mixture and blend well. Shape dough into ball. Roll out as desired.
*Sarah Lee Switzer*

## Meringue Shell

4 egg whites
1/2 tsp. cream of tartar
1/4 tsp. salt
1 cup sugar
1 tsp. vanilla

Beat whites, cream of tartar, and salt until stiff. Gradually beat in sugar, adding 1 Tbsp. at a time. Continue beating until very stiff and shiny. Blend in vanilla. Spread in bottom and sides of buttered 9-inch pie plate. Bake at 375° for about 1 hour. Turn off heat, open oven door, and leave in over 1/2 hour. Cool thoroughly before filling.
*Annabelle Gish*

# Cream, Custard, and Icebox Pies

## Apple Butter Pie

1/2 cup plus 2 Tbsp. water
1/2 cup plus 2 Tbsp. sugar
1 cup apple butter
1/2 cup raisins, chopped
1 tsp. lemon rind
1 Tbsp. cornstarch
2 eggs, separated
1 8-inch baked pie shell

Reserving 2 Tbsp. water and 2 Tbsp. sugar for later, cook first 6 ingredients in top of double boiler until thick. Beat egg yolks well and add to mixture. Cook 10 minutes longer. Add 2 Tbsp. water. Pour into baked pie shell. Beat egg whites with 2 Tbsp. sugar. Bake until topping browns slightly.
*Muriel Onkst*

## Apple Custard Pie

1 8-inch unbaked pie shell
1 cup sugar
2 Tbsp. flour
Pippin apples, pared and halved
cream
cinnamon
butter

Mix sugar and flour together; put small amount of mixture in bottom of shell. Prepare apples and lay cut side down. Sprinkle rest of sugar mixture over apples. Fill shell full of cream. Sprinkle cinnamon over top and dot with butter. Bake 15 minutes at 425° and then 45 minutes at 350°.
Note:
Use canned cream, if preferred.
*Emma Lynch*

## Bob Andy Pie

1 cup white sugar
1 cup brown sugar
3 rounded Tbsp. flour
1 tsp. cinnamon
2 1/2 cups milk
2 Tbsp. butter, melted
3 eggs, separated
1/4 tsp. salt

Beat all ingredients together except for egg whites. Then beat egg whites separately and fold into mixture. Continue stirring as mixture is poured into pie shells. Bake at 350° for 45 minutes. Makes 2 pies.
*Nina Austin*

## Banana Pie Supreme

6 Tbsp. cake flour
2/3 cup sugar
1/4 tsp. salt
1 3/4 cups milk
1 1/4 tsp. vanilla
2 egg yolks, slightly beaten
1 tsp. vanilla

1 cup whipped cream
1 9-inch, baked pie shell

Mix flour, sugar, salt, and milk. Cool in double boiler over boiling water until thick. Add egg yolks and cook 1 minute longer. Cool. Add vanilla. Chill. When chilled, fold in whipped cream. Layer pudding and sliced bananas in pie shell.
*Daisy Frantz*

## Mile-High Berry Pie

1 10-oz. pkg. frozen strawberries or raspberries, thawed
1 cup sugar
2 egg whites, at room temperature
1 Tbsp. lemon juice
dash of salt
1/2 pint whipped cream
1/4 cup roasted and chopped almonds, (optional)
1 8-inch, baked pie shell

Reserving a few berries for garnish, combine berries, sugar, whites, juice, and salt in electric mixing bowl. Beat for 15 minutes at high speed or until stiff. Fold in whipped cream and almonds, if desired. Fill pie shell made with 1/2 tsp. almond extract added to dough. Freeze until firm. Garnish with berries and sprigs of mint. Serve frozen; do not thaw.
*Eunice Grover*

## Blueberry Ice Cream Pie

1 1/3 cups fine
  graham cracker
  crumbs
1/4 cup butter
1/4 cup sugar
1 qt. vanilla ice cream,
  softened
1 1/2 cups blueberries
3 egg whites, at room
  temperature
1 tsp. vanilla
1/2 tsp. cream of tartar
6 Tbsp. sugar

Mix crumbs, butter, and sugar until crumbly. Press crumbs firmly against sides and bottom of unbuttered 9-inch pie plate. Bake at 375° for 8 minutes. Cool. Spread half of ice cream in cooled crumb shell. Mix remaining ice cream with blueberries. Fill pie; freeze until firm. Beat egg whites, vanilla, and cream of tartar until soft peaks form. Gradually add sugar, beating until stiff and glossy. Cover entire surface of ice cream with meringue. Place in 475° oven about 2 or 3 minutes. Serves 6 to 8.
*Treva Aukerman*

## Butterscotch Pie 1

2 egg yolks
1 Tbsp. butter
1 cup brown sugar
2 Tbsp. flour
1 1/2 cups milk
1 tsp. vanilla
1 8-inch, baked pie
  shell

Cream first 4 ingredients together; then add milk. Cook slowly until thick. Add vanilla and pour into pie crust. Top with meringue or whipped cream. Serves 6.
Note:
This makes a delicious pudding with whipped cream. Use whole eggs for pudding.
*Iva Bauman*

## Butterscotch Pie 2

1 cup brown sugar
1/2 cup cream
1 1/2 Tbsp. butter
2 Tbsp. flour
milk
2 eggs, separated
1 cup water
pinch of salt
1/2 tsp. vanilla
3 Tbsp. white sugar
1 8-inch, baked pie
  shell

Put brown sugar, cream, and butter in skillet or saucepan, and let boil well. Mix flour with a little milk and add egg yolks. Beat well. Add water and stir in boiled sugar mixture. Cook until thick. Add salt and vanilla. Fill pie shell. Beat egg whites, adding white sugar; spoon on top of pie. Bake in 325° oven for about 12 minutes or until lightly browned.
*Inez Oyler*

## Cherry Supreme Pie

1/2 pt. whipping cream
1 3-oz. pkg. cream
  cheese
1/2 cup powdered
  sugar
1 cup cherry pie filling
1 9-inch baked pie
  shell

Whip cream. Blend cheese and sugar; fold into whipped cream. Fill pie shell. Put cherries on top. Chill. Serves 6.
*Suzanne Overholtzer*

## Chocolate Pie

2 cups milk
3/4 cup sugar
2 eggs
1 rounded Tbsp. flour
1 rounded Tbsp. cornstarch
1 rounded Tbsp. cocoa
1 Tbsp. butter
1 tsp. vanilla
1 8-inch, baked pie
  shell

Combine first 6 ingredients and cook until thick, stirring constantly. Remove from heat; add butter and vanilla. Chill and pour into pie shell. Serve with whipped cream or plain.
*Katherine Jarboe*

## Chocolate Chip Pie

2 9-inch baked pie
  shells
6 egg yolks
3 cups sugar
1 pt. cream
2 cups milk
3 Tbsp. unflavored
  gelatin
water
1 tsp. vanilla
1 pt. light cream
flaked sweet chocolate

Combine yolks, sugar,
cream, and milk.
Cook in double boiler
just until thickened.
Dissolve gelatin in
water. Remove cus-
tard mixture from
heat and add gelatin.
Cool and flavor with
vanilla. Refrigerate
overnight. Let stand
1 hour at room tem-
perature. Then whip
cream; add to mix-
ture and whip to-
gether. Pour into pie
shells. Let stand in
the refrigerator until
ready to serve. Add
whipped cream on
top. Cover with flaked
sweet chocolate.
*Betty King*

## Cloud Nine Pie

1 9-inch, baked pie
  shell
1 cup sugar
1 envelope plain
  gelatin
1/4 tsp. salt
3/4 cup milk
3 egg yolks, slightly
  beaten
1 tsp. grated orange
  peel
3/4 cup orange juice
1/2 tsp. grated
  lemon peel
1/4 cup lemon juice
1 cup whipping cream,
  whipped or
  non-dairy topping

Combine sugar,
gelatin, and salt in
saucepan. Add milk
and egg yolks. Cook
over medium heat,
stirring constantly,
until mixture thickens
slightly. Remove from
heat; add juices and
peels. Chill until par-
tially set. Fold in
whipped cream. Chill
until mixture mounds
when spooned. Pile
into baked pie shell.
Chill. Add whipped
cream on top to
serve. Freezes well.
*Pearl Howser*

## Bavarian Coconut Pie

1 9-inch baked pie
  shell
1 envelope unflavored
  gelatin
1/4 cup sugar
3 eggs, separated
1 1/4 cups milk
1/4 tsp. salt
1/4 cup sugar
1 tsp. vanilla
2 cups coconut,
  shredded

1 cup whipping cream,
  whipped

Combine gelatin
with sugar; set aside.
In top of double
boiler, beat egg yolks;
add gelatin mixture
and milk. Cook over
hot, but not boiling,
water until mixture
coats spoon. Refrig-
erate, stirring occa-
sionally, until custard
mounds. Beat just
until smooth. Then
beat egg whites with
salt until stiff, grad-
ually adding sugar.
Fold into custard
mixture. Combine
whipped cream,
vanilla, and 1 cup
coconut. Add to
custard. Pour into pie
shell, reserving 1/3 of
mixture. Refrigerate
pie and extra filling
until almost set.
Heap on remaining
filling and garnish
with remaining
coconut. Refrigerate
until serving time.
*Leona Selby*

## Cream Pie 1

1/2 cup brown sugar
2/3 cup white sugar
1/4 cup flour
1/2 tsp. nutmeg
pinch of salt
1 egg yolk, beaten
1 cup cream
1 cup milk
1 egg white, stiffly
  beaten
1 9-inch, unbaked pie
  shell

Mix dry ingredients
together well. Then
add remaining ingre-
dients. Pour into pie
shell. Bake at 350°
for 30 or 40 minutes.
*Esther Gish*

## Cream Pie 2

1/2 cup butter or
   margarine
1 cup sugar
1/4 cup cornstarch
2 cups milk
1 tsp. vanilla
1 8-inch, baked pie
   shell

Melt butter and sugar in saucepan. Dissolve cornstarch in small amount of milk. Add milk to butter mixture. Gradually add cornstarch mixture. Cook until thick. Remove from heat and add vanilla. Pour into pie shell.
*Peggy Wise*

## Cream Pie 3

1 cup sugar
1/4 cup flour
1 cup milk
1 egg
1/4 cup butter or
   margarine
1 tsp. vanilla
1 8-inch, unbaked pie
   shell

Combine sugar and flour well; add egg and enough cold milk to make a smooth batter. Heat rest of milk, adding butter. When milk foams, stir in flour mixture. Stir over medium heat until slightly thickened. Add vanilla; then pour into shell. Bake at 450° for 15 minutes; then reduce heat to 350° for 10 minutes or until set. Center will look soft, but will thicken as it cools.
*Gladys Beachler*

## Crumb Pie 1

Filling:
2 cups water
1 cup brown sugar
1/3 cup flour
1/2 cup dark corn
   syrup
2 eggs, beaten
1 tsp. vanilla
2 8-inch, unbaked pie
   shells

Crumb Topping:
2 cups flour
1/2 cup white sugar
1/2 cup brown sugar
1/2 cup margarine,
   melted
1 tsp. baking soda

Heat water. Mix sugar, flour, and syrup, adding small amount extra water. Stir mixture into hot water; cook until thick. Remove from heat. Add eggs and vanilla. Beat well. Pour into pie shells.
   Make *Crumb Topping* by mixing topping ingredients together until crumbly. Sprinkle on top of filled pies. Bake at 350° for 30 to 40 minutes.
*Marietta Pegg*

## Crumb Pie 2

Filling:
1 cup light corn syrup
1 cup boiling water
1/3 cup sugar
1 tsp. baking soda
2 8-inch, unbaked pie
   shells

Crumb Topping:
2 cups flour
1/2 cup margarine
1/2 cup sugar
1/2 tsp. salt

Mix filling ingredients. Pour into pie shells. Make *Crumb Topping* by combining ingredients until crumbly. Sprinkle over filled pies. Let pies set 15 or 20 minutes; then bake about 45 minutes at 325°.
*Lydia Wolf*

## Golden Pie

Crust:
2 boxes Zwieback
  cookies or graham
  crackers, crumbled
1 cup sugar
1/2 cup butter, melted
1 tsp. cinnamon
1 whole egg plus 2 egg
  yolks

Custard Filling:
3 Tbsp. flour
1 cup sugar
3 cups milk
5 eggs, separated
1 tsp. vanilla
1 large can crushed
  pineapple, undrained
7 Tbsp. sugar

Combine crust ingredients, reserving 1 cup of crumbs. To the remaining crumbs, add eggs. Pat crust 1/2-inch thick in bottom of baking pan. Bake about 10 minutes. Cook flour, sugar, milk, yolks, and vanilla until thick; cool. Add pineapple and juice. Pour mixture over baked crust. Beat egg whites, adding 7 Tbsp. sugar. Spread over custard. Then sprinkle reserved crumbs over top and brown in 350° oven for 12 minutes or so. Serve with whipped cream.
*Orpha Barton*

## Golden Treasure Pie

Fruit Filling:
2 8-1/2-oz. cans
  crushed pineapple,
  undrained
1/2 cup sugar
2 Tbsp. cornstarch
2 Tbsp. water

Custard Filling:
2/3 cup sugar
1 Tbsp. butter
1/4 cup flour, sifted
1 cup cottage cheese
1 tsp. vanilla
1/2 tsp. salt
2 eggs, slightly beaten
1 1/4 cups milk
1 10-inch unbaked pie
  shell

Combine pineapple, sugar, cornstarch, and water in small saucepan. Bring to a boil. Cook 1 minute, stirring constantly. Cool. Make custard. Blend sugar and butter; add flour, cheese, vanilla, and salt. Beat until smooth. Slowly add eggs and then milk to cheese mixture, beating constantly. Pour pineapple filling into pie shell, spreading evenly. Gently pour custard over pineapple, being careful not to disturb first layer. Bake at 450° for 15 minutes; then reduce heat to 325° and bake 45 minutes longer. Makes 8 to 10 servings.
*Lois Garber*

## Lemon Chiffon Pie

1 1/2 tsp. plain gelatin
1/3 cup cold water
4 eggs, separated
5/6 cup sugar
1 Tbsp. lemon rind,
  grated
1/4 cup lemon juice
1/4 tsp. salt
1/2 cup whipping
  cream
1 8-inch, baked pie
  shell

Add gelatin to water; set aside. Put egg yolks in double boiler and stir in 1/3 cup sugar, lemon rind, and juice. Cook over boiling water, stirring constantly, until thickened. Stir in gelatin until melted. Remove from heat. Beat egg whites and salt until they form peaks; then add remaining 1/2 cup sugar and beat until stiff. Gently fold in hot mixture. Pour into baked shell. Chill until set. Serve with whipped cream.
*Leona Selby*

## Lemon Ice Cream Pie

6 Tbsp. butter, melted
grated rind of 1 lemon
1/8 tsp. salt
1/4 cup lemon juice
1 cup sugar
2 whole eggs plus 2
  yolks, beaten slightly
1/2 pt. vanilla ice
  cream
1 9-inch, baked pie
  shell, cooled
3 egg whites
1/4 cup sugar

Meringue:
3 egg whites
1/4 cup sugar
Combine first 5 ingredients. Add eggs to lemon mixture. Cook over low heat until smooth. Cool. Put 1/2 pint vanilla ice cream in pie shell and freeze. Add layer of lemon sauce and freeze. Add layer of 1/2 pint ice cream and freeze. Add layer of lemon sauce and freeze. Cover with meringue made from beating egg whites and sugar together until stiff. Bake at 475° for 5 minutes to brown slightly. Freeze.
*Lois Bauman*

## Lemon Meringue Pie Supreme

7 Tbsp. cornstarch
1 1/2 cups sugar
1/4 tsp. salt
1 1/2 cups hot water
3 eggs, separated
2 Tbsp. butter or margarine
1 tsp. grated lemon peel
1/2 cup fresh lemon juice
1 9-inch, baked pie shell
1/4 tsp. cream of tartar
6 Tbsp. sugar

Mix cornstarch, sugar, and salt in saucepan; gradually stir in water. Cook over direct heat, stirring until thick and clear, about 10 minutes. Remove from heat. Stir 1/2 cup of the hot mixture into the egg yolks and then add remaining hot mixture. Cook over low heat, stirring 2 to 3 minutes. Remove from heat; stir in butter, lemon peel, and juice. Cool. Pour mixture into baked pie shell. Beat whites with cream of tartar until frothy, adding sugar gradually. Continue beating until meringue stands in firm peaks. Spread over filling, making sure meringue touches crust all around. Bake at 350° for 15 minutes or until delicately browned. Cool.
*Phyllis Rumble*

## Lemon Mist Pie

3 eggs, separated
10 Tbsp. sugar
1/4 tsp. salt
3 tsp. grated lemon rind
juice of 1 lemon
3 Tbsp. lemon gelatin
1/2 cup hot water
1/4 tsp. cream of tartar
1 8-inch, baked pie shell

Beat yolks; add 8 Tbsp. (or 1/2 cup) sugar, salt, rind, and juice. Cook until thick. Mix gelatin and water; beat with beater into lemon custard. Then chill. Beat egg whites and cream of tartar with rest of sugar. Fold into custard mixture.

Pour mixture into pie shell. Chill several hours until set. Top with whipped cream.
*Betty Lou Garber*

## Mother Bowman's Lemon Pie

1 lemon
2 cups sugar
3 eggs, separated
1 Tbsp. butter
2 Tbsp. cornstarch or flour
2 cups hot water
1 8-inch, baked pie shell, cooled

Grate lemon; add sugar to rind. Squeeze out lemon juice into rind mixture; make a paste. Add yolks, butter, and cornstarch, stirring until smooth. Add hot water, while beating slowly. Set on stove and boil until thick. Then add well beaten whites of eggs. Pour into pie shell.
*Mary Filbrun*

## Baked Lemon Pie 1

1 cup sugar
3 Tbsp. flour
1 rounded Tbsp. butter
2 eggs, separated
1 cup milk
juice and rind of
  1 lemon
1 8-inch, unbaked pie
  shell

Cream sugar, flour, and butter together. Beat egg yolks and add to creamed mixture. Slowly and alternately add milk, lemon rind, and juice. Beat egg whites until stiff. Fold into lemon mixture. Pour into pie shell and bake 40 minutes at 350° or until center is done.
*Ethel Rumble*

## Baked Lemon Pie 2

Crust:
1 1/2 cups Zwieback
  or graham cracker
  crumbs
1/2 cup walnuts,
  chopped fine
1/2 cup sugar
1/2 cup butter, melted
1 egg white, beaten
Custard:
3 egg yolks

1 can sweetened
  condensed milk
juice of 2 lemons
1/4 cup grated rind
2 egg whites, beaten

Combine crust ingredients, except egg white. Reserve 1/2 cup crumbs for top. Then add egg white to remaining crumbs; line pie pan with crumbs and pat smoothly on bottom and sides.

Prepare custard. Beat egg yolks and add milk, lemon juice, and rind. Fold in beaten egg whites very carefully. Pour into pie crust and sprinkle 1/2 cup crumbs on top. Bake 25 minutes at 325° or 350°.
*Emma Blickenstaff*

## Lime Chiffon Pie

1 6-oz. pkg. lime
  gelatin
1/2 cup sugar
1 cup hot water
1 9-oz. can crushed
  pineapple
1 cup whipped cream
1/4 tsp. salt
1/2 cup flaked coconut
1 9-inch crumb crust

Dissolve gelatin and sugar in hot water; add crushed pineapple and chill until syrupy. Whip gelatin mixture and fold in whipped cream, salt, and flaked coconut. Pour mixture into chilled crumb crust; garnish with plain or toasted coconut. Chill thoroughly before serving.
*Ellen Reece*

## Mary's Simple Pie

1/2 cup sugar
4 1/2 Tbsp. flour
2 cups milk
2 egg yolks
1 8-inch, unbaked pie
  shell

Meringue:
2 egg whites
2 Tbsp. sugar

Mix flour and sugar together. Add just enough milk to moisten. Then add egg yolks. Heat remaining milk. Add egg mixture to milk, stirring constantly. Cook over medium heat until consistency of pie filling. Pour into pie shell. Make meringue by beating whites stiff and adding sugar. Spoon over filling and bake 10 to 15 minutes at 350°.
*Alice Kline*

## Mocha Pie

1 1/2 lbs. marsh-
  mallows
1 1/2 cups strong,
  perked coffee
1 tsp. instant coffee
1 qt. non-dairy topping
  *or* 1 pt. whipping
  cream, whipped
1 cup nuts, chopped
1 cup milk chocolate
  shavings
3 8-inch, baked pie
  shells

Melt marshmallows in double boiler. Add coffees. Cool until mixture begins to set. Add topping and nuts, blending well. Pour into pie shells. Add milk chocolate shavings on top.

Note:
This pie freezes well.
*Annie Bowman*
Variation:
Omit the chocolate.
*Mary Gish*

## Molasses Pie

Filling:
1 1/2 cups molasses
1 tsp. baking soda
1 cup boiling water
1 tsp. vanilla
3 8-inch *or* 2 9-inch,
  unbaked pie shells
Crumb Topping:
6 cups flour
3 cups sugar
1 1/2 cups butter and
  lard

Combine filling ingre-
dients and pour into
pie shells. Blend
topping ingredients
and sprinkle over fill-
ing. Bake 30 to 40
minutes at 350°.
*Deanna Davison*

Variation:
Sprinkle 1 tsp. cinna-
mon over crumb
topping.
*Maudia Onkst*

## Oatmeal Pie

3/4 cup sugar
1/2 cup margarine
2 eggs, beaten
3/4 cup dark corn
  syrup
3/4 cup quick rolled
  oats
1/2 cup coconut,
  flaked
chopped nuts,
  (optional)
1 9-inch, unbaked pie
  shell

Cream sugar and
margarine. Add eggs,
mixing well. Then,
add other ingredients.
Pour into pie shell.
Bake 45 minutes at
350°.
*Lydia Wolf*
*Esther Flora*

## Parfait Pie

1 3-oz. pkg. gelatin
  (any flavor)
1 cup boiling water
1 pt. vanilla ice cream
fruit of choice (straw-
  berries, etc.)
1 9-inch, baked pie
  shell *or* graham
  cracker crust

Dissolve gelatin in
boiling water. Chill;
then blend into ice
cream. Add fruit.
Pack mixture into pie
shell. Serve immedi-
ately or freeze.
*Ethel Rumble*

## Peachy Cream Pie

1 8-oz. pkg. cream
  cheese, softened
2 Tbsp. sugar
2 Tbsp. milk
1/4 tsp. almond extract
1 9-inch, baked pie
  shell
2 10-oz. pkgs. frozen
  peaches, thawed
Glaze:
1 Tbsp. cornstarch
1/4 cup sugar
1 Tbsp. lemon juice
2/3 cup peach juice
1 Tbsp. butter or
  margarine

Combine cheese,
sugar, milk, and
extract; mix until well
blended. Spread on
pie shell. Chill. Drain
peaches, reserving

juice. Arrange slices
on cream cheese. For
*Glaze*, combine corn-
starch and sugar;
add juices. Stir over
medium heat, cook-
ing until clear and
thick. Add butter and
cook 2 minutes. Cool
and pour over
peaches.
*Eunice Grover*

## Pear Cream Pie

fresh pears, pared,
  cored, and halved
1 9-inch, unbaked pie
  shell
1 cup sugar
3 rounded Tbsp. flour
3/4–1 cup half-and-
  half
nutmeg

Line pie shell with
pears cut-side up.
Mix sugar and flour
together. Sprinkle
over pears in alter-
nate layers with the
half-and-half.
Sprinkle with nut-
meg. Bake 10
minutes at 375° and
30 to 40 minutes at
350° or until pears
are tender. Best
served slightly warm.
*Eva R. Landes*

## Pecan Pie 1

3 eggs
1 cup light corn syrup
1/4 tsp. salt
1 tsp. vanilla
1 cup sugar
2 Tbsp. butter or
  margarine
1 cup pecan halves
1 9-inch, unbaked pie
  shell
whipped cream

In medium bowl, beat
eggs slightly. Add
corn syrup, salt,
vanilla, sugar, and
butter; mix well. Stir
in pecans. Pour into
pie shell and bake 15
minutes at 400°.
Reduce heat to 350°
and bake 30 to 35
minutes or until edge
of filling is set. Cool;
before serving, put
whipped cream on
top.
*Genevieve Barber*

## Pecan Pie 2

3 eggs, beaten
1/2 cup sugar
1 cup dark corn syrup
1/2 tsp. salt
1 tsp. vanilla
1 cup pecans
3 Tbsp. butter or
  margarine
1 9-inch, unbaked pie
  shell

Combine ingredients,
except butter. Fill
shell to within 3/8".
Dot with butter. Bake
for 45 minutes at
350°.
*Connie Reece*

## Peanut Butter Pie

Crust:
1 1/2 cups flour
1/2 tsp. salt
2 Tbsp. milk
1/2 cup oil
2 Tbsp. sugar
Fillings:
1/2 cup chunky
  peanut butter
3/4 cup powdered
  sugar
  *and*
1 pkg. vanilla pudding
Topping:
1 small container non-
  dairy frozen topping
  *or* 1 pkg. whipped
  topping

Mix crust ingredients
together and shape
into a ball. Using
fingers, press crust
into 9-inch pie plate.
Bake at 400° for 10
to 12 minutes. Cool.
Make one filling by
crumbling peanut
butter and sugar to-
gether. Make second
filling of pudding
according to package
directions for pie.
Cool. Put peanut
butter crumbs in
bottom of cooled pie
crust, reserving 1/4
cup for garnish. Pour
pudding over crumbs
in pie crust. Prepare
whipped topping or
use prepared topping.
Spoon on top of
pudding. Sprinkle
with remaining
crumbs. Chill in re-

frigerator until
serving time.
Note:
Regular pie crust
may be used.
*Ruth Wise*

## Pineapple Pie

1 cup evaporated milk
1 1/4 cups crushed
  pineapple
1 3-oz. pkg. lemon
  gelatin
1 cup sugar
2 8-inch or 1 10-inch,
  baked pie shell

Chill evaporated milk
15 to 20 minutes in
ice cube tray until ice
crystals form around
edges. Meanwhile,
bring crushed pine-
apple to a boil and
dissolve gelatin in it.
Then add sugar. Cool
mixture in refrig-
erator until almost
stiff. Next, whip
chilled milk until it
stands in stiff peaks.
Pour whipped milk
over cooled gelatin
mixture and beat
with mixer at low
speed. Pour into pie
shell; chill at least 1
hour. Garnish with
drained, crushed
pineapple, if desired.
*Doris Moore*
*Dorothy Moore*

## Pumpkin Pie 1

Part 1:
1/4 cup butter
1 cup brown sugar
1 cup hot water
1 can sweetened,
  condensed milk

**Part 2:**
3 1/2 cups (1 large can) pumpkin
1 tsp. salt
3 eggs, separated
3 rounded Tbsp. flour
1 tsp. cinnamon
1/2 tsp. ginger
1 cup sugar
3/4 cup milk
3 8-inch, unbaked pie shells

Brown butter and brown sugar in skillet or pan; add hot water and milk. Turn off burner and let stand. Mix pumpkin, salt, egg yolks, flour, and spices. Add mixture from Part 1 plus sugar and milk. Beat egg whites and fold in last. Pour into pie shells. Bake for 10 minutes at 400° to set crust; then decrease heat to 325° or 350°. When just about done, sprinkle tops with coconut, chopped walnuts, or *Pumpkin Topping* (see next column).
*Rachel Shoup*

## Pumpkin Pie 2

1 1/2 cups pumpkin, cooked
1 cup brown sugar
1/2 tsp. cloves
1/4 tsp. allspice
1 tsp. cinnamon
1/4 tsp. ginger
1 tsp. salt
3 eggs, separated
3/4 cup milk, scalded
3 8-inch, *or* 2 10-inch, unbaked pie shells

Prebake pie shells for 8–10 minutes at 350°. Meanwhile, mix pumpkin with sugar, spices, salt, and egg yolks. Scald milk and add to pumpkin mixture. Beat egg whites, and add to pumpkin mixture. Beat until smooth and pour into partially baked shells. Bake about 30 minutes at 325° until filling is firm to touch.
*Flossie Rumble*

## Pumpkin Pie Topping

About 10 minutes before pie finishes baking, sprinkle the top with this mixture. Blend together:
1 Tbsp. butter
2 Tbsp. brown sugar
1 Tbsp. grated orange rind
3/4 cup whole pecans
*Fern Boyd*

## Quakertown Pie

Filling:
1 cup brown sugar
1/2 cup molasses
2 cups hot water
1 large Tbsp. flour
1 egg
1 tsp. vanilla
2 8-inch, unbaked pie shells

Topping:
2 cups flour
1 tsp. baking powder
1 tsp. baking soda
1/2 cup shortening or margarine

Boil filling ingredients, except vanilla, until thick like cream. Add vanilla. Pour into pie shells. Make *Topping* by crumbling ingredients together. Sprinkle over filling. Bake 40 minutes at 350°.
*Frances Kelley*
*Mary Ellen Miller*

## Raisin Cream Pie 1

1 cup raisins
1/2 cup sugar
1 cup cream *or* half-and-half
2 Tbsp. flour
1 egg yolk
1 tsp. vinegar
1 8-inch, baked pie shell

Cook raisins in water until liquid is absorbed. Mix sugar, cream, and flour. Cook until thick. Add raisins and then egg yolk. Remove from heat. Add vinegar. Pour into baked pie shell. Top with a meringue and brown lightly in 350° oven for 8 minutes.
*Anna Brubaker*

Variation:
Use 2 eggs.
*Ethel Rumble*

## Raisin Cream Pie 2

2 Tbsp. butter
1 cup sugar
2 eggs
1/2 cup milk
1 cup raisins
3/4 cup nuts, chopped
1 8-inch, unbaked pie
   shell

Cream butter and sugar; add eggs and beat well. Add milk and stir together. Then add raisins and nuts. Pour mixture into pie shell. Bake open-faced or with a lattice top crust, for 15 minutes at 400°; then bake 20 minutes or more at 325°.
*Ruby Bowman*

## Raisin Cream Pie 3

1 cup raisins
1 1/2 rounded Tbsp.
   flour
3/4 cup sugar
1 1/2 cups cream
3 egg yolks
pinch of salt
1 9-inch, baked pie
   shell

Cook raisins in a little water until liquid is absorbed. Add remaining ingredients except vanilla.

Cook until thick. Add vanilla. Pour into pie shell. Top with a meringue and brown lightly in 350° oven about 8 minutes. Serves 6.
*Martha Gish*

## Raisin Cream Pie 4

1 4-oz. pkg. vanilla
   pudding mix
1/4 cup sugar
1/8 tsp. salt
1 1/3 cups water
1/3 cup seeded
   muscat raisins
2/3 cup sour cream
1 9-inch, baked pie
   shell

Combine pudding mix, sugar, salt, and water; blend well and stir in raisins. Cook as directed on pudding package. Remove from heat and cool 5 minutes, stirring once or twice. Stir in sour cream. Pour into pie shell and sprinkle with nutmeg and top with whipped cream, if desired.
*Ruth Long*

## Raisin Mocha Meringue Pie

1 1/2 cups seedless
   raisins
1 cup water
2 tsp. instant coffee
1 6-oz. pkg. semi-sweet
   chocolate pieces
1/2 pt. whipping
   cream
1 9-inch meringue
   shell

Simmer raisins, water, and instant coffee 5 minutes. Cover and let stand until cold; drain. Melt chocolate over warm water. Whip cream until barely stiff. Fold warm chocolate into cream slowly. Fold in raisins. Turn into meringue shell. Chill thoroughly.
*Annabelle Gish*

## Raspberry Cream Pie

1 cup sugar
4 rounded Tbsp. flour
   or cornstarch
1/2 cup hot water
2 cups cream
3–4 cups raspberries,
   fresh *or*
   frozen and thawed
2 8-inch, unbaked pie
   shells

Mix sugar, flour, and water together in small bowl; add cream. Gently fold in raspberries. Pour into pie shells and bake at 350° for 40 minutes or until filling is set.
*Alice Kline*

## Rhubarb Custard Pie

1 1/2 cups rhubarb,
   cut fine
1 cup sugar
1 Tbsp. flour
1/2 tsp. cinnamon
1 Tbsp. butter, melted
2 eggs, separated
1 cup milk
1 8-inch, unbaked pie
   shell

Mix rhubarb, sugar, flour, and cinnamon; then add melted butter. Put into pie shell. Beat egg yolks well and add milk to them. Pour egg mixture over rhubarb mixture. Bake at least 1 hour at 350°. When done, make meringue from whites. Spoon on pie and bake at 325° for 8 minutes or until meringue is lightly browned.
*Ethel Rumble*

## Southern Nut Pie

1/2 cup crunchy cereal
1/2 cup warm water
1 cup light brown sugar
1 cup dark corn syrup
1/2 cup butter
1/8 tsp. salt
3 eggs, slightly beaten
1/2 cup pecans, chopped
1 tsp. vanilla
1 9-inch, unbaked pie shell

Mix cereal with warm water; let stand until water is absorbed. Meanwhile, combine sugar, syrup, butter, and salt. Bring quickly to a boil over high heat, stirring until sugar is dissolved. Add small amount syrup to eggs, beating well. Then add rest of syrup, mixing well. Stir in softened cereal, nuts, and vanilla. Pour into pie shell. Bake at 375° for 45 to 50 minutes or until filling is puffed across top. Cool before serving.
*Karen L. Miller*

## Southern Chess Pie

1 cup brown sugar
1/2 cup white sugar
1 Tbsp. flour
2 eggs
2 Tbsp. milk
1 tsp. vanilla
1/2 cup butter, melted
1 cup pecans or walnuts, chopped
1 8-inch, unbaked pie shell

Combine sugars and flour. Beat in other ingredients, except nuts. Then fold in nuts. Pour into pie shell and bake at 375° for 40 minutes or just until filling sets.
*Emma Blickenstaff*
*Joyce Peters*

## Fresh Strawberry Pie 1

4 cups strawberries, washed and hulled
1 cup sugar
2 tsp. cornstarch
pinch of salt
2 Tbsp. lemon juice
1 Tbsp. butter
several drops red food coloring
1 9- or 10-inch, baked pie shell

Mash 2 cups strawberries. Add sugar, cornstarch, salt, and lemon juice. Cook until clear, stirring constantly. Add butter and coloring. Remove from heat. Cool completely. Pour over 2 cups fresh strawberries, folding gently. Pour into pie shell.

Chill. Garnish with whipped cream to serve.
*Annie Silvers*
*Ruth Yost*
*Phyllis Denlinger*

## Fresh Strawberry Pie 2

Glaze:
1 cup sugar
2 Tbsp. cornstarch
pinch of salt
1 3/4 cups cold water
1 3-oz. pkg. strawberry gelatin
1 tsp. vanilla
4 drops red food coloring
2 pts. strawberries, washed and hulled
1 9-inch, baked pie shell

Mix sugar, cornstarch, and salt. Add cold water and cook, stirring constantly, until clear. While still hot, add gelatin, vanilla, and coloring. Cool until mixture starts to thicken. Slice strawberries and arrange in shell; then pour on glaze. Chill. Top with whipped cream when serving.
*Barbara Gish*

## Fresh Strawberry Pie 3

1 3-oz. pkg. strawberry gelatin
1/2 cup plus 2 Tbsp. sugar
1/4 tsp. salt
1 1/2 cups boiling water
2 Tbsp. lemon juice
1/2 pt. whipping cream *or* 1 envelope whipped topping mix
1 9-inch, baked pie shell
1 box fresh strawberries, stemmed

Dissolve gelatin, 1/2 cup sugar, and salt in boiling water. Add lemon juice and set aside 1/2 cup for glaze. Chill remainder until lightly thickened. Whip cream, adding 2 Tbsp. sugar. Reserve 1/4 cup whipped cream, folding remaining whipped cream into slightly thickened gelatin. Spoon into pie shell. Chill until set.
Meanwhile, chill reserved glaze until slightly thickened. Arrange whole or halved strawberries over top of pie filling. Spoon glaze evenly over strawberries.

Chill until firm. Garnish with remaining whipped cream.
*Lou Rumble*

## Strawberry Freezer Pie

2 egg whites
1 scant cup sugar
1/2 tsp. salt
1 Tbsp. lemon juice
1 pt. strawberries, sliced
1/2 pt. whipping cream, whipped
1 8-inch, baked pie shell

Beat whites, sugar, salt, and lemon juice for 15 minutes. Fold in strawberries and whipped cream. Pour into pie shell and freeze.
*Ruthanne Wise*

## Surprise Beauty "Pie"

Crust:
2 cups vanilla wafers, crushed
1/2 cup butter, melted
Filling:
1 8-oz. pkg. cream cheese, softened
1 cup sugar
1 tsp. vanilla
2 cups miniature marshmallows
chopped nuts, (optional)
Topping:
1 box Junket Danish dessert
1 small box frozen berries
Combine crust in-

gredients and press into 13x9x2-inch pan or 3 8-inch pie pans. Combine cream cheese, sugar, and vanilla. Add marshmallows and nuts. Pour over crust.
Make topping according to package directions, except use 1 1/4 cups water instead of 2 cups. Combine topping with berries, reserving a few for garnish. Spoon topping over filling and garnish with remaining berries. Refrigerate.
Variation:
Use regular, baked pie crusts.
*Gay Bauman*

## Vanilla Pie

Syrup:
1 egg
1 cup sugar
2 cups cold water
1 cup dark corn syrup
1 tsp. vanilla
4 8-inch, unbaked pie shells
Cake Mixture:
1 egg
1/2 cup shortening
2 cups sugar
1 tsp. baking soda
3 cups flour
pinch of salt
1 cup buttermilk

Mix syrup ingredients together and set aside. For cake mixture, cream egg, shortening, and sugar. Sift dry ingredients and add alternately with buttermilk to creamed mixture; set aside. Pour syrup mixture into pie shells.

Top with about 6 Tbsp. cake mixture per pie. Bake in 350° oven for 40 minutes or until done, testing as for a cake.
*Lola Miller*

## White Christmas Pie

1 Tbsp. unflavored gelatin
1/4 cup cold water
1/2 cup sugar
4 Tbsp. flour
1/2 tsp. salt
1 1/2 cups milk
3/4 tsp. vanilla
1/4 tsp. almond extract
1/2 cup whipping cream
3 egg whites (3/8 cup)
1/4 tsp. cream of tartar
1/2 cup sugar
1 9-inch, baked pie shell
1 cup coconut, moist and shredded

Soften gelatin in cold water; set aside. Mix sugar, flour, and salt together in saucepan. Slowly stir in milk; cook over low heat, stirring until mixture boils. Boil 1 minute; remove from heat. Stir in softened gelatin. Cool. When partially set, beat with egg beater until smooth. Blend in vanilla and extract. Whip cream until stiff and gently fold into gelatin mixture. Then make a meringue of egg whites, cream of tartar, and sugar; fold into mixture. Then add coconut. Pile into pie shell. Sprinkle

with coconut. Chill until set, about 2 hours.
Note:
Double this recipe to make 3 8-inch pies.
*Leah Garber*

# Fruit Pies

## Apple Crumb Pie

4 large apples, pared and sliced
1 cup sugar
1 tsp. cinnamon
3/4 cup flour
1/2 cup butter
1 9-inch, unbaked pie shell

Mix apples, 1/2 cup sugar, and spice together. Mix remaining 1/2 cup sugar, flour, and butter until crumbly; pour on top of apples. Bake in pie shell at 450° for 10 minutes. Reduce heat and bake until apples are soft.
*Rhonda Landes*

## Apple Pizza Pie

Crust:
1 1/4 cups flour, sifted
1 tsp. salt
1/2 cup shortening
1 cup Cheddar cheese, shredded
1/4 cup ice water
Topping:
1/2 cup powdered non-dairy creamer
1/2 cup brown sugar
1/2 cup white sugar
1/3 cup flour, sifted
1/4 tsp. salt

1 tsp. cinnamon
1/2 tsp. nutmeg
1/4 cup butter
6 cups apple slices, 1/2" thick
2 Tbsp. lemon juice

Combine flour, salt, and shortening until crumbly. Add cheese, mixing well. Add ice water. Roll on floured board to 15-inch circle. Pat in pizza pan and flute edges. Mix dry topping ingredients together. Sprinkle 1/2 of dry mixture over pastry in pan. Cut butter into rest of crumbs until crumbly. Overlap apple slices and sprinkle with lemon juice. Add remaining crumbs on top. Bake 30 minutes at 450°. Serves 12.
*Miriam Blocher*

## Mock Apple Pie

1 1/2 cups sugar
1 1/2 cups water
1 1/2 tsp. cream of
  tartar
1 tsp. cinnamon
nutmeg, (optional)
1 tsp. lemon juice
12 soda crackers
butter

Boil first 5 ingredients 5 minutes. Add lemon juice. Cool. Pour over 12 crackers lining pie pan. Dot with butter. Then break crackers in about 3 or 4 pieces; mixture will look soupy. Bake at 375° for 25 minutes.
*Leah Garber*

## Blueberry Pie

1 scant cup sugar
1/3 cup flour
2 9-inch, unbaked pie
  shells
4 cups blueberries,
  washed and drained
pinch of salt
1 1/2 Tbsp. lemon
  juice
6 Tbsp. water
butter

Mix 1/2 of sugar and flour in bottom of pie shells. Add berries, remaining flour and sugar, salt, lemon juice, and water. Dot with butter. Add top pie shell. Bake at 350° for 45 minutes or until done.
*Nellie Miller*

## Peach Crumb Pie

1 9-inch, unbaked pie
  shell
3/4 cup sugar
3 Tbsp. flour
5 cups fresh peaches,
  peeled and sliced
1 1/2 tsp. lemon juice
3 Tbsp. butter
1/4 cup flour
1/3 cup brown sugar

Mix together sugar, flour, peaches, and lemon juice. Pour into pie shell. Combine butter, flour, and brown sugar until crumbly and sprinkle over peaches. Bake at 400° for 40 minutes.
*Joan Cover*

## Apple Pie Deluxe

1 cup sugar
2 Tbsp. flour
1/8 tsp. salt
1/2 tsp. cinnamon
4 cups (5 or 6) tart
  apples, pared and
  diced
4 canned pear halves
1 tsp. rum flavoring
2 Tbsp. butter

Mix together sugar, flour, salt, and cinnamon. Add to prepared apples and mix thoroughly. Set aside. Crush 4 canned pear halves and spread on bottom of a 9-inch pie shell. Sprinkle with rum flavoring. Heap apple mixture over pears; dot with butter. Put on top crust, seal, and crimp edges. Cut open design for steam to escape. Bake at 400° for 45 minutes or until apples are tender. Best served warm.
*Eunice Grover*

Source:                              Who Likes It:

Source:                              Who Likes It:

Source:                              Who Likes It:

## PLAY-DOUGH

1 cup flour
1/2 cup salt
2 tsp. cream of tartar
2 Tbsp. salad oil
1 cup water
color with food coloring

Mix all ingredients together in saucepan. Cook over medium heat, stirring constantly, until "dough" sticks together. Store in a plastic container when cool.

Note: *This is not to be eaten.*

# Cake Collectibles and Frosting Finds

*When wealth is lost,*
*nothing is lost;*
*when health is lost,*
*something is lost;*
*when character is lost,*
*all is lost.*
GERMAN PROVERB

*Forgetting what is behind . . .*
*I press on*
*toward the goal*
*to win the prize*
*for which God*
*has called me heavenward*
*in Christ Jesus.*
PHILIPPIANS 3:13, 14 (NIV)

# Cake Collectibles

Angel Food, Chiffon, and Sponge Cakes

## Chocolate Angel Food Cake

3/4 cup cake flour, sifted
4 Tbsp. cocoa powder
1 1/4 cups egg whites (10 to 12 whites)
1/4 tsp. salt
1 tsp. cream of tartar
1 1/4 cups sugar, sifted
1 tsp. vanilla

Sift flour and cocoa 4 times; set aside. In a large bowl beat egg whites and salt until foamy; add cream of tartar. Continue beating eggs until stiff enough to hold up in peaks, but not dry. Fold in sugar, 2 Tbsp. at a time. Add vanilla. Fold in flour, 2 Tbsp. at a time. Pour mixture into ungreased angel food cake pan. Bake at 275° for 30 minutes. Increase to 325° and bake 1 hour. Remove from oven and invert pan; remove cake when completely cooled.
*Rachel Shoup*

## Feather Sponge Cake

6 eggs, separated
1/2 cup cold water
1 1/2 cups sugar
1/2 tsp. vanilla
1/2 tsp. lemon or orange extract
1 1/2 cups cake flour
1/4 tsp. salt
3/4 tsp. cream of tartar

Beat egg yolks until thick and lemon colored; add water gradually and continue beating until very thick. Gradually beat in sugar and then extracts. Fold in flour sifted with salt, a little at a time. Beat egg whites until foamy; add cream of tartar and beat until whites form moist glossy peaks. Fold in egg yolk mixture. Pour into tube pan and bake at 325° for 1 hour and 10 minutes. Cool. Split cake into 3 equal layers. Spread with a lemon pie filling or pudding. Frost with whipped cream; then sprinkle on *Crisp Coffee Topping*.

Crisp Coffee Topping:
3/4 cup sugar
2 Tbsp. coffee, liquid
2 Tbsp. light corn syrup
1 1/2 tsp. baking soda

Bring sugar, coffee, and syrup to a boil; cook to hard crack stage. Remove from heat and add baking soda. Stir vigorously until well blended, but not enough to destroy foam made by soda. Turn at once into ungreased shallow pan. Let set without moving until completely cold. Knock out of pan and crush between sheets of waxed paper to make coarse crumbs.
*Ada Wise*

## Filled Chiffon Cake

1 frozen chiffon cake
1 pkg. instant vanilla pudding mix
1 small can crushed pineapple, undrained
2 cups cream, whipped

Combine pudding mix and pineapple. Fold 1 cup whipped cream into pineapple-pudding mixture. Slice cake in 3 layers. Put mixture between layers of cake. Freeze. Frost with 1 cup whipped cream, when ready to serve.
Variation:
Use frozen angel food cake or pound cake instead.
*Ruth Wise*

# 172
CAKE
COLLECTIBLES
AND
FROSTING
FINDS

## Glorious Sponge Cake

6 eggs, separated
1/2 tsp. cream of tartar
1/2 tsp. salt
1 cup sugar
1 cup flour
1/4 cup water
1 tsp. vanilla

Beat egg whites, cream of tartar, and salt together in large bowl for 5 minutes. Add 1/2 cup sugar; set aside. Beat egg yolks for 5 minutes; add remaining 1/2 cup sugar, flour, water, and vanilla. Fold in egg whites. Bake in tube pan at 325° for 60–70 minutes. Cool. Make *Penuche Icing*.

Penuche Icing:
1/4 cup butter
1/2 cup brown sugar, packed
2 Tbsp. milk
1 cup powdered sugar
1/4 cup nuts, chopped

Melt butter; add brown sugar and boil 2 minutes, stirring constantly. Add milk; return to boil, stirring constantly. Add powdered sugar and nuts. Spread thinly over cake.
*Ruth Balsbaugh*

## Quick Sponge Cake

1 cup cake flour
1 tsp. baking powder
1/4 tsp. salt
7/8 cup sugar
3 eggs
1 1/2 Tbsp. water
1 tsp. vanilla

Measure dry ingredients into bowl. Make a hole in the center of ingredients. Place eggs, water, and vanilla in hole. Beat until smooth. Bake in 9-inch square pan at 350° for 20 minutes. Frost if desired. Serve warm or cold with fruit and milk or cream.
*Marjorie Miller*

## CAKE MIXERS
### Breakfast Cake

1 large pkg. yellow cake mix
4 eggs
3/4 cup oil
1 cup cold water
1/2 cup sugar
2 tsp. cinnamon
1/2 cup nuts, chopped

Combine all ingredients and beat 8 minutes. Layer cake batter alternately with sugar, cinnamon, and nuts in Bundt or angel food pan. Bake at 350° for 1 hour. Top with *Drizzle Frosting*.

Drizzle Frosting:
1 cup powdered sugar
2 Tbsp. butter
3 Tbsp. milk
1 tsp. vanilla

Beat ingredients together well.
*Margaret Brubaker*

## Strawberry Gelatin Cake

1 large pkg. white cake mix
1 6-oz. pkg. strawberry gelatin
2 cups hot water
1 box strawberry whipped topping mix *or* non-dairy frozen topping *or* real whipped cream

Bake cake as directed. When done, make deep holes all through cake with fork. Dissolve gelatin in 2 cups hot water (no cold water). Pour or spoon it over hot cake. Place in refrigerator and chill. Prepare topping; spread on cake. Chill until firm. Serve with mound of whipped cream on top.
*Arleen Peters*
*Donna Rumble*

## Easy Lemon Bundt Cake 1

1 small pkg. lemon gelatin
3/4 cup water
3/4 cup oil
1 large pkg. lemon cake mix
4 eggs

Combine ingredients; beat 2 minutes on medium speed. Pour into 13x9x2-inch pan or Bundt pan. Bake at 350° for 30 minutes. Combine topping ingredients.

Topping:
2 cups powdered sugar
1/2 tsp. lemon juice
3 Tbsp. milk
1/2 cup butter

After cake is done, poke holes in top with a fork. Pour topping over cake and return to oven for 5 minutes.
*Phyllis Denlinger*
Variation:
Use a white cake mix and orange or cherry gelatin.
*Janice Root*

## Easy Lemon Bundt Cake 2

1 large pkg. white cake mix
1 pkg. lemon gelatin
4 eggs
3/4 cup apricot nectar
3/4 cup oil
1 can frozen lemonade concentrate, thawed

Mix first five ingredients and beat 4 minutes. Pour into greased and floured Bundt pan. Bake for 30 to 45 minutes in 350° oven. Pour lemonade concentrate on cake while warm.
*Myrtle Bashor*

## Pecan Cinnamon Cake

Cake:
1 large pkg. yellow cake mix
1 small pkg. instant vanilla pudding mix
3/4 cup water
3/4 cup less 2 Tbsp. oil
4 eggs
1 tsp. vanilla
Filling:
3/4 cup pecans, chopped
1/2 cup sugar
1 tsp. cinnamon

Mix cake ingredients and beat. Put alternately in tube pan with filling, ending with batter on top. Bake at 350° for 45 to 50 minutes. Cool 15 minutes; then invert on serving plate and glaze.
Glaze:
3/4 cup powdered sugar
1/2 tsp. vanilla
1/4 tsp. cinnamon
3 tsp. water
Combine ingredients, beating until smooth.
*Karen L. Miller*
*Iva Bauman*

## Sherry Cake

1 large pkg. yellow cake mix
1 small pkg. instant vanilla pudding
4 eggs
3/4 cup sherry wine
3/4 cup oil
1 tsp. nutmeg

Mix all ingredients together for 5 minutes. Bake in greased and floured tube or Bundt pan at 350° for 45 minutes.
*Mina Benedict*

## Valentine Delight

1 large pkg. white cake mix
1 cup boiling water
1 3-oz. pkg. cherry gelatin
1/2 cup fruit juice or water
1/2 cup crushed pineapple, drained
1/4 cup nuts, chopped
a few drops lemon juice
1 cup whipping cream, chilled

1/4 cup powdered sugar

Bake cake mix in heart-shaped pans. Cool 10 minutes; remove from pans. Pour boiling water over gelatin; stir in fruit juice. Chill until slightly thickened. Stir in pineapple, nuts, and lemon juice. For later ease of lifting, place in each pan 2 strips of foil, extending over pan edges. Put cooled layers back in pans, one layer right side up and the other layer upside down. Spoon gelatin mixture evenly over tops of layers. Chill until firm. Beat cream and powdered sugar. Carefully lift cake out and put on serving plate. Stack layers with gelatin side up. Frost sides with whipped cream. Decorate with red hots.
Variation:
Use lime gelatin, instead of cherry, and round cake pans.
*Leah Garber*

# 174
CAKE
COLLECTIBLES
AND
FROSTING
FINDS

## Van Gogh Cake

4 eggs
1 large pkg. yellow
  cake mix
1 3-oz. pkg. instant
  lemon pudding mix
3/4 cup water
3/4 cup oil

Put all ingredients in
mixer at once and
beat well. Pour into
greased tube or
Bundt pan. Bake 50
minutes at 325°.
Pour *Orange Glaze*
on cake while hot.
Orange Glaze:
1 1/2 cups powdered
  sugar
2 Tbsp. butter, melted
1/3 cup orange juice
  concentrate, thawed
Combine ingredients,
beating until smooth.
*Nellie Miller*

## CHOCOLATE CAKES
## Carob Cake

1/2 cup butter or
  margarine
1 cup brown sugar
2 eggs
1 cup whole wheat
  flour
1/2 tsp. salt
1/4 cup carob powder
1/4 tsp. cinnamon
1/2 tsp. baking powder
1/2 tsp. baking soda
1/2 cup buttermilk

Cream butter and
sugar together. Add
eggs and beat well.
Sift dry ingredients
together 3 times and
add to creamed mix-
ture alternately with
1/2 cup buttermilk,
beating well. Put into
8-inch square or
round pan. Bake at
350° for 25 to 30
minutes. Cool and
frost.
Carob Frosting:
1/3 cup carob powder
2/3 cup milk powder
4 tsp. vanilla
2 Tbsp. oil
1/4 cup honey
Beat ingredients
thoroughly until light
and creamy. Will frost
two 8" layers.
Note:
A natural chocolate
substitute, carob
powder comes from
the dried pods of the
carob tree. Its use
dates back to Bible
days. When substi-
tuting it for chocolate,
use brown sugar in-
stead of white.
*Eunice Grover*

## Chocolate Applesauce Cake

1 cup shortening
2 cups brown sugar,
  packed
2 eggs
2 2/3 cups canned
  applesauce
3 1/2 cups flour
6 Tbsp. cocoa
2 tsp. baking soda
1 tsp. salt
2 tsp. cinnamon
1/2 tsp. nutmeg
1/2 tsp. cloves

Beat shortening and
sugar until light and
fluffy. Add eggs and
applesauce. Combine
remaining ingre-
dients and sift into
creamed mixture.
Mix until well blended.
Spoon into well-
greased 13x9x2-inch
pan. Bake 35 to 40
minutes at 350°.
*Maralee Oyler*

## Chocolate Buttermilk Cake 1

1/2 cup shortening
1 1/2 cups white
  sugar and 1/2 cup
  brown *or*
  2 cups white sugar
4 Tbsp. cocoa
1 tsp. salt
2 eggs
2 cups buttermilk
2 tsp. baking soda
2 1/2 cups flour
1 tsp. vanilla

Cream shortening,
sugar, cocoa, and salt.
Add eggs, one at a
time, beating well.
Combine buttermilk
and baking soda; add
to creamed mixture
alternately with flour.
Add vanilla. Bake in
13x9x2-inch pan at
350° until done.
Frost as desired.
*Lola Miller*

## Chocolate Buttermilk Cake 2

1/2 cup shortening
2 cups sugar
2 eggs, beaten
1/2 cup buttermilk
2 tsp. vanilla
2 1/2 cups flour
3 tsp. baking soda
1/2 tsp. salt
1/2 cup cocoa
1 cup boiling water

Cream shortening; add sugar gradually, creaming well. Add beaten eggs, buttermilk, and vanilla, beating well. Sift together dry ingredients, including cocoa, and add to creamed mixture. Add boiling water and beat again. Pour into two 9-inch greased cake pans. Bake at 350° for 30 minutes or until done. Cool and frost. Note:

Use sour milk if buttermilk is not available. Make yours by adding a teaspoon or so of vinegar per cup of regular milk; let mixture stand several minutes.
*Betty King*

## Chocolate Buttermilk Cake 3

2 cups flour
2 cups sugar
1/2 cup margarine
1/2 cup shortening
4 Tbsp. cocoa
1 cup water
1/2 cup buttermilk
2 eggs, beaten
1 tsp. baking soda
1 tsp. cinnamon
1 tsp. vanilla

Combine flour and sugar; set aside. In saucepan, bring margarine, shortening, cocoa, and water to a boil. Pour cocoa mixture over flour and sugar; stir. Then add remaining ingredients. Mix well and pour into a greased jelly roll pan. Bake at 400° for 20 minutes. Ice while hot.

Icing:
1/2 cup margarine
4 Tbsp. cocoa
6 Tbsp. milk
1 box powdered sugar
1 tsp. vanilla

Bring margarine, cocoa, and milk to a boil. Add sugar and vanilla, beating well.
*Nancy Layman*

## Chocolate Chip Date Cake

1 cup dates, chopped
1 1/2 cups boiling water
1 tsp. baking soda
1/2 cup shortening
1 cup sugar
2 eggs, well beaten
1 1/4 cups plus 3 Tbsp. flour
1/4 tsp. salt
3/4 tsp. baking soda
Topping:
1 pkg. chocolate chips
1/2 cup sugar
1/2 cup nuts

Combine dates, water, and baking soda; let cool. Cream shortening, sugar, and eggs; add to date mixture. Sift dry ingredients and add to date-sugar mixture. Pour into a 13x9x2-inch pan. Combine topping ingredients and sprinkle on top of cake. Bake at 350° for 40 mintues.
*Chloie King*

## Chocolate Cupcakes

1/2 cup unsweetened cocoa
1 cup hot water
1 2/3 cups flour
1 1/2 cups sugar
1/2 tsp. baking powder

1 tsp. baking soda
1/2 tsp. salt
1/2 cup shortening, softened
2 eggs
1 tsp. vanilla

Line 24 muffin cups. Mix cocoa and water until smooth. Cool. Sift dry ingredients together. Add shortening and cooled cocoa mixture. Beat 2 minutes at medium speed. Add eggs and beat 2 more minutes. Stir in vanilla. Fill baking cups half full. Bake at 400° for 15 to 20 minutes. Frost as desired.
*Nancy Bowman*

## Chocolate Mayonnaise Cake 1

3 cups flour
1 1/2 cups sugar
1/3 cup cocoa
2 1/4 tsp. baking powder
1 1/2 tsp. baking soda
1 1/2 cups mayonnaise
1 1/2 cups water
1 1/2 tsp. vanilla

Combine all ingredients together. Pour into 13x9x2-inch pan. Bake at 350° for 30 minutes or until cake springs back from light finger touch. Cool and frost as desired.
*Jill Bauman*

# 176

CAKE
COLLECTIBLES
AND
FROSTING
FINDS

## Chocolate Mayonnaise Cake 2

2 cups flour, sifted
4 Tbsp. cocoa
pinch of salt
1 cup sugar
2 tsp. baking soda
1 cup mayonnaise or
  salad dressing
1 cup warm water
1 tsp. vanilla

Combine and sift flour, cocoa, and salt. Combine sugar and baking soda in mixing bowl; mix in mayonnaise and water. Add dry ingredients and beat until smooth. Add vanilla. Bake in loaf pan at 350° for 30 minutes.
*Mildred Davison*

## Dark Chocolate Cake

1/2 cup shortening
2 cups sugar
2 eggs
1/2 cup cocoa
1/2 cup hot coffee
2 cups flour
1/2 tsp. salt
1/2 tsp. baking
  powder
1 tsp. baking soda
1 cup milk
1 tsp. vanilla

Cream shortening and sugar together. Add eggs and beat. Add cocoa and coffee.

Combine dry ingredients and add to creamed mixture alternately with milk. Bake at 350° in 2 layer pans for 20 to 25 minutes or in 13x9x2-inch pan for 30 to 40 minutes.
*Cora Eller*

## Devil's Food Cake

2 cups sugar
1/2 cup shortening *or*
  butter
2 eggs
1 cup milk
1 tsp. baking soda
2 cups flour
1/2 cup cocoa
1/2 cup boiling water
1 tsp. vanilla

Cream sugar and shortening; add eggs and beat well. Dissolve cocoa in boiling water; beat to smooth paste. Sift baking soda and flour together. Add cocoa, vanilla, and flour mixture to creamed mixture. Beat well. Pour into 9-inch square pan. Bake in 350° oven for 30 minutes or until done. Cool and frost as desired.
Note:
If shortening is used, add pinch of salt.
*Flossie Rumble*

## Lazy Day Chocolate Cake 1

3 cups flour
2 cups sugar
2 tsp. baking soda
1/2 tsp. salt
6 Tbsp. cocoa
3/4 cup (12 Tbsp.) oil
2 Tbsp. vinegar

2 tsp. vanilla
2 cups water

Sift dry ingredients into mixing bowl; add liquids and mix. Pour into ungreased 13x9x2-inch pan and bake at 350° for 35 minutes.
*Lois Rumble*

## Lazy Day Chocolate Cake 2

1/2 cup chocolate
1/2 cup hot water
2 cups sugar
1/2 cup shortening
2 eggs
1 cup milk
1 tsp. vanilla
2 cups flour
1 tsp. baking soda
pinch of salt
1/2 tsp. baking powder

Dissolve chocolate in hot water. Then, combine all ingredients together, blending well. Bake 30 minutes at 350° in large pan.
*Paula Beachler*

## Quickie Brownie Cake

1/2 cup margarine
1/2 cup oil
4 Tbsp. cocoa
1 cup cold water
2 cups flour
2 cups sugar
2 eggs
1/2 cup buttermilk
1 tsp. baking soda
1 tsp. vanilla
1/4 tsp. salt

Heat margarine, oil, and cocoa until dissolved. Add water, flour, and sugar, beating well. Add remaining ingredients and blend thoroughly.

Bake in 13x9x2-inch pan at 425° for 20 minutes. Cool. Make icing.

Icing:
1/2 cup margarine
4 Tbsp. cocoa
1/4 cup milk
1 tsp. vanilla
1 box powdered sugar
1/2 cup nuts, chopped

Heat margarine and cocoa. Add remaining ingredients. Ice while cake is hot.
*Marietta Pegg*

## Sour Cream Chocolate Cake 1

4 squares baking
   chocolate
1/2 cup butter or
   margarine
1 cup boiling water
2 cups sugar
2 cups flour
1/2 tsp. salt
1 1/2 tsp. baking soda
1 cup sour cream
2 eggs, beaten slightly

Combine chocolate, butter, and water; stir until melted. Then sift dry ingredients together. Combine chocolate mixture and flour mixture. Beat well. Then add sour cream and beat. Add eggs and beat well. Bake at 375° in 13x9x2-inch glass pan or in 2 large layer pans or cupcake pans. Adjust baking time according to pan size used; generally 25–40 minutes.
*Daisy Frantz*

## Sour Cream Chocolate Cake 2

1 cup sugar
2 eggs, beaten
1 cup sour cream
dash of salt
1 tsp. baking soda
4 Tbsp. cocoa
1 cup cake flour

Mix together sugar, eggs, and sour cream. Sift dry ingredients and add to creamed mixture. Beat well. Bake at 350° in an 8-inch square pan for about 40 minutes.
*Linda Lavy*

## Sour Cream Chocolate Chip Cake

6 Tbsp. butter,
   softened
1 cup plus 1 Tbsp.
   sugar
2 eggs
1 1/3 cups flour
1 1/2 tsp. baking
   powder
1 tsp. cinnamon
1 tsp. baking soda
1 cup sour cream
1 small pkg. chocolate
   chips

Cream butter with 1 cup sugar until blended. Blend in eggs, one at a time. Combine dry ingredients. Blend with creamed mixture. Mix in sour cream. Pour batter into greased and floured 13x9x2-inch pan. Scatter chocolate chips evenly over batter and sprinkle with 1 Tbsp. sugar. Bake at 350° for 35 minutes. Serve warm or cooled.
*Eileen Barton*

## White Chocolate Cake

1/2 lb. white chocolate
1/2 cup hot water
1 cup butter or
   margarine
1 cup sugar
4 eggs, separated
1 tsp. vanilla
2 1/2 cups flour
1 tsp. baking soda
1 cup buttermilk
1/2 cup nuts, chopped
1 cup coconut, flaked

Mix chocolate and water; let cool. Cream butter and sugar until fluffy, adding egg yolks one at a time; beat well. Add melted chocolate and vanilla to creamed mixture. Sift together flour and baking soda; add alternately to creamed mixture with buttermilk or sour milk. Beat egg whites and add to mixture. Stir in nuts and coconut. Pour into 4 8-inch layer pans and bake at 350° for 30 minutes. Cool and frost with *Coconut Cream Frosting*. (See next page.)

# 178
CAKE
COLLECTIBLES
AND
FROSTING
FINDS

Coconut
Cream Frosting:
1 small can evaporated
  milk
1 cup sugar
1 Tbsp. butter
3 egg yolks, beaten
  slightly
1 tsp. vanilla
1 cup coconut
1 cup nuts, chopped

Bring milk, sugar, and butter to a boil, stirring constantly. Add beaten egg yolks and bring to a boil again after about 15 minutes. Mix in vanilla, coconut, and nuts. Cool and spread on cake.
Note:
This frosting is excellent on dark chocolate cakes, too!
*Eunice Grover*

## COFFEE KLATSCH CAKES
### Buttermilk Cake
3/4 cup margarine
2 1/2 cups sugar
3 eggs
3 1/2 cups flour
2/3 tsp. baking soda
1 1/2 tsp. baking
  powder
1 tsp. salt
2 cups buttermilk
2 tsp. vanilla

Cream margarine, sugar, and eggs.

Combine with unsifted dry ingredients. Add buttermilk and vanilla. Bake in greased 13x9x2-inch glass baking dish at 350° for 1 hour. Cool. Frost with *Cooked Coconut Frosting.*

Cooked
Coconut Frosting:
1 small can evaporated
  milk
1/2 cup sugar
2 egg yolks
1/4 cup margarine
1 tsp. vanilla
3/4 cup coconut, flaked
3/4 cup nuts, chopped

Cook milk, sugar, egg yolks, and margarine, stirring over medium heat until thickened, about 12 minutes. Add vanilla, coconut, and nuts.
Variation:
If halving the recipe, use one egg.
Note:
This frosting is excellent as a filling for chocolate layer cakes.
*Mary Gish*
*Daisy Frantz*

### Crumb Coffee Cake
1/2 cup shortening or
  margarine
1 cup sugar
2 cups flour
1/2 tsp. cloves
1 tsp. cinnamon
1/2 tsp. salt
2 tsp. baking powder
1 egg
1/2 tsp. baking soda
1 cup hot water or
  buttermilk or sour
  milk
chopped nuts or
  coconut

Combine first **7** ingredients and work into crumbs. Reserve 1 cup crumbs for top of cake. Add egg. Dissolve baking soda in hot liquid and add to remaining mixture. Beat until smooth. Pour into greased, 8-inch square pan; add crumbs and chopped nuts or coconut on top. Bake at 325° for 25 minutes.
*Barbara Rumble*

### Maudia's German Crumb Cake
1 tsp. salt
3 cups flour
2 cups sugar
1 tsp. cinnamon
1 tsp. nutmeg
1/2 cup shortening
2 cups buttermilk
1 Tbsp. baking soda
  dissolved in buttermilk

Combine dry ingredients. Cut in shortening. Reserve 1/2 cup of the dry mixture. Add buttermilk, mixing well. Then, add dissolved baking soda. Blend until smooth. Pour into 8-inch square pan. Sprinkle 1/2 cup of dry mixture on top of cake. Bake at 350° for 25 minutes.
*Muriel Onkst*

## Lazy Daisy Cake

2 eggs
1 cup sugar
1 cup flour
1 tsp. baking powder
1 tsp. vanilla
1/2 cup boiling milk
1 Tbsp. butter

Mix eggs and dry ingredients; beat 1 minute. Add vanilla, milk, and butter, beating well. Pour thin batter into greased 8-inch square pan. Bake at 325° until brown. Add topping.

Topping:
5 Tbsp. brown sugar
3 Tbsp. butter
2 Tbsp. milk

Boil and pour on hot cake. Serves 9 to 12.
*Linda Lavy*
*Edna Thompson*

## Nutmeg Coffee Cake

2 cups flour, sifted
2 tsp. baking powder
1 tsp. baking soda
1/2 cup white sugar
1 cup brown sugar
1 tsp. nutmeg
1/2 tsp. salt
1/2 cup salad oil
1/2 cup nuts, chopped
2 eggs, slightly beaten
1 cup buttermilk
1 cup raisins

Mix all ingredients together, except last three. Reserve 1 cup for topping. To rest of dry mixture, add eggs, buttermilk, and raisins. Pour into greased 13x9x2-inch metal pan. Sprinkle reserved crumbs over top. Bake at 450° for

10 minutes. Reduce heat to 350° and bake for 30 minutes.
*Dorothy Root*

## Oatmeal Cake 1

1 cup rolled oats
1 1/3 cups boiling water
1/2 cup butter
1 cup brown sugar
1 cup white sugar
2 eggs
1 1/3 cups flour
1 tsp. baking soda
1/2 tsp. salt
1 tsp. cinnamon

Combine rolled oats and boiling water; let cool. Beat the butter into oatmeal and water mixture. Combine both sugars, and add to oatmeal mixture, beating well. Add eggs and beat well. Sift flour, baking soda, salt, and cinnamon; add to oatmeal mixture, beating well. Pour and bake at 350° for 35 to 40 minutes. When done, add topping.

Topping:
6 Tbsp. butter
1/2 cup brown sugar
1 cup coconut, shredded
1/2 tsp. vanilla
1/2 cup nuts, chopped
1/3 cup cream or evaporated milk
Note:
Broil topping slightly, if desired.
*Martha Cover*
*Claudia Flory*
*Ann Crawmer*

## Oatmeal Cake 2

1 cup boiling water
1 cup quick rolled oats
1/2 cup shortening
1 cup brown sugar
1/2 cup white sugar
2 eggs
1 cup flour
1 tsp. salt
1 tsp. baking soda
1/2 tsp. cinnamon
1/2 tsp. cloves
1/2 cup nuts, chopped
1/2 cup dates, chopped

Pour boiling water over oats and set aside. Cream shortening, sugars, and eggs. Add dry ingredients. Add oats. Bake in 12x8x2-inch pan at 350° for 45 minutes or until done.
*Marianne Bowman*

# 180

CAKE
COLLECTIBLES
AND
FROSTING
FINDS

## Quick Coffee Cake

1/2 cup butter or
 margarine
1 cup white sugar
2 eggs
1/2 tsp. salt
1 tsp. vanilla
2 cups flour
1 tsp. baking powder
1 tsp. baking soda
1 cup buttermilk

Crumb Topping:
1/2 cup brown sugar
1/4 cup white sugar
1/2–1 tsp. cinnamon
2 Tbsp. flour
2 1/2 Tbsp. butter or
 margarine
1/2 cup nuts, chopped

Mix butter and sugar
well; add eggs. Mix
well. Sift dry ingredients together and
add to creamed mixture alternately with
buttermilk. Pour 1/2
of the batter into
9-inch square pan.
Combine crumb topping ingredients.
Sprinkle 1/2 of the
crumb mixture over
cake. Add remaining
cake mixture and
rest of crumbs on
top. Pat crumbs lightly into cake mixture.
Cut with knife 3
times through mixture. Bake at 350°
for 35 to 40 minutes.
Good warm or cold.
*Nellie Miller*

## Sour Cream Coffee Cake 1

1/2 cup brown sugar
1 cup white sugar
1/2 cup shortening
2 eggs
1 cup sour cream
1/2 tsp. salt
2 tsp. cinnamon
1 tsp. baking soda
1 tsp. baking powder
2 1/4 cups flour
2 cups raw apples,
 pared and grated

Topping:
1/4 cup brown sugar
1/4 cup white sugar
1/2 tsp. cinnamon
1/2 cup walnuts,
 chopped

Cream together
sugars and shortening. Add remaining
ingredients. Pour into
greased and floured
spring tube pan.
Combine topping ingredients and sprinkle on top. Bake at
350° for 50 to 60
minutes.
*Virginia Skiles*

## Sour Cream Coffee Cake 2

4 eggs
1 cup sugar
1 cup sour cream
1/4 tsp. baking soda
1 tsp. baking powder
1 1/2 cups flour
1/2 tsp. salt
1/2 tsp. vanilla

Topping:
6 Tbsp. sugar
1 1/2 tsp. cinnamon
1 Tbsp. butter
1/2 cup nuts, finely
 chopped

Beat eggs until light;
add sugar and continue beating for 1
minute. Add sour
cream. Sift dry ingredients together and
add to sour cream
mixture. Add vanilla.
Turn into buttered
13x9x2-inch pan.
Sprinkle with topping. Bake at 375°
for 35 minutes.
Serves 12.
Note:
The topping will go to
bottom of cake during
baking.
*Esther Gish*

## Sour Cream Coffee Cake 3

1/2 cup margarine
1 1/2 cups sugar
2 eggs
1 tsp. vanilla
2 cups flour
1/2 tsp. baking soda
1 tsp. baking powder
1 small carton
 sour cream

Topping:
1 cup sugar
4 tsp. cinnamon
nuts, chopped

Cream cake ingredients together.
Combine topping
ingredients, blending
well. Spread 1/2 of
batter in greased
13x9x2-inch pan.
Sprinkle with 1/2 of
topping mixture.
Repeat again. Top
with nuts.
Bake for 45 minutes
at 350°.
*Suzanne Overholtzer*

## Sour Cream Coffee Cake 4

1 cup margarine
1 1/2 cups white sugar
3 eggs
1 cup sour cream
1 tsp. baking soda
1 tsp. baking powder
2 1/2 cups flour
1 tsp. almond flavoring
Topping:
1/2 cup brown sugar
2 Tbsp. cinnamon
1/2 cup pecans or
  walnuts, chopped

Cream margarine and sugar. Add eggs. Sift dry ingredients and add to creamed mixture alternately with sour cream. Add almond flavoring. Combine brown sugar, cinnamon, and nuts. Pour a thin layer of batter into greased and floured 13x9x2-inch pan. Sprinkle with part of the topping. Pour in rest of the batter. Top with remaining topping. Bake at 350° for 25 minutes or longer until done. Serve warm or cold.
*Ruth Bowman*

## Toffee Delight

2 cups flour
1 cup white sugar
2 tsp. baking powder
1 tsp. salt
1 3 3/4-oz. pkg. dry
  instant vanilla
  pudding mix
1 3 3/4-oz. pkg. dry
  instant butterscotch
  pudding mix
1 cup water
3/4 cup cooking oil
1 tsp. vanilla
4 eggs

Topping:
1 1/2 cups brown
  sugar
1 cup nuts, chopped
1 Tbsp. cinnamon

In large mixing bowl, combine all ingredients. Beat 2 minutes at medium speed. Pour 1/3 batter into greased and floured 13x9x2-inch pan. Combine topping ingredients. Alternately layer remaining two-thirds batter with topping mixture, ending with *Topping*. Bake at 350° for 40 to 45 minutes or until top springs back when touched lightly in center.
*Phyllis Boyd*

## CORNUCOPIA CAKES
Fruit-Based
## Apple Cake 1

2 cups sugar
1/2 cup shortening
2 eggs
1 tsp. cinnamon
1/4 tsp. allspice
1/4 tsp. nutmeg
2 cups flour
2 tsp. baking soda
1/2 tsp. salt
1/2 cup nuts, chopped
4 cups raw apples,
  cored and chopped

Cream together sugar and shortening. Beat in eggs. Sift dry ingredients together and add to creamed mixture. Add nuts and apples. Bake in 13x9x2-inch pan at 350° for 40 to 45 minutes.
*Fern Boyd*

## Apple Cake 2

1 1/4 cups oil
2 cups sugar
2 eggs
1 cup nuts, chopped
3 cups apples,
  cored and diced
1 tsp. cinnamon
3 cups flour
1 tsp. baking soda
1/2 tsp. salt
2 tsp. vanilla

Mix first 6 ingredients. Then sift remaining ingredients together, and add to first mixture. Add vanilla, blending well. Bake in tube pan at 350° for 45 minutes to 1 hour.
*Ella Huffman*
Variation:
Grate apples and add 1 tsp. nutmeg.
*Becky Layman*
*Shirley Denlinger*

# 182
CAKE
COLLECTIBLES
AND
FROSTING
FINDS

## Apple Cake 3

4 cups apples, chopped
2 cups sugar
2 eggs, slightly beaten
1/2 cup salad oil
2 tsp. vanilla
2 cups flour
1 or 2 tsp. cinnamon
2 tsp. baking soda
1 tsp. salt

Combine apples and sugar; let stand. Combine eggs, oil, and vanilla. Sift dry ingredients together. Combine all together. Put into 9-inch square pan. Bake at 375° for 1 hour.
*Anna E. Brubaker*

## Applesauce Cake 1

2 cups sugar
1 cup shortening
2 tsp. baking soda
2 cups sour applesauce
water
4 cups flour, sifted
1 tsp. baking powder
2 cups raisins, floured
1 tsp. cloves
1 tsp. cinnamon

Cream sugar and shortening. Dissolve baking soda in small amount of water and add to creamed mixture. Add remaining ingredients. Bake in greased and floured 13x9x2-inch pan at 325° or 350° until tested done.
*Mary Heinrich*

## Applesauce Cake 2

1/2 cup shortening or margarine, softened
1 cup brown or white sugar
1 cup applesauce
1 1/2 cups flour
1 tsp. cinnamon
1 tsp. cloves
1/2 tsp. salt
1 tsp. baking soda
1 tsp. cocoa
1 cup raisins
1 cup chopped nuts, (optional)

Cream together shortening and sugar. Add remaining ingredients. Pour into 13x9x2-inch pan and bake at 375°. Make *Applesauce Frosting* and frost cake.

Applesauce Frosting:
1 1/2 cups powdered sugar
2 Tbsp. margarine, melted
enough applesauce to make desired thickness

Combine ingredients, beating well.
Note:
This is a very moist cake and will freeze well.
*Jane Layman*

## Applesauce Cake 3

2 1/2 cups flour
1 1/2 cups sugar
1/4 tsp. baking powder
1 1/2 tsp. baking soda
1 1/2 tsp. salt
3/4 tsp. cinnamon
1/2 tsp. cloves
1/2 tsp. allspice
1/2 cup shortening, softened
1/2 cup water
1/2 cup walnuts, chopped
1 1/2 cups applesauce, sweetened
1 large egg

Sift dry ingredients together. Add shortening, water, and walnuts; beat for 2 minutes. Add applesauce and egg; beat 2 minutes. Place in 13x9x2-inch pan. Bake at 350° for 45 to 50 minutes.
*Janet Rumble*

## Apricot Cake

3 cups flour
2 1/2 cups sugar
1 3/4 tsp. baking soda
1 tsp. salt
2 tsp. cinnamon
3 eggs
1 cup canned apricots, drained and cut up
1 cup oil
3/4 cup apricot juice
1 cup nuts, chopped

Mix dry ingredients; make a well and add eggs and apricots. Beat well. Add oil and juice; mix thoroughly. Add nuts. Bake in 3 loaf pans lined with waxed paper at 350° for 60 minutes or until done; for tube pan, bake at 325° for 75 minutes.
*Verna Kinze*

## Banana Cake 1

2 cups cake flour, sifted
1 tsp. baking soda
3/4 tsp. salt
1 1/3 cups sugar
1 tsp. baking powder
1/2 cup butter or shortening, softened
1/2 cup sour milk or buttermilk
1 cup ripe bananas, mashed
2 eggs
1/2 cup nuts, chopped

Sift dry ingredients into shortening. Add 1/4 cup milk and mashed bananas; mix until flour is moistened. Then beat 2 minutes, scraping bowl often. Add eggs, nuts, and remaining milk. Beat 1 minute longer at low speed of electric mixer. Pour into 2 greased and floured 8-inch layer pans. Bake at 350° for 25 minutes or until done. Cool and frost.
*Betty King*

## Banana Cake 2

1/2 cup butter
1 1/2 cups sugar
2 eggs
1 cup bananas, mashed
1/2 tsp. lemon juice
1 tsp. vanilla
4 tsp. sour cream
1/2 cup nuts, chopped
1 3/4 cups flour
1 tsp. baking powder
1/2 tsp. baking soda
pinch of salt

Cream butter; add sugar, mixing well. Add eggs, blending well; then add bananas. Add remaining ingredients. Bake in large loaf pan for 35 minutes at 350°.
*Joan Howser*

## Banana Cake 3

1/2 cup shortening
1 1/2 cups sugar
2 eggs, beaten lightly
1 cup bananas, mashed
1 3/4 cups flour
4 Tbsp. sour milk
1 tsp. baking soda
1 tsp. baking powder
1 tsp. vanilla
1 cup nuts, chopped

Cream shortening and sugar. Add eggs and mix well. Then add bananas. Combine flour and baking powder. Combine sour milk and baking soda. Add flour and sour milk alternately to banana mixture. Add vanilla and nuts last. Bake in 2 8-inch layer pans at 350° for 30 minutes. or as cupcakes at 375° for 20 minutes.
*Ella Huffman*
*Edna Stamy*

## Date Cake

2 cups dates, chopped
1 1/2 cups boiling water
3 cups flour
1 Tbsp. butter
1 egg
2 tsp. baking soda
1 cup nuts, chopped

Pour boiling water over dates and set aside to cool. Combine remaining ingredients. Add to dates. Pour into 13x9x2-inch pan. Bake at 350° for 1 hour.
*Ida Garber*

## Fruit Cake

1 1/2 cups raisins
1 1/2 cups dates
2 cups sugar
2 cups boiling water
3 cups flour
1 tsp. baking powder
3/4 tsp. salt
1 tsp. cloves
1 tsp. baking soda
2 tsp. cinnamon
1 cup nuts, floured
1 cup candied fruit

Combine first 4 ingredients and simmer 20 minutes. Cool. Add dry ingredients to cooked mixture. Then add nuts and candied fruit. Pour into 2 loaf pans. Bake 1 1/2 hours at 300°.
*Dorothy Gish*

# 184
CAKE
COLLECTIBLES
AND
FROSTING
FINDS

## Fruit Cocktail Cake

2 cups flour
1 1/2 cups brown
    sugar
2 tsp. baking soda
1/4 tsp. salt
2 cups fruit cocktail,
    undrained
1 cup nuts, chopped

Mix dry ingredients by hand in large bowl. Add fruit and nuts. Pour into 8-inch square baking dish or larger pan to make bars; bake at 350° for 35 minutes. Cool; make frosting and frost.

Boiled Frosting:
1/2 cup margarine
1/3 cup canned milk
3/4 cup brown sugar
1 cup coconut
1 tsp. vanilla

Boil margarine, milk, and sugar to soft ball. Stir in coconut and vanilla.
*Linda Thompson*

## Gumdrop Fruit Cake

4 cups flour
1/4 tsp. salt
1 tsp. cinnamon
1/4 tsp. cloves
1/4 tsp. nutmeg
1 lb. raisins
1–2 lbs. large
    gumdrops, cut up*

1 cup walnuts,
    chopped
1 cup butter
1 tsp. baking soda
1 tsp. hot water
2 cups sugar
1 1/2 cups applesauce
1 tsp. vanilla

Sift first 5 ingredients together. Dredge raisins and gumdrops in flour mixture. Gently sauté nuts in butter. Dissolve baking soda in hot water; add to buttery nuts, sugar, and eggs. Then fold in applesauce, vanilla, and dry ingredients. Pour batter into 3 small loaf pans, lined with greased paper. Bake 2 hours at 300°.
*Omit black gumdrops
*Lois Root*
*Ruby Bowman*

## Jam Cake 1

1 cup shortening
1 1/2 cups sugar
2 eggs
1 cup jam, *any kind*
3 cups flour
1 tsp. baking soda
1 1/2 tsp. nutmeg
1 Tbsp. cinnamon
1 cup sour milk

Cream shortening and sugar. Add eggs and jam to creamed mixture. Then add remaining ingredients. Pour into 13x9x2-inch pan and bake at 350° for 20 minutes.
Note:
Good as cupcakes, too.
*Lois Cover*

## Jam Cake 2

3/4 cup butter
1 cup sugar
3 eggs, separated
3/4 cup fruit jam
2 cups cake flour
1/2 cup sour milk
1 tsp. cinnamon
1 1/2 tsp. nutmeg

Cream butter and sugar; add egg yolks and then jam. Add a little flour to hold mixture together; then add sour milk. Add remaining flour and spices, beating well. Beat egg whites until stiff and add last. Bake in 9-inch square pan at 350° for 40 minutes or until done.
*Alice Kline*

## Jam Cake 3

1 lb. brown sugar
1/2 cup shortening
1 cup buttermilk
4 eggs
1 cup strawberry
    preserves
4 cups flour
3/4 tsp. salt
2 tsp. cinnamon
2 tsp. nutmeg
1 tsp. cloves
1 tsp. baking soda
1 lb. raisins
4 cups walnuts, halved

Combine all ingredients and mix well. Pour into tube pan. Bake slowly at 350° for 1/2 hour. Reduce heat to 325° and finish baking, close to 2 hours.
*Sarah Lee Switzer*

## Orange Slice Cake

1 cup butter
2 cups sugar
4 eggs
3 1/2 cups flour
1 pkg. dates, chopped
1 lb. candy orange
  slices, chopped
1 tsp. baking soda
1/2 cup buttermilk
2 cups nuts, chopped
1 can coconut, flaked

Orange Glaze:
1 cup fresh orange
  juice
2 cups powdered
  sugar

Cream butter and sugar; add eggs, one at a time. Dredge dates, orange slices, and nuts in flour; add to creamed mixture. Dissolve baking soda in buttermilk; add to batter, beating well. Blend in coconut. Pour into large tube pan and bake at 250° for 2 1/2 hours. While cake is hot, pour *Orange Glaze* on top. Let stand overnight. Then remove cake from pan.
*Ruth Bowman*
*Ruth Wise*
*Fern Boyd*

## Palmetto Cake

1 cup butter
1 box powdered sugar
5 eggs, beaten
2 tsp. coconut milk
2 tsp. baking powder
3 1/2 cups flour
1 coconut, ground
1 box white raisins
1/4 lb. candied cherries
1/4 lb. citron
1/4 lb. candied pine-
  apple
1 cup almonds, sliced

Cream butter and sugar; add beaten eggs and coconut milk. Next, add dry ingredients and mix well. Add fruits and nuts. Pour batter into greased and floured tube pan, lined with heavy brown paper. Bake at 275° for 2 1/2 to 3 hours. If browning too fast, put a pan of water in the oven.
*Mina Benedict*

## Fresh Peach Cake

1 cup shortening
2 eggs
1 1/2 cups sugar
2 cups fresh peaches,
  mashed *or* liquefied
  in blender
2 1/2 cups flour, sifted
1 tsp. allspice
1 tsp. cloves
1 tsp. cinnamon
2 tsp. baking soda
2 tsp. cocoa, (optional)
1 cup raisins, floured

Cream shortening, eggs, and sugar. Add mashed peaches to creamed mixture. Sift together flour, spices, baking soda, and cocoa; blend in well. Add raisins dredged in flour. Pour into a greased 13x9x2-inch pan, and bake at 350° for 30 minutes. Cool and frost with *Brown Sugar Frosting*.
Note:
This is a moist cake so be sure it is well baked.

Brown Sugar
Frosting:
1/2 cup butter or
  margarine
1 cup brown sugar
1/4 cup milk
1 3/4 cups powdered
  sugar

Melt butter; add brown sugar and boil over low heat 2 minutes, stirring constantly. Add milk and bring to a boil, stirring constantly. Cool to lukewarm. Add powdered sugar (more if needed) and beat until smooth.
*Mary Heinrich*

# 186
CAKE
COLLECTIBLES
AND
FROSTING
FINDS

## Prune Cake 1

1/2 cup shortening
1 1/2 cups sugar
3 eggs, well beaten
2 cups flour
1 tsp. baking powder
1 tsp. baking soda
1 tsp. cinnamon
1 tsp. nutmeg
1 tsp. allspice
1 cup sour milk
1 cup prunes, pitted
  and stewed

Cream shortening and sugar; add beaten eggs. Sift flour, baking powder, baking soda, and spices together; add to creamed mixture alternately with sour milk. Add prunes. Pour into greased and floured Bundt pan or 2 loaf pans. Bake at 350° for 50 minutes or until cake is done. Cool and frost with *Mocha Frosting*.

Mocha Frosting:
6 Tbsp. butter
1 egg yolk
3 cups powdered sugar
1 1/2 Tbsp. cocoa
1 1/2 Tbsp. hot coffee

Combine ingredients, beating until smooth.
*Flossie Rumble*

## Prune Cake 2

1 cup salad oil
2 cups sugar
3 eggs
1 tsp. vanilla
2 cups flour
1 tsp. salt
1 tsp. baking soda
1 tsp. nutmeg
1 tsp. cinnamon
1 tsp. allspice
1 cup buttermilk
1 cup nuts, chopped
1 cup pitted prunes,
  chopped

Blend oil, sugar, eggs, and vanilla, beating until smooth. Mix flour, salt, baking soda, and spices. Stir into creamed mixture. Add buttermilk and mix. Stir in nuts and prunes. Pour into a greased and floured 13x9x2-inch pan or 2 loaf pans. Bake in 350° oven for 40 to 50 minutes or until cake is done. Cool 5 minutes. Make *Buttermilk Topping*.

Buttermilk Topping:
1 cup sugar
1/2 cup buttermilk
1/2 tsp. baking soda
1 Tbsp. light corn
  syrup
1/2 tsp. vanilla
1/2 cup margarine

Combine all ingredients in saucepan. Bring to a boil and let mixture reach the soft ball stage, 234° to 240° after about 20 minutes. Mixture will be reddish-brown. Puncture top of cake with fork. Pour hot topping over cake. Cool before slicing. Serve with ice cream balls, if desired. Makes 10 to 12 servings.
*Bethel Hinkle*

## Prune Cake 3

1/2 cup shortening
1 1/4 cups sugar
3 eggs, well beaten
2 cups flour, sifted
1 tsp. baking soda
1 tsp. baking powder
1 tsp. cinnamon
1 tsp. nutmeg
1 tsp. allspice
1 cup sour milk
1 cup stewed prunes,
  pitted and chopped
  fine

Cream shortening and sugar; add beaten eggs. Sift together flour, baking soda, baking powder, and spices; add to creamed mixture alternately with sour milk. Add prunes. Pour into greased and floured Bundt pan or 13x9x2-inch pan. Bake at 375° for about 50 minutes or until done. Cool slightly and cover with icing.

Icing:
2 Tbsp. butter
3 cups powdered sugar
1 egg yolk
1 1/2 Tbsp. cocoa
1 1/2 Tbsp. boiling
  water

Cream butter, sugar, and egg yolk. Combine with cocoa dissolved in boiling water. Beat well.
*Flossie Rumble*

## Scripture Cake

4 1/2 cups flour
(1 Kings 4:22)
1 cup milk
(Judges 5:25)
1 cup butter
(Psalm 23:5)
2 cups sugar
(Jeremiah 6:20)
2 Tbsp. honey
(1 Samuel 14:25)
2 cups figs, chopped
(Nahum 3:12)
2 cups almonds,
chopped
(Numbers 17:8)
2 tsp. baking powder
(Amos 4:5)
2 tsp. baking soda
(1 Corinthians 5:6)
2 tsp. salt
(Leviticus 2:13)
6 eggs (Jeremiah 17:11)
season to taste with
spices (2 Chronicles
9:9)

Combine dry ingredients; set aside. Cream butter, sugar, and honey. Gradually add eggs one at a time, beating well. Combine with dry ingredients. Blend well. Add fruits and nuts, mixing well. Line 2 loaf pans with foil and bake at 350° for 1 hour or until done.
Note:
Bible references are from the KJV.
*Vertrilla Overholtzer*

CORNUCOPIA
CAKES
Vegetable-Based
## Beet Cake

1 cup oil
1/2 cup butter, melted
2 cups sugar
3 eggs
2 1/2 cups flour
2 tsp. cinnamon
2 tsp. baking soda
1 tsp. salt
2 tsp. vanilla
1 cup Harvard beets,
chopped
1/2 cup creamed
cottage cheese
1 cup crushed pineapple, drained
1 cup nuts, chopped
1/2 cup coconut,
shredded

Cream first 3 ingredients. Add eggs, beating well. Mix flour, cinnamon, baking soda, salt, vanilla, and beets. Add to creamed mixture, blending well. Add remaining ingredients. Pour into 13x9x2-inch pan. Bake at 350° for 45 to 50 mintues. Cool. Make *Cream Cheese Frosting.*
Cream
Cheese Frosting:
1 box powdered sugar
1/2 cup butter, melted
several drops orange
juice
1 8-oz. pkg. cream
cheese
vanilla
Combine ingredients, beating well. Frost cooled cake. Refrigerate leftover portion.
*Marjorie Miller*

## Carrot Cake 1

1 1/3 cups brown
sugar
1 1/2 cups raw carrots,
grated
1/2 tsp. cloves
1 tsp. cinnamon
1 1/2 cups cold water
1 tsp. nutmeg

2 Tbsp. shortening
1/4 tsp. salt
1 cup raisins
2 tsp. baking soda
2 cups flour
1 cup nuts, chopped

In a saucepan combine all ingredients, except last three. Boil 5 minutes; cool. Sift flour and baking soda. Add to boiled mixture, blending well. Add nuts. Pour into tube pan and bake at 350° for 50 to 60 minutes. Serve with or without frosting.
*Mary Howser*

# 188
CAKE
COLLECTIBLES
AND
FROSTING
FINDS

## Carrot Cake 2

2 cups flour
2 tsp. baking soda
1/2 tsp. salt
3 eggs
3/4 cup oil
3/4 cup buttermilk
2 cups sugar
2 tsp. vanilla
2 cups carrots, grated
1 small can crushed
  pineapple, drained
1 cup nuts, chopped
1 3 1/2-oz. can coconut

Sift dry ingredients;
set aside. Beat eggs;
add oil, buttermilk,
sugar, and vanilla.
Mix well; add to dry
ingredients. Mix in
carrots, pineapple,
nuts, and coconut.
Pour into greased
13x9x2-inch pan.
Bake at 350° for 50
minutes or until
done. Frost if
desired.
*Mildred Moore*

## Carrot Cake 3

2 cups sugar
3 cups flour
1 tsp. baking soda
2 tsp. cinnamon
1/2 tsp. salt
1 1/2 cups oil
1 tsp. vanilla
3 eggs
1 cup walnuts,
  chopped
2 cups carrots, coarsely
  grated

1 small can crushed
  pineapple, well
  drained

Mix dry ingredients
in large bowl. Add
remaining ingre-
dients. Beat well.
Pour into 2 greased
and floured loaf pans
and bake at 350°.
Bake for 1 hour and
15 minutes.
*Joy Thompson*
*Laurel Balsbaugh*

## Carrot Cake 4

2 1/2 cups flour, sifted
1 1/2 tsp. baking soda
1/2 tsp. salt
1 1/2 tsp. cinnamon
1/4 tsp. nutmeg
1 1/2 cups carrots,
  grated
1/4 cup buttermilk
1 cup butter or
  margarine
2 cups sugar
4 eggs
1 tsp. vanilla
6 oz. chopped pecans
powdered sugar

Sift flour, baking
soda, salt, cinnamon,
and nutmeg; set
aside. Combine
carrots and butter-
milk. In large bowl,
beat butter and sugar
at medium speed
until light. Add eggs
and vanilla; beat until
smooth and fluffy. At
low speed, lightly beat
in flour mixture alter-
nately with carrot
mixture, beginning
and ending with flour
mixture. Stir in nuts.
Turn into greased
and floured 10-inch
tube pan. Bake at
350° for 60 to 65
minutes or until cake

tester inserted in
middle comes out
clean. Cool in pan 15
minutes. Turn out on
rack. To serve, sift
powdered sugar on
top.
*Lois Shirk*

## Pumpkin Cake

1 1/2 cups sugar
1/2 cup shortening
2 eggs
2 cups flour
1/2 tsp. salt
1/2 tsp. baking soda
1 Tbsp. baking
  powder
1/2 tsp. cinnamon
1/2 tsp. nutmeg
1/2 tsp. ginger
3/4 cup milk
1 tsp. vanilla
1 cup pumpkin
1/2 cup nuts, chopped

Cream sugar and
shortening together.
Add eggs. Sift dry
ingredients together
and add to creamed
mixture. Add remain-
ing ingredients. Bake
in greased and
floured 13x9x2-inch
pan at 350° for 25 to
30 minutes. Cool and
prepare *Broiled Icing*.

Broiled Icing:
3 Tbsp. butter
1/4 cup nuts, chopped
1/3 cup brown sugar

Boil ingredients to-
gether. Spread on top
of cake and put
under broiler for a
couple of minutes.
*Mary Howser*

## Rhubarb Cake

1 1/2 cups brown sugar
1/2 cup shortening
1 egg
1 tsp. baking soda
1 cup sour milk
1 cup nuts, chopped
1 tsp. vanilla
1/2 tsp. salt
2 cups flour
1 1/2 cups rhubarb, chopped
Topping:
1/2 cup sugar
1/2 cup nuts, chopped
1 tsp. cinnamon

Cream sugar and shortening; add egg. Combine baking soda and sour milk; add to creamed mixture. Add remaining ingredients. Pour into 13x9x2-inch pan and sprinkle with topping. Bake at 350° for 35 to 40 minutes.
*Alice Kline*

## Sauerkraut Cake

2/3 cup margarine or butter
1 1/2 cups sugar
3 eggs
1 tsp. vanilla
1/2 cup cocoa
2 1/4 cups flour, sifted
1 tsp. baking powder
1 tsp. baking soda
1/2 tsp. salt
1 cup water
2/3 cup sauerkraut, rinsed, drained, and chopped

Cream butter and sugar; beat in eggs and vanilla. Sift dry ingredients and add alternately with water to creamed mixture. Stir in sauerkraut.

Turn into 2 greased and floured 8-inch round pans. Bake at 350° for 30 minutes. Cool and frost with *Mocha Whipped Cream Frosting.*

Mocha Whipped Cream Frosting:
1 1/2 cups heavy cream
3 Tbsp. sugar
1 Tbsp. instant coffee
2 tsp. cocoa
2 Tbsp. rum *or* rum extract

Whip all ingredients together until soft peaks form; spread over cake. Refrigerate leftover portion.
*Mary Angle*

## Sweet Potato Cake

2 cups raw sweet potatoes or yams, shredded
1 1/3 cups water
2 cups raisins
1 1/3 cups sugar
3 Tbsp. butter or margarine
1/2 tsp. allspice
1/2 tsp. cinnamon
1/4 tsp. cloves
2 cups flour
2 tsp. baking soda
1/2 tsp. salt
2 cups nuts, chopped

Combine raw sweet potatoes, water, raisins, sugar, butter, and spices in a saucepan. Bring to a boil and cook 5 minutes. Put into pan of cold water until cooled completely. Sift flour, baking soda, and salt together; add to cooled mixture. Beat well. Add chopped nuts and mix well. Bake in greased and

floured 8-inch or 9-inch or 2-qt. pan at 325° for 40 to 50 minutes.
*Mary Ann Fall*

# NOVELTY CAKES
## Cocoa-Cola Cake

2 cups flour
2 cups sugar
1 cup butter or margarine
2 Tbsp. unsweetened cocoa
1 cup cola soda
1/2 cup buttermilk
2 eggs, beaten
1 tsp. baking soda
1 tsp. vanilla
1 1/2 cups miniature marshmallows

Combine flour and sugar in large mixing bowl; set aside. Melt butter; add cocoa and cola; heat to boiling point. Cool slightly. Pour over flour-sugar mixture; stir until well blended. Add buttermilk, eggs, baking soda, and vanilla. Mix well. Stir in marshmallows and pour into greased and floured 13x9x2-inch pan. Bake for 40 minutes at 350°. Frost while cake is warm.
*Katherine Wolf*

# 190
CAKE
COLLECTIBLES
AND
FROSTING
FINDS

## Red Velvet Cake

1/2 cup shortening
1 1/2 cups sugar
2 eggs
2 oz. red food coloring
1 tsp. vanilla
1 tsp. salt
1 tsp. baking soda
1 Tbsp. vinegar
2 1/2 cups cake flour, sifted
1 cup buttermilk

Cream shortening and sugar. Add eggs, coloring, vanilla, and salt, mixing well. Mix baking soda and vinegar together; add to creamed mixture. Add sifted flour and buttermilk alternately to creamed mixture. Bake in two 9-inch layers or 13x9x2-inch pan at 350° for about 40 minutes or until tested done. Cool and make *Fluffy Frosting*.

Fluffy Frosting:
5 Tbsp. flour
1 cup milk
1/2 cup shortening
1/2 cup margarine
1/2 tsp. vanilla
1 cup sugar

Make a paste of flour and milk, cooking until very thick and smooth. Cool to lukewarm. Cream other ingredients together and add paste. Beat until fluffy. Frost cake.
*Connie Reece*

## Texas Sun Cake

2 cups sugar
2/3 cup shortening
4 eggs, separated
3 cups flour
3 tsp. baking powder
pinch of salt
1 cup milk
1 tsp. vanilla
1 cup coconut

Cream sugar and shortening; add egg yolks. Beat until light. Sift together flour, baking powder, and salt. Add flour mixture and milk alternately to creamed mixture. Add vanilla. Beat egg whites lightly and add to batter. Blend in coconut. Pour batter into 2 layer pans or a 13x9x2-inch pan. Bake at 350° until tested done. Cool cake and cover with *Boiled Icing*.

Boiled Icing:
1 2/3 cups sugar
1/2 cup water
pinch of cream of tartar
2 egg whites, beaten
flaked coconut

Boil sugar, water, and cream of tartar to soft ball stage. Pour over beaten egg whites, beating well. Pour over cake; sprinkle coconut on top.
*Mary Heinrich*

## Tomato Soup Cake

2 Tbsp. butter or margarine
1 cup sugar
2 cups cake flour, sifted
1 tsp. cloves
1 tsp. cinnamon
1 tsp. nutmeg
1/4 tsp. salt
1 tsp. baking soda
1 10-oz. can tomato soup

Cream butter and sugar well. Sift flour; measure and sift again 3 times with spices and salt. Mix baking soda and soup; add to creamed mixture alternately with dry ingredients. Pour into greased medium-sized loaf pan. Bake 50 to 60 minutes in 350° oven. Cool 5 minutes in pan. Make *Chocolate-Cream Cheese Frosting*.

Chocolate-Cream Cheese Frosting:
1 3-oz. pkg. cream cheese, softened
3 Tbsp. milk
3 cups powdered sugar, sifted
2 squares semi-sweet chocolate, melted
1/2 tsp. salt
1 tsp. vanilla

Mash cheese; add milk gradually, beating until blended. Add sugar slowly, blending thoroughly. Add melted chocolate, salt, and vanilla, beating until smooth. Apply to top and sides of loaf cake.
*Florence Crawmer*

# POUND CAKES

## Brown Sugar Pound Cake

1 1/2 cups shortening (part butter)
1 lb. light brown sugar
1/2 cup sugar
5 egg yolks, well beaten
3 cups flour
1/2 tsp. baking powder
1 cup milk
1 cup nuts, chopped
1 tsp. vanilla
5 egg whites, stiffly beaten

Cream shortening; add brown and white sugars and cream again. Stir in beaten egg yolks. Add flour and baking powder alternately with milk. Add nuts and vanilla; lastly, fold in egg whites. Bake in greased and floured Bundt pan for 1 1/2 hours at 325°.
*Doris Boyd*

## Caramel Nut Pound Cake

1 cup butter or margarine
1/2 cup shortening
1 box light brown sugar
1 cup white sugar
5 large eggs
3 cups cake flour
1/2 tsp. baking powder
1 cup milk
1 tsp. vanilla
1 cup walnuts, pecans, or black walnuts, chopped

Cream butter, shortening, and brown sugar. Add white sugar; beat until light and fluffy.

Add eggs; beat 3 minutes. Sift dry ingredients together; add to creamed mixture alternately with milk. Add vanilla and nuts. Bake in tube pan or Bundt pan for 1 hour and 30 minutes or until done at 325°.
*Ruth Bowman*

## Chocolate Bar Pound Cake

8 small, plain chocolate bars
1 cup margarine
2 cups sugar
4 eggs
2 tsp. vanilla
2 1/2 cups cake flour
1/2 tsp. salt
1/4 tsp. baking soda
1 cup buttermilk
2 cups nuts, chopped and floured

Soften chocolate bars and margarine at room temperature. Cream bars, margarine, sugar, eggs, and vanilla. Sift flour, salt, and baking soda. Add flour mixture and buttermilk alternately to creamed mixture, beating well after each addition. Blend in nuts. Pour into tube pan. Bake at 325° for 1 hour and 10 minutes or until done.
*Ruth Bowman*

## Orange Bundt Cake

1 cup butter
1 cup sugar
3 eggs, separated
1 cup sour cream
grated rind of 1 orange
1 3/4 cups flour
1 tsp. baking powder
1 tsp. baking soda

Cream butter and sugar; add egg yolks, sour cream, and orange rind. Beat until light and fluffy. Sift together dry ingredients and stir into first mixture. Beat egg whites stiff and fold in. Turn batter into oiled and floured Bundt mold; bake at 325° for 1 hour. Remove from oven and let stand for 10 minutes. Loosen carefully around edge and turn out on plate with a rim. Pour hot *Orange Syrup* over top of cake.

Orange Syrup:
juice of 2 oranges
3/4 cup sugar
juice of 1 lemon
dash of salt

Combine and boil 3 to 4 minutes.
*Lorraine Grover*

# 192
CAKE
COLLECTIBLES
AND
FROSTING
FINDS

## SPICE CAKES
### Gingerbread 1
1 cup molasses or
  honey
1 egg
pinch of salt
1 tsp. baking soda
1 tsp. ginger
1 1/2 cups flour
1/4 cup salad oil
2/3 cup warm water

Combine ingredients,
adding water last.
Pour into 8-inch
square pan. Bake in
325° oven for about
3 minutes or until
center of cake springs
back after light touch.
*Freeda Beachler*

### Gingerbread 2
2 1/2 cups flour
1 tsp. baking powder
1 1/2 tsp. baking soda
1/2 tsp. salt
1/2 cup sugar
1 tsp. cinnamon
1/4 tsp. nutmeg
1/4 tsp. cloves
1/4 tsp. allspice
1 tsp. ginger
1/2 cup shortening
1 egg
1 cup molasses
1 cup hot water

Sift dry ingredients
together. Add
shortening, egg, and
molasses to dry in-
gredients. Beat 2
minutes; then add
hot water. Bake at

350° for 35 minutes
in 13x9x2-inch bak-
ing dish. Cool cake
for 5 minutes. Add
*Broiled Topping*.

Broiled Topping:
6 Tbsp. butter, softened
2/3 cup brown sugar,
  packed
4 Tbsp. cream
1/2 cup nuts, chopped
1 cup coconut flakes

Combine ingredients
and spread on top of
cake. Then put under
broiler until bubbly.
*Ruth Balsbaugh*

### Gingerbread 3
1 cup sugar
1 cup molasses
1 cup oil
3 eggs
2 cups flour
2 tsp. baking soda
1/4 tsp. salt
1 tsp. cinnamon
1 tsp. ginger
1 cup boiling water

Cream first 4 ingre-
dients together. Add
dry ingredients to
creamed mixture.
Quickly stir in boil-
ing water. Bake in 8-
inch square pan at
325° for 35 to 40
minutes.
*Ann Crawmer*

### Spice Cake
2 cups white sugar
2 cups brown sugar
2 cups raisins
2 cups salad oil
4 cups water
2 tsp. cloves
2 tsp. nutmeg
4 tsp. cinnamon
2 tsp. salt
6 cups flour
4 tsp. baking soda
1 tsp. vanilla

2 cups walnuts,
  chopped

Mix all but last four
ingredients in large
kettle and boil 1 or 2
minutes. Cool. Add
remaining ingre-
dients. Pour into
greased 13x9x2-inch
pan. Bake at 325° for
1 1/2 hours. Freezes
well.
Variation:
Add 1/2 cup butter
or margarine to
heated mixture.
*Mildred Moore*

# Frosting Finds
### Banana Frosting
2 ripe bananas,
  mashed
1 tsp. lemon juice
2 Tbsp. oil
1/2 tsp. vanilla
1/4 tsp. salt
3/4 cup honey

Whip ingredients
until fluffy. Will frost
two 9-inch layers.
*Eunice Grover*

### Broiled
### Coconut Frosting
4 Tbsp. butter
4 Tbsp. cream or
  canned milk
10 Tbsp. brown sugar
1 cup coconut

Melt butter in a pan.
Add other ingredi-
ents. Stir until well
blended. Pour on
cake hot from the
oven. Broil about 5
minutes until frost-
ing bubbles and
browns.

Note:
This is tasty on banana or applesauce cake.
*Mary Heinrich*
*Emma Bowman*

## Caramel Frosting

1/2 cup butter
1 cup brown sugar
1/2 cup milk
1 3/4–2 cups powdered sugar, sifted

Melt butter and add brown sugar. Cook over low heat 2 minutes, stirring constantly. Add milk and continue stirring until mixture comes to a boil. Remove from heat and cool. Add the powdered sugar until frosting is the right consistency for spreading.
*Janice Root*

## Coconut Frosting

2 cups sugar
1/2 cup water
1 tsp. butter
1 tsp. vanilla
1/2 cup shredded or grated coconut

Boil sugar and water to the soft ball stage, 238°. Add butter and cook until mixture is thick enough to spread. Add vanilla. When cool, spread on cake and sprinkle coconut over the top.
*Edna Thompson*

## Cream Cheese Frosting

1 6-oz. pkg. cream cheese
1/2 cup margarine
1 box powdered sugar

2 tsp. vanilla
1 cup nuts, chopped
milk

Mix all ingredients together. Add milk for desired consistency. Refrigerate when storing.
*Joy Thompson*

## Mock 7-Minute Frosting

1 egg white
1/2 cup light corn syrup
1/4 tsp. cream of tartar
1 tsp. vanilla
food coloring, (optional)

Combine all ingredients, beating until stiff. Spread on cake only a few hours before serving.
*Deanna Davison*

## Perfection Frosting

1-1b. box powdered sugar
1/4 cup (2 medium) egg whites
1 tsp. vanilla
1/8 tsp. salt
1 Tbsp. water
1/3 cup butter or margarine, softened
food coloring

Combine all ingredients, except coloring, in small mixer bowl. Blend at low speed; then beat at high speed until smooth and fluffy, about 5 minutes, scraping bowl often. Beat in food coloring a drop or two at a time until frosting is desired tint. (If too stiff, beat in a few drops of

water.) Frosts top and sides of two 8-inch or 9-inch layers.
*Ada Wise*

## Pineapple Cream Frosting

1 cup crushed pineapple
1 cup sugar
1 pkg. gelatin
1/4 cup cold water
1/4 cup boiling water
2 pkgs. cream topping mix
2 tsp. Maraschino cherries, chopped
food coloring

Bring pineapple and sugar to a boil. Soak gelatin in cold water; then add boiling water. Combine the pineapple and gelatin mixtures; cool. Prepare topping mix as directed. Combine with cherries and gelatin-fruit mixtures. Tint as desired.
Note:
This can double as a cake filling. Use angel food or pound cake.
*Mary Gish*

# 194
CAKE
COLLECTIBLES
AND
FROSTING
FINDS

## Raisin-Yogurt Frosting

1/4 cup yogurt
1 tsp. lemon juice
1/4 cup unsweetened
  orange juice
3/4 cup honey
1/2 cup seedless
  raisins

Combine yogurt, juices, and honey, beating well. Add raisins.

*Eunice Grover*

## Strawberry Frosting

1 3-oz. pkg. strawberry
  gelatin
1/2 cup hot water
1 pkg. frozen straw-
  berries, partially
  thawed
1 cup canned milk,
  chilled
1 cup whipping cream

Dissolve gelatin in hot water; add strawberries. Beat the canned milk and whipping cream until stiff. Fold into strawberry mixture. Frost cake. Keep in refrigerator.
Variation:
Use 2 cups whipping cream instead of canned milk.
Note: This can double up as a cake filling. Use angel food or pound cake.

*Marjorie Bauman*

## Never-Fail Meringue

2 Tbsp. sugar
1 Tbsp. cornstarch
1/2 cup water
3 egg whites
1/8 tsp. salt
1/2 tsp. vanilla
6 Tbsp. sugar

Combine sugar and cornstarch in small saucepan. Add water. Cook over low heat until thick and clear. Cool. Beat egg whites with salt and vanilla. Beat until soft mounds form. Add sugar gradually, beating well. Add cornstarch mixture and continue beating until it stands in stiff peaks. This will cover one 9-inch pie. To brown, bake in 350° oven for 12 to 15 minutes.

*Chloie King*

*Extra Recipes*

_____
_____
_____
_____
_____
_____
_____
_____
_____
Source: _____  Who Likes It: _____

_____
_____
_____
_____
_____
_____
_____
_____
_____
Source: _____  Who Likes It: _____

_____
_____
_____
_____
_____
_____
_____
_____
_____
Source: _____  Who Likes It: _____

## A LOVE CAKE FOR MOTHER

1 can obedience
several lbs. affection
1 pt. neatness
some holiday, birthday, and everyday surprises
1 cup running errands
1 box powdered get-up (I-should-be-willing brand)
1 bottle of keep-sunny-all-day-long
1 can pure thoughtfulness

Mix well and bake in a hearty warm oven and serve to Mother in big slices every day.

# Blooming Desserts

*She who would thrive,*
*must rise at five;*
*She who hath thriven,*
*may lie till seven.*
ANONYMOUS

*Jesus said,*
*"I have come*
*that they may have life,*
*and have it*
*to the full."*
JOHN 10:10

# Ice Cream

## Add-A-Flavor Ice Cream

1 qt. half-and-half
1 pt. whipping cream
1 can sweetened
  condensed milk
dash of salt
1 1/2 cups sugar
5-eggs
1 1/2 Tbsp. vanilla

Mix all ingredients together. Choose flavor, adding it to cream mixture. Pour into 1 1/2-gallon freezer and fill it with extra milk. Freeze according to freezer directions.

Suggested Flavors:
*Banana*—mash 3 to 4
  ripe bananas
*Chocolate*—use 1 can
  chocolate syrup
*Fruit*—mash 2 qts.
  ripe fruit

## FRUITED Banana and Fruit Ice Cream

1 cup orange juice
1/2 cup lemon juice
3 or 4 bananas,
  mashed
4 eggs
3 cups sugar
3 cups cream
3 cups milk

Combine eggs, sugar, cream, and milk, blending well. Freeze. Stir in fruit juices and bananas when cream mixture is slushy. Refreeze. Makes 1 1/2 gallons.
*Suzanne Overholtzer*

## Boysenberry Ice Cream

(For 1 1/2-gallon freezer)

1 cup honey
2 cups sugar
1 qt. boysenberries,
  fresh or frozen,
  sweetened
1 pt. cream
milk
1 1/2 tsp. vanilla
salt

Mix honey, sugar, and berries together until sugar and honey are dissolved. Add cream and pour into freezer container. Add enough milk to fill freezer to within 2 inches from top. Add vanilla and a sprinkle of salt; stir well. Freeze according to freezer directions.
*Naomi Bauman*

## Peach or Apricot Ice Cream

8 eggs, beaten
3 cups sugar
2 cans evaporated milk
1 Tbsp. vanilla
8 cups peaches or
  apricots, chopped
  finely *or* pureed
extra milk

Combine all ingredients, except fruit and extra milk. Add fruit, mixing well. Add enough extra milk to fill a 1 1/2-gallon freezer. Freeze according to freezer directions.
*Naomi Barton*

## Strawberry Ice Cream

6 eggs
4 cups sugar
1 qt. half-and-half
4 tsp. vanilla
1 can evaporated milk
4 boxes berries,
  crushed
red food coloring
extra milk

Combine all ingredients, except extra milk. Fill a 2-gallon container, adding extra milk to fill it. Freeze.
*Janet Rumble*

## NON-FRUITED
### Peppermint Ice Cream
(low-calorie)

3 qts. whole milk
1 1/2 cups sugar
6 Tbsp. flour
1 tsp. salt
2 envelopes unflavored gelatin, softened in 1/3 cup cold water
1 1/2 cups peppermint stick candy, crushed
1/4 tsp. red food coloring
8 eggs, beaten slightly
1 cup heavy cream, (optional)

Scald 1 qt. milk in top of double boiler. Mix dry ingredients, except candy, and add part of hot milk. Blend. Return to double boiler and cook over boiling water until slightly thickened. Remove from heat; add some of hot liquid slowly to eggs. Return to double boiler and cook over simmering water, stirring constantly, until mixture coats a wooden spoon. Remove from heat; gradually stir hot mixture into gelatin, stirring until gelatin completely dissolves. Strain into 5-qt. freezer can and refrigerate.

Add candy, food coloring, and cream; fill rest of container with milk. Chill thoroughly before freezing. Makes about 1 gallon.
Note: This keeps well in the freezer without forming ice crystals. The flavor can be varied to suit. Use 1/2 cup more sugar if candy is omitted.
*Clara Belle Barton*

### Vanilla Ice Cream 1

12 eggs
1 1/2 cups sugar
2 cans sweetened condensed milk
1 can evaporated milk
3 Tbsp. vanilla

Beat eggs until thick. Add sugar, beating 3 minutes longer. Then add remaining ingredients. Fill a 1 1/2-gallon freezer; add milk to fill container. Freeze according to container directions.
*Mary Gish*

### Vanilla Ice Cream 2

2 1/2 qts. half-and-half
1 3/4 cups sugar
1 pt. whipping cream
1 1/2 Tbsp. vanilla

Mix all ingredients in a 1-gallon freezer.
Note:
No milk is used.
Variations:
Use 1 cup white sugar and 1 cup brown sugar, or use 2 cups brown sugar.
*Edna Thompson*

### Vanilla Ice Cream 3

6 eggs
1 cup sugar
1 pt. half-and-half
1 can evaporated milk
1 box instant vanilla pudding
1 Tbsp. vanilla

Beat eggs and sugar together. Add remaining ingredients. Pour into a 1-gallon freezer and fill with milk. Freeze according to freezer directions.
*Ida Garber*

General Note:
Recipes for sauces and toppings are on pages 116 and 117.

### Chocolate Ice Cream

6 eggs, well beaten
3 cups sugar
2 pkgs. instant chocolate pudding
1 pkg. sweet chocolate, melted
1 qt. half-and-half *or* 1 pt. whipping cream
2 cans sweetened condensed milk
milk

Beat eggs; add sugar and continue to beat. Then add chocolate pudding, melted chocolate, half-and-half, and condensed milk. Pour into 2-gallon freezer can; add milk to fill. Freeze according to freezer directions.
*Leona Selby*

## Milk Chocolate Chip Ice Cream

1/4 cup cocoa
1 cup boiling water
4 eggs
3 cups sugar
1 can evaporated milk
4 squares semi-sweet
  chocolate, grated
dash of salt
2 Tbsp. vanilla

Dissolve cocoa in boiling water; cool. Combine with remaining ingredients, blending well. Fill a 1 1/2-gallon ice cream freezer and add milk to fill freezer. Freeze according to freezer directions.
*Linda Thompson*

# Custards

## Baked Custard 1

4 eggs
1/2 cup sugar
salt to taste
vanilla
1 qt. milk

Beat eggs slightly; add sugar, salt, and vanilla, blending in until smooth. Gradually add milk. Pour into 6 moistened custard cups and set in pan of water. Bake at 350° for 35 minutes until custard is firm. Serve cold.
*Myrtle Landes*

## Baked Custard 2

9 eggs, slightly beaten
1 cup sugar
3/4 tsp. salt
6 cups milk, scalded
3 tsp. vanilla
nutmeg

Combine eggs, sugar, and salt. Slowly stir in slightly cooled milk and vanilla. Pour into baking dish. Sprinkle with nutmeg. Set in pan of hot water 1-inch deep. Bake 1 1/2 hours at 325° until knife inserted near center comes out clean. Serve warm or chilled.
*Rachel Miller*

## Bread Custard

1 egg
1 Tbsp. sugar
1 cup milk
1 tsp. vanilla
bread, cut into 2-inch
  squares
1/4 tsp. cinnamon
frozen non-dairy
  topping *and* whipped
  cream

Beat egg; add sugar and beat again. Add milk and vanilla. Beat until frothy. Pour into shallow pan set in a larger pan containing water 1 inch below top of shallow pan. Lay bread on top of custard. Sprinkle with cinnamon. Bake at 325° until knife inserted shows custard has congealed. Remove from water and cool quickly. Turn into bowl. Mix equal amounts frozen topping and whipped cream; cut into custard, without actually stirring. Yields 1 serving.
Note: Multiply proportions of ingredients according to number of people served.
*Mildred Beachler*

## Lemon Custard Surprise

1 cup sugar
1/4 cup flour
1/8 tsp. salt
2 Tbsp. butter, melted
5 Tbsp. lemon juice
grated peel of 1 lemon
3 eggs, separated
1 1/2 cups milk,
  scalded

Combine sugar, flour, salt, and butter; add lemon juice and peel. Combine egg yolks and milk; mix well and add to sugar mixture. Beat egg whites until stiff and fold into mixture. Pour into greased custard cups. Bake in pan of hot water at 325° for 45 minutes. When baked, each dessert will have a custard on the bottom and sponge cake on top.
Serves 8.
Note: This may also be baked in greased shallow baking dish.
*Virginia Peters*

## Honey Custard

3 cups milk, scalded
4 Tbsp. honey
3 eggs, beaten
1/4 tsp. salt
dash of nutmeg
dash of cinnamon
hot water

Combine scalded milk and honey in a bowl. In another bowl, combine beaten eggs and salt. Stir into milk mixture. Divide custard among 6 cups. Sprinkle with spices. Place cups in pan of hot water. Bake at 375° for 30 to 40 minutes. Serve warm or chilled.
*Ruth Bauman*

## Rhubarb Custard

1 1/2 cups raw
   rhubarb
2 eggs, separated
1 cup sugar
butter, size of hickory
   nut
2 tsp. sugar

Combine fruit, beaten yolks, sugar, and butter. Pour into small baking dish. Bake at 325° for about 40 minutes. Beat the egg whites stiff with sugar. Brown top in oven. Serve cold.

Note:
Can be used as a pie filling.
*Alice Kline*

# Puddings
## Banana Pudding

1 cup brown sugar
4 rounded Tbsp. flour
2 eggs
1 cup milk
1 can peanuts,
   crushed
sliced bananas, cut in
   fourths

Combine first 3 ingredients, gradually adding milk; cook until thick, stirring constantly. Cool. Add crushed peanuts. Layer bananas, pudding, and nuts alternately in a serving dish.
Variation:
Use instant butterscotch pudding instead of making your own.
*Bonnie Long*

## Brownie Nut Pudding

1 1/2 cups baking mix
1 1/2 cups sugar
4 Tbsp. cocoa
1/2 cup nuts, chopped
3/4 cup evaporated
   milk
1 tsp. vanilla
1 1/4 cups boiling
   water

Combine mix, only 1/2 cup sugar, 2 Tbsp. cocoa, and nuts. Stir in 1/2 cup milk and vanilla.

Spread batter in greased 8-inch square dish; set aside. Mix remaining 3/4 cup sugar, 2 Tbsp. cocoa, 1/4 cup milk, and boiling water in bowl. Pour mixture on top of batter. Do not stir. Bake at 350° for 40 minutes. Pudding will go to the bottom.
*Linda Thompson*

## Buttermilk Pudding

1 cup brown sugar
1 egg
1 cup buttermilk
1 tsp. baking soda,
   dissolved in buttermilk
2 1/2–3 cups flour

Combine all ingredients in stainless steel bowl or baking dish; mix well. Place bowl on a rack or on an inverted lid, and put both in a pan. Fill pan with water to 1 inch from top of bowl. Bring to a boil. Lower heat, cover pan, and steam for 1 hour or until done.
To serve:
Cut in wedges and crumble into cereal bowl. Eat with milk and sugar for an old-fashioned "bread and milk" supper.
*Dorla Shuman*

## Chocolate Pudding

1 qt. milk
1 1/2 cups sugar
2 rounded Tbsp. flour
2 rounded Tbsp. corn-starch
2 rounded Tbsp. cocoa
pinch of salt
4 eggs
1 tsp. vanilla

While milk is heating, mix together remaining ingredients, except vanilla. Add mixture to milk and cook until thick. Add vanilla.
Note:
This can be used as pie filling for two 9-inch pies.
*Mary Howser*

## Cinnamon Pudding

1 1/2 cups cold water
2 cups brown sugar
4 Tbsp. butter
1 cup nuts, chopped
1 cup white sugar
1 cup milk
2 cups flour
2 tsp. baking powder
1 tsp. cinnamon

Bring water, brown sugar, and 2 Tbsp. butter to a generous boil. Add chopped nuts; set aside. Make a batter of remaining 2 Tbsp. butter and other ingredients. Pour batter into greased 12x8x2-inch baking dish. Pour syrup mixture with nuts over top. Bake at 375° for 20 to 30 minutes. Serve with ice cream, if desired.
*Carolyn Fisher*
*Peggy Wise*

## Date Pudding 1

1 cup nuts, chopped
1 cup dates, chopped
1 cup brown sugar
3 Tbsp. flour
1 tsp. baking powder
3 eggs, separated

Mix together all ingredients, except whites. Beat egg whites and fold into mixture. Put into large greased and floured baking dish. Bake at 350° for 20 minutes. When cold, cut into squares and serve with whipped cream.
*Carla Miller*

## Date Pudding 2

2 cups brown sugar
2 cups hot water
1 cup white sugar
1 3/4 cups flour
1 tsp. baking powder
1/2 tsp. baking soda
1/8 tsp. salt
1 cup milk
1/2 cup dates, chopped
1/2 cup nuts, chopped
1 tsp. vanilla

Mix brown sugar and water together in a 13x9x2-inch baking pan. In mixer bowl, sift dry ingredients together. Then add milk and remaining ingredients. Pour over brown sugar mixture without stirring. Bake at 325° for 45 minutes.
*Leah Garber*

## Fruit Bowl Pudding

1 can pineapple chunks
1 small box vanilla pudding
1 cup dried apricots
bananas, sliced
Cheddar cheese, grated

Drain pineapple juice to make 2 cups and cook with pudding. Add apricots and pineapple to hot pudding. Slowly stir in bananas and grated cheese.
*Phyllis Flory*

Variation:
Use orange juice, apples, oranges, and fresh pineapple, instead of apricots and cheese.
*Martha Gish*

## Persimmon Pudding 1

1 1/2 cups flour
3/4 tsp. salt
1 1/2 tsp. baking soda
1/2 tsp. cinnamon
1 1/4 cups plus 1 Tbsp. sugar
1 1/2 tsp. vanilla
1 1/2 cups persimmon pulp
3/4 cup milk
3/4 cup nuts, chopped
3/4 cup raisins

Sift dry ingredients. In preparing pulp, peel persimmons and force through coarse sieve; add sugar and vanilla. Add dry ingredients alternately with milk. Blend in nuts and raisins. Pour into greased 2-qt. baking dish placed in larger baking dish partially filled with water. Bake at 325° for about 70 minutes.
*Mary Gish*

## Persimmon Pudding 2

4 persimmons, peeled
2 eggs
1 cup milk
1 cup sugar
2 cups flour
1 tsp. baking powder
pinch of salt
1 tsp. baking soda
1 tsp. vanilla
1 cup nuts, chopped
1 cup dates, chopped
1 cup raisins

Mash persimmons; add eggs, milk, and sugar. Sift flour, baking powder, salt, and baking soda; add to persimmon mixture. Add vanilla, nuts, dates, and raisins. Pour into a 2-qt. baking dish set in pan partially filled with water. Bake at 325° for about 1 hour or until firmly set.
*Irene Faye Gish*

## Persimmon Pudding 3

1 cup sugar
2 Tbsp. butter or margarine
1 egg, well beaten
1 cup flour, sifted
1/2 tsp. salt
1/4 tsp. cinnamon
1/2 cup milk
1 cup persimmon pulp
2 tsp. baking soda
1 cup nuts, chopped

Cream sugar and butter; add beaten eggs. Beat well. Sift flour, salt, and cinnamon together; add alternately with milk. Add baking soda to persimmon pulp; combine with flour mixture. Then, add nuts. Steam, covered, for 2 hours.
*Wilma Filbrun*

## Tapioca Pudding

6 cups milk
9 Tbsp. sugar
dash of salt
9 Tbsp. tapioca
3 eggs, separated
2 Tbsp. vanilla
2 Tbsp. sugar

Cook first 4 ingredients in double boiler until tapioca is clear. Stir 3 egg yolks with a little of the hot mixture. Then add to pudding. Continue stirring until pudding coats the spoon. Remove from heat and add vanilla. Beat egg whites with 2 Tbsp. sugar for meringue. Pour hot mixture over meringue and stir in gently.
*Virginia Skiles*

## Tapioca Fruit Finlandia

1 cup dried apricots
1 cup water
1/3 cup quick-cooking tapioca
1/8 tsp. salt
1 cup water
4 cups orange juice
1 cup Mandarin orange sections
sliced bananas
12 or more large prunes, cooked
1 cup seedless grapes (in season)

Heat covered apricots and water to boiling; uncover and let stand 1 hour. Stir together tapioca, salt, water, and 1 cup of orange juice in small pan. Heat, stirring constantly, until mixture comes to a full boil. Pour into large bowl.

Cool 15 minutes. Stir in remaining 3 cups orange juice, apricots, and liquid. Add fruits. Refrigerate.
Note:
The orange juice helps to keep the bananas from darkening for a day. Serve cold. Keeps well when fixed ahead.
*Eunice Grover*

## Tapioca Fruit Treat 1

3 qts. water
1 cup tapioca
1/2 tsp. salt
1 cup whipping cream, whipped
1 cup sugar
1 can fruit cocktail, drained
2 bananas, sliced
1 1/2 cups small marshmallows

Soak tapioca in water 12 hours or overnight. Cook slowly about 30 minutes in same water with salt, stirring occasionally. Drain through colander but do not rinse. Cool completely. Add remaining ingredients. Let set for 2 or 3 hours or until sugar dissolves.
*Martha Blom*

## Tapioca Fruit Treat 2

1 cup pearl tapioca
3 cups water
1/4 cup milk
1/2 cup sugar
1/2 tsp. salt
3/4 cup nuts, chopped
1/2 cup dates, chopped
1/2 pt. whipping cream, whipped

Put tapioca and water in top of double boiler. Let soak 4 hours or overnight. Cook tapioca until partially clear. Cool. Stir milk, sugar, and salt into tapioca, mixing well. Add nuts and dates. Fold in whipped cream and serve.
*Edith L. Deeter*

## Tapioca Fruit Treat 3

2 large cans plums, pitted and cut up
7 Tbsp. quick-cooking tapioca
1 pkg. whipped topping mix
1 small carton sour cream

Cook plums and tapioca together until thickened. Cool. Prepare topping and combine with sour cream. Fold into tapioca mixture.
*Rosemary Denlinger*

## Yummy Vanilla Pudding

1 cup sugar
4 Tbsp. cornstarch
4 egg yolks
2 cups milk
1 tsp. vanilla
1/2 pt. whipping cream

Combine sugar, cornstarch, yolks, and milk in saucepan; cook until thick and creamy. Add vanilla. Cool; then beat lightly. Whip and sweeten cream; fold into pudding.
*Naomi Barton*

# Special Baked Desserts
FRUIT-BASED
Apples

## Cran-Apple Crisp

2 cups cranberries
3 cups apples, cored, pared, and sliced
1 cup sugar
1 Tbsp. lemon juice
1/4 tsp. salt
Topping:
1 cup brown sugar, packed
1 cup quick-cooking rolled oats
1/2 cup flour
1/3 cup margarine

Combine non-topping ingredients and place in a 2-qt. casserole. Combine topping ingredients, blending well. Sprinkle over cranberry mixture. Bake at 325° for 45 minutes. Serve warm with whipped cream, ice cream, or sour cream.
*Barbara Basore*

## Apple Dumplings

Crust:
2 cups flour
1 tsp. salt
2/3 cup shortening
1/4 cup water

Syrup:
1 cup sugar
2 cups water
1/4 tsp. cinnamon
3 tsp. butter

Filling:
6 apples, halved and
  cored
1/2 cup sugar
1 1/2 tsp. cinnamon
butter

Mix flour, salt, and shortening together. Add water. Divide into 6 pieces and roll out. Prepare syrup by boiling ingredients for 3 minutes. Prepare *Filling*. Fill apple cavities with a mixture of sugar and cinnamon. Dot each apple with 1 tsp. butter. Wrap apples in dough. Place in pan and pour syrup over apples. Bake in 425° oven for 40 to 45 minutes.
*Paula Beachler*

Variation:
Use finely cut rhubarb instead of apples, and use pinch of ginger instead of cinnamon.
*Gladys Bleachler*

## Schnitz Un Knepp
(Apple Dumplings)

1 cup snits (dried
  apples)
1 pt. water
1/2 Tbsp. shortening
1 Tbsp. sugar
Dumpling Batter:
2 cups flour
4 tsp. baking powder
1/2 tsp. salt
1 Tbsp. sugar
1 Tbsp. shortening
1 cup milk

Cook snits, water, shortening, and sugar 5 minutes in saucepan. For batter, sift dry ingredients together. Blend in shortening; add milk. Drop batter by spoonfuls into boiling broth of cooked apple snits. Cover tightly and cook for 18 minutes. Serve warm with cream or plain.
*Betty Eller*

## Apple Round-Ups

Syrup:
1 cup sugar
1 1/2 cups water
2 Tbsp. butter
1/8 tsp. cinnamon
1/8 tsp. nutmeg
1/8 tsp. red food
  coloring
Dough:
3 cups dough (any
  biscuit recipe will do)
Filling:
3 cups ground apples
1/2 cup sugar
cinnamon

Combine syrup ingredients and bring just to boiling. Roll dough into an 18x13-inch rectangle. Spread with mixture of apples, sugar, and cinnamon. Roll as for jelly roll. Cut 1-inch slices and place cut-side down in a greased 13x9x2-inch baking dish. Pour syrup over top and bake at 350° for 35 to 40 minutes. Serve hot with ice cream.
*Mary Gish*

## Baked Apples 1

apples, cored, pared,
  and halved
1 3/4 cups sugar
3 Tbsp. flour
cinnamon
2 cups water
several large
  marshmallows

Line a 13x9x2-inch baking dish with prepared apples. Mix dry ingredients and water, until smooth. Pour over apples and bake at 350° for 1 hour. Just before done, place 1/2 large marshmallow in center of each half. Remove from oven when marshmallows start to brown.
*Mary Gish*

## Baked Apples 2

2 cups sugar
1 cup water
12 small red apples,
  preferably Winesap
1/3 cup red hots
red food coloring

Boil sugar and water. Add whole red apples and red hots. Boil just a few minutes or until red hots start to soften. Add red food coloring to desired shade. Place in baking pan and bake at 325° until tender.
*Eunice Grover*

## Wacky Crust Apple Cobbler

1 cup flour
1 tsp. baking powder
1/2 tsp. salt
1 Tbsp. sugar
1 egg
2/3 cup shortening
3/4 cup water
1 21-oz. can apple pie
  or fruit filling
1 Tbsp. lemon juice
1/2 tsp. apple pie
  spice or cinnamon

In small mixer bowl, combine first 7 ingredients. Blend well. Beat 2 minutes at medium speed of mixer. Pour batter into 9-inch pie pan. Combine pie filling, lemon juice, and spice; pour into center of batter. Do not stir. Bake at 325° for 45 to 50 minutes.
*Lydia Wolf*

# Berries
## Berry Cobbler 1

1/2 cup butter or
  margarine
1 cup flour
1 1/2 cups sugar
1/2 tsp. salt
3 tsp. baking powder
milk
1/4 cup lemon juice
4 cups berries,
  prepared

Melt butter in baking dish. Combine 3/4 cup sugar, flour, salt, and baking powder. Add enough milk to make a pouring batter. Pour batter over melted butter. Mix juice, remaining 3/4 cup sugar, and berries together. Spoon over batter in baking dish. Bake at 350° for 1 hour or until done.
*Mary Martin*

## Berry Cobbler 2

1/2 cup butter
1 cup flour
1/2 cup sugar
3 tsp. baking powder
1/8 tsp. salt
2/3 cup milk
2 cups fruit or berries,
  sweetened

Melt butter in 8-inch round or square baking dish. Sift together flour, sugar, baking powder, and salt. Add milk, stirring until just blended. Spoon over butter; do not stir. Pour sweetened fruit over batter and bake at 375° for 35 minutes. Serve warm with cream. Makes 6 servings.
*Virginia Trussel*

## Berry Nice Dessert

Crust:
1 cup flour
1/4 cup brown sugar
3/4 cup nuts, chopped
1/2 cup butter

Fillings:
30 large marshmallows
2/3 cup milk
1 cup whipping cream
  *and*
1 6-oz. pkg. strawberry
  gelatin
2 cups boiling water
1 lb. frozen berries

Mix crust ingredients and pat lightly in 13x9x2-inch baking dish. Bake at 325° for 15 minutes. Cool. Melt marshmallows and milk in double boiler; cool. Whip cream and fold into marshmallow mixture. Spread on crust. Combine gelatin and water, mixing well; add frozen berries. Mash berries in hot gelatin. When partially jelled, spoon on top of marshmallow layer.
*Ruthanne Wise*
*Sarah Lee Switzer*

## Berry Crisp

1 qt. berries
1/3 cup white sugar
1/4 cup butter
1/3 cup flour
1/3 cup brown sugar
3/4 cup rolled oats

Sprinkle berries with white sugar in 9-inch square pan. Blend butter, flour, brown sugar, and rolled oats. Sprinkle over berries. Bake at 350° about 30 minutes. Makes 6 servings.
*Dorothy Moore*

## Blueberries
## Blueberry Buckle

1/2 cup shortening
1 cup sugar
1 egg
2 1/2 cups flour, sifted
2 1/2 tsp. baking powder
1/4 tsp. salt
1/2 cup milk
2 tsp. lemon juice
2 cups blueberries, fresh or frozen
1/2 tsp. cinnamon
1/4 cup butter or margarine

Cream shortening and 1/2 cup sugar; add egg and beat until light. Add flour, baking powder, and salt to creamed mixture; add milk. Spread in greased 9-inch square pan. Toss lemon juice with blueberries; sprinkle over batter. Make crumb topping with remaining 1/2 cup flour, 1/2 cup sugar, and other ingredients. Cover berries. Bake at 350° for 45 minutes or until done. Serve warm.
*Marietta Pegg*

## Cherries
## Cherry Cobbler

1 1/4 cups sugar
1 rounded cup flour
1 rounded tsp. baking powder
1/2 cup milk
1 egg
3 Tbsp. butter
2 cups pitted cherries
1 1/2 cups boiling water

Reserving 3/4 cup sugar, sift dry ingredients in a bowl. Add milk, egg, and butter, mixing well. Pour into greased 1-qt. baking dish. Combine remaining 1/2 cup sugar, cherries, and water; pour over batter. Bake at 350° for about 40 minutes. Note:
Reduce amounts of sugar if desired.
*Esther Gish*

## Cherry Torte

1 cup graham cracker crumbs
1/3 cup butter, melted
1 cup sugar
1 8-oz. pkg. cream cheese, softened
2 eggs
1 22-oz. can cherry pie filling

Blend butter, crumbs, and 1/2 cup sugar thoroughly. Place in 8-inch square or round baking pan. Beat cheese with beater until smooth. Beat in remaining 1/2 cup of sugar gradually. Add eggs, one at a time, beating hard after each addition. Beat until mixture is very smooth. Pour over crumbs and bake at 325° for 25 minutes. Remove from oven and cool. Spoon cherry pie filling over top and chill in refrigerator 3 hours or overnight.
*Alia Flory*

## Dates
## Date
## Crumble Torte

Crumb Mixture:
1 14-oz. pkg. date bar mix
1/2 cup walnuts, chopped
2 Tbsp. butter
a large container frozen non-dairy topping
walnut halves

Combine date bar mix, nuts, and butter; spread in large baking dish. Bake at 400° for 10 minutes. Break into pieces with fork. Cool; then crumble. Alternately layer crumbs and thawed topping in a 2 1/2-qt. or 10x6x2-inch baking dish, ending with topping. Chill several hours or

overnight. Garnish with walnut halves. Serves 8.
*Edna Thompson*

## Miscellaneous Fruits
### Fruit Cobbler 1
1/3 cup butter
3/4 cup milk
1 cup sugar
1 cup flour
2 tsp. baking powder
1/2 tsp. salt
1 large can peaches, apricots, or bing cherries, drained

Melt butter in 1-qt. baking pan. Combine milk and dry ingredients together. Pour over butter. Mix thoroughly. Place fruit over batter. Bake at 350° for 1 hour. Serve with ice cream or whipped cream.
*Mary Ann Fall*
*Claudia Flory*

### Fruit Cobbler 2
1 qt. fruit with juice
1/2 cup sugar
1/4 cup butter
1 cup flour
1 cup sugar
1 tsp. baking powder
1/4 tsp. salt
1/4 cup oil
1/2 cup milk

Pour fruit and sugar into 1 1/2 or 2-qt. baking dish. Dot with butter. Mix remaining ingredients together and pour over fruit. Bake at 350° to 375° until done for 30 to 45 minutes. Serve warm.
*Doria Shuman*

## Fruit Dumplings
1 qt. canned or fresh fruit
1/3 cup sugar
1/2 cup water
Batter:
1 cup flour
1 tsp. baking powder
1/2 cup sugar
1/2 cup milk
pinch of salt

Mix fruit, sugar, and water in large saucepan; bring to a boil. Combine batter ingredients, blending until smooth. Drop dumpling batter on hot fruit and cook 15 to 20 minutes on low heat. Good hot or cold.
*Mary Heinrich*
Variation:
Add 2 Tbsp. melted butter or shortening to the batter. Serve with cream or ice cream.
*Mary E. Davidson*

## Peaches
### Peaches 'N Crepes
Crepe Batter:
1/2 cup flour, sifted
2 eggs
3/4 cup milk
dash of salt
3 drops vanilla
1 1/2 Tbsp. sugar
sliced peaches

Combine crepe ingredients and beat with rotary beater until smooth. Refrigerate the batter several hours to thicken. Heat a heavy 6-inch skillet until a drop of water dances on it. Then grease lightly and pour in

2 Tbsp. batter. Lift skillet off heat and tilt from side to side until batter covers bottom evenly. Now cook until underside of crepe is lightly browned; cooking should take only seconds. Roll up crepes; place in chafing dish or skillet with peach slices. To serve, pour hot *Crepe Sauce* over crepes and fruit. Heat through. Makes about 10 crepes.

Crepe Sauce:
1/3 cup sugar
1 Tbsp. cornstarch
dash of salt
1 1/2 cups orange juice
1/4 cup butter
1/2–1 tsp. orange peel

Mix together sugar, cornstarch, and salt. Blend in 1/4 cup orange juice. Heat remaining 1 1/4 cups orange juice to boiling; stir in sugar mixture. Cook and stir until clear. Remove from heat; add butter and orange peel. Stir until butter melts. Serve over crepes.
*Danielle Boone*

## Peachy Keen Bake

4 cups freestone
  peaches, sliced
1 pkg. yellow or white
  cake mix
1/2 cup butter, melted
1/2 cup nuts, chopped

Spread sliced peaches
in the bottom of a
13x9x2-inch baking
dish. Sprinkle dry
cake mix on top.
Drizzle melted butter
over top of dry mix.
Sprinkle chopped
nuts and bake about
35 minutes at 375°.
Serve warm or cold
with ice cream or
whipped cream
*Mary Howser*
*Joan Howser*

## Pineapple
### Pineapple-Cherry Cobbler

1 can pineapple
  tidbits, drained
1 can cherry pie filling
1 cup nuts, chopped
2 cups (1/2 box) yellow
  cake mix
1/2 cup margarine or
  butter
whipped cream,
  (optional)

Dump first 3 ingre-
dients into shallow
2-qt. dish. Sprinkle
with dry cake mix.
Dot with margarine.

Bake at 350° for 50
minutes or until
crusty and golden.
Top with whipped
cream.
*Ruthanne Wise*

Variation 1:
Use 3/4 cup margar-
ine or butter and
melt it. Pour over
cake mix.
*Eunice Grover*

Variation 2:
Use 4 cups drained
and sliced Elberta
peaches, instead of
the pineapple and
the pie filling.
*Doris Boyd*

## Strawberry
### Strawberry Shortcake

2/3 cup shortening
2 cups flour
3 tsp. baking powder
1/2 cup sugar
1/2 tsp. salt
milk

Mix dry ingredients
together with pastry
blender until crumbly.
Add enough milk to
make a stiff dough.
Bake in muffin tins
for 20 minutes at
350°. Serve with
fresh or frozen straw-
berries. Yields 12
muffins.
*Marietta Pegg*

# Special Baked Desserts
VEGETABLE-
BASED
## Pumpkin
### Pumpkin Pie Squares

Crust:
1 cup flour
1/2 cup quick rolled
  oats
1/2 cup brown sugar
1/2 cup butter

Filling:
2 cups pumpkin
1 13 1/2-oz. can
  evaporated milk
2 eggs
2 Tbsp. butter, melted
3/4 cup sugar
1/2 tsp. salt
1 tsp. cinnamon
1/2 tsp. ginger
1/4 tsp. cloves

Topping:
1/2 cup nuts, chopped
1/2 cup brown sugar
2 Tbsp. butter

To make crust, blend
together crust ingre-
dients in mixing
bowl; use mixer on
low speed until
crumbs form. Press
into ungreased
13x9x2-inch pan.
Bake at 350° for 15
minutes. To make
filling, combine all
filling ingredients in
mixing bowl; beat
well. Pour into crust
evenly. Bake at 350°
for 20 minutes.

For *Topping*, combine ingredients and sprinkle over baked filling. Return to oven for another 15 to 20 minutes until filling is firm. Cool in pan. Cut into squares. Serve with whipped cream.
*Nancy Layman*

## Rhubarb
## Rhubarb Shortcake

4 cups rhubarb, diced
1 1/2 cups sugar
2 Tbsp. flour
1/4 tsp. nutmeg
butter

Batter:
1 1/2 cups flour
3/4 cup sugar
2 tsp. baking powder
1/4 cup oil
5/8 cup milk
1/4 tsp. salt
1 egg

Combine rhubarb, sugar, flour, and nutmeg. Spread evenly into 13x9x2-inch baking dish. Dot with butter. Combine batter ingredients, mixing well. Spread over rhubarb mixture and bake at 350° about 35 minutes.
*Iva Jamison*

## CREAM-BASED
## Cheese Cake

Crust:
1 pkg. graham crackers, crushed
1 Tbsp. sugar
1/4 cup margarine

Filling:
1 8-oz. pkg. cream cheese
6 eggs, separated
2 cups sugar
1 tsp. salt
2 tsp. vanilla
2 pkg. whipped topping mix, prepared

Mix crust ingredients together and press on bottom of 13x9x2-inch pan, reserving some crumbs for top. Bake 8 minutes at 350°. Cool. Make filling. Cream the cheese, egg yolks, sugar, and salt; add vanilla. Beat egg whites until stiff and fold into creamed mixture. Then fold in whipped topping. Pour mixture over crust and sprinkle remaining crumbs on top. Freeze. Serve frozen.
*Mary Gish*

## Cheese Treat

Crust:
3 egg whites
1 cup sugar
1/2 tsp. baking powder
1/2 tsp. vanilla
36 round crackers, crushed
3/4 cup chopped nuts
Topping:
1 pkg. whipped topping mix
1 3-oz. pkg. cream cheese, softened
1 cup crushed pineapple, drained
Maraschino cherries

Beat egg whites until medium stiff; add sugar, baking powder, and vanilla. Fold in crushed crackers and nuts. Pour into greased 9-inch square baking dish. Bake at 325° for 30 minutes or less, until lightly browned.

Prepare *Topping* mix. Add cream cheese to crushed pineapple; fold into whipped topping and pour on top of cooled crust. Refrigerate. Cut into squares and serve with Maraschino cherries on top. Best made 48 hours before serving.
*Esther Flora*

## Cream Puffs

1 cup flour
1/4 tsp. salt
1/2 cup shortening (at
  least 1/4 cup butter)
1 cup boiling water
4 eggs

Sift flour and measure; add salt and sift again. Combine shortening and boiling water in saucepan; keep over low heat until butter melts. Add flour at one time and stir vigorously over low heat. Add unbeaten eggs, one at a time, beating thoroughly after each addition. Continue beating until a thick dough forms. Drop by tablespoon onto a greased baking sheet about 2 inches apart. Bake in a hot 425° oven about 50 minutes or until beads of moisture no longer appear on dough surfaces. Do not open oven door during early part of baking! When cool, cut off tops and fill bottoms with cream filling or sweetened whipped cream. Replace tops and sprinkle with powdered sugar. Yields 12 large puffs.
*Gladys Metzger*

## Ice Cream Toffee Dessert

1 cup flour
1/4 cup brown sugar
1/2 cup nuts, chopped
1/4 cup butter,
  softened
vanilla ice cream
fruit pie filling

Mix flour, brown sugar, and nuts together. Blend in soft butter. Place mixture in a baking pan and bake at 350° until lightly browned. Stir frequently. Remove from oven and cool. Then line the bottom of a 13x9x2-inch baking dish with crumbs, reserving 2 Tbsp. or so. Spread softened vanilla ice cream on crumbs. Sprinkle remaining crumbs on top and freeze. To serve, cut in squares and garnish with a spoonful of fruit pie filling.
Variation:
Substitute other ice cream flavors for the vanilla.
*Virginia Wolf*

🌷
# Special No-Bake Desserts
## FRUIT-BASED
### Apricot Whirl

3 cups graham
  cracker crumbs
1/2 cup butter
2 cups powdered
  sugar
1 egg, beaten
1 pt. whipping cream
1-lb. pkg. dried
  apricots*

Line 12-inch or slightly smaller oblong glass dish with 1 cup graham cracker crumbs. Mix together butter, sugar, and beaten egg. Whip cream and add to egg-sugar mixture. Add layer of cream mixture over top of crumbs in pan. Alternate with layers of apricot, crumbs, and cream mixture, ending with crumbs on top. Refrigerate several hours before serving.
*Soak dried apricots overnight. Cook and sweeten to taste; then mash.
*Emma Lynch*

## Janet's Blueberry Delight

1 1/2 cups blueberries
1 1/2 Tbsp. cornstarch
1 3/4 cups sugar
1 pkg. graham
  crackers, crushed
  fine
1/2 cup margarine,
  melted
1 8-oz. pkg. cream
  cheese
1 pkg. whipped
  topping mix,
  prepared

Thicken berries with cornstarch and 1 cup sugar; cool. Mix crumbs and melted margarine. Pat into 8-inch square pan. Mix cream cheese with remaining 3/4 cup sugar; fold into prepared topping. Pour cheese mixture into crumb-lined pan.

Top with cooled berry mixture. Chill several hours. Freezes well.
*Kathleen Barnhart*

## Cherry Mallow Delight 1

3 cups graham cracker crumbs
1/2 cup butter or margarine, melted
1/4 cup sugar
1 pt. whipping cream
1 pkg. miniature marshmallows
3 cans cherry pie filling

Combine crumbs, melted butter, and sugar. Line a 13x9x2-inch pan with 1/2 the crumb mixture. Whip the cream, and add less than whole package of marshmallows. Divide cream mixture in half. Alternately layer cream mixture and pie filling, ending with extra marshmallows and remaining crumbs on top. Refrigerate for at least 5 hours. Serves 18.
*Linda Thompson*

## Cherry Mallow Delight 2

Crust:
1 1/2 cups graham crackers or vanilla wafers, crushed
1/2 cup butter, melted
Fillings:
30 large marshmallows
1/2 cup milk
1/2 cup heavy cream, whipped
1 can cherry pie filling

1/8 tsp. almond flavoring

Combine crumbs and butter; reserve 1/4 cup. Press remaining crumb mixture in bottom of large, flat pan. Melt marshmallows in milk over medium heat, stirring often. Cool. Fold the whipped cream into marshmallow mixture. Spread over crumbs. Combine pie filling and flavoring; spread evenly over marshmallows. Sprinkle rest of crumbs on top and chill.
Note:
Substitute raspberry, apricot, or blueberry pie fillings, omitting almond flavoring from the last two.
*Ina Bauman*

## Cherry Rice Dessert

2 3-oz. pkgs. cherry gelatin
1 1/2 cups water (3/4 cup hot, 3/4 cup cold)
1 can crushed pineapple, undrained
1/2 cup rice, cooked
2 pkgs. whipped topping mix, prepared

Mix together all ingredients, except topping. Pour into large mold or bowl. Refrigerate until thickened. Fold in prepared topping. Let set until firm.
*Darleen Layman*

## Frozen Fruit 1

5 ripe bananas, mashed
1 large can crushed pineapple
2 cups orange juice
1 cup water
1 cup sugar

Mix all ingredients together. Pour into 13x9x2-inch pan. Freeze. Very refreshing.
*Jane Layman*

## Frozen Fruit 2

2 eggs, beaten
5 Tbsp. sugar
4 Tbsp. lemon juice
25 large marshmallows
2 Tbsp. butter
1 can fruit cocktail, drained
nuts, (optional)
1 can crushed pineapple
1 small can Maraschino red cherries, cut up
1 cup cream, whipped

Cook first 5 ingredients together in double boiler until marshmallows are melted. When cool, add fruits and nuts. Fold in whipped cream. Pour into mold or casserole and freeze. Cut and serve.
*Dorothy Root*

## Fruit Compote

6 cups assorted fresh
   fruit
1 cup sparkling white
   grape juice
2 Tbsp. orange liqueur
2 Tbsp. orange juice
1/2 gallon pineapple
   sherbet

Combine all but
sherbet. Place sherbet
in large decorative
bowl or small punch
bowl. Pour fruit mix-
ture on top.
Note:
This is good for
showers.
*Janice Jarboe*

## Fruit Delight

Crust:
12 double graham
   crackers, crushed
1/2 cup margarine,
   melted
Fillings:
2 pkgs. whipped
   topping mix
1 8-oz. pkg. cream
   cheese, softened
1 cup powdered sugar
1 can fruit pie filling

Combine crumbs
with melted mar-
garine. Press into
bottom of 13x9x2-
inch pan. In one
bowl, prepare whipped
topping mix accord-
ing to package di-
rections. In another
bowl, combine soft-
ened cream cheese
and powdered sugar.
Then combine
whipped topping
with cheese-sugar
mixture; mix well
using beater. Spread
over crumb layer in
pan; then spread pie
filling to make a
third layer. Refrig-
erate several hours
before serving.
*Anita Angle*
*Rachel Shoup*

## Fruit Torte

Crust:
2 cups graham
   cracker or vanilla
   wafer crumbs
9 Tbsp. butter, melted
Fillings:
1 1/2 cups powdered
   sugar
1 or 2 eggs
1 Tbsp. water
1 can pie filling
1 cup walnuts, ground
1 pkg. whipped
   topping mix

Mix crumbs and 3
Tbsp. melted butter
together. Pour re-
maining melted but-
ter into 8-inch square
pan. Spread crumb
mixture on bottom of
pan, reserving 1/4
cup for top. Cream
sugar and egg thor-
oughly. Add water
and beat well. Spread
creamed mixture over
crumbs. Add pie
filling. Cover with
ground walnuts. Pre-
pare topping mix and
spread topping over
nuts. Sprinkle re-
served crumbs over
nuts.
*Arlene Boone*

## Orange Cream Dessert

1 Tbsp. unflavored
   gelatin
1 Tbsp. water
2 tsp. cornstarch
2 Tbsp. flour
3/4 cup sugar
1 cup boiling water
1 Tbsp. butter
3 egg yolks
2 Tbsp. orange juice
grated rind of 1 orange
3 Tbsp. lemon juice
1/2 pt. whipping
   cream
angel food cake or
   pound cake, broken
   up

Soak gelatin in water
for 5 minutes. Sift
dry ingredients in
top of double boiler.
Add boiling water,
stirring until smooth.
Add butter and yolks,
stirring until thick.
Add juices and rind.
Cool and chill 1 hour.
Whip the cream and
fold into orange mix-
ture. Place cake
pieces in 8-inch
square pan. Pour
orange cream mix-
ture on top. Refriger-
ate several hours. Cut
into squares. Garnish
with Mandarin
orange slices.
Variation:
Spoon orange cream
mixture on sliced
cake.
*Eunice Grover*

## Lime Sherbet Delight

2 3-oz. pkgs. lime gelatin
2 cups boiling water
2 pts. lime sherbet
1 cup whipped cream
bananas or pineapple, (optional)

Dissolve gelatin in boiling water; add sherbet and stir until melted. Fold in whipped cream. Add bananas or pineapple, if desired.

*Shirley Denlinger*

Variation:
Use orange gelatin and orange sherbet; then add Mandarin oranges and marshmallows. Omit whipped cream.

*Ruth Long*

## Pineapple Dessert

1 lb. vanilla wafers, crushed
1/2 cup butter
1 1/2 cups powdered sugar
2 eggs, well beaten
1 cup crushed pineapple, drained
1 cup whipping cream, whipped
1/2 cup nuts, chopped

Spread 1/2 crushed wafers in bottom of 13x9x2-inch pan. Cream butter and sugar; add beaten eggs and mix well. Spread over crumbs. Spread pineapple over creamed mixture; then spread whipped cream on pineapple. Sprinkle nuts and remaining crumbs on top. Chill 2 hours. Cut into squares.

*Martha Reece*

## Strawberry Squares

Crumb Crust:
1 cup flour
1/2 cup nuts, chopped
1/4 cup brown sugar
1/2 cup margarine, melted

Filling:
3 egg whites
3 Tbsp. lemon juice
1 1/2 cups white sugar
3 cups strawberries, fresh or frozen
1 1/2 cups whipping cream

Combine crust ingredients. Bake on cookie sheet at 350° for 20 minutes, stirring occasionally. Cool; then press 2/3 crumbs into 13x9x2-inch dish. Beat egg whites until frothy. Add lemon juice and sugar. Thaw and drain strawberries if frozen. Add to egg mixture. Whip cream and add to strawberry-egg mixture. Pour on top of crumbs. Sprinkle remaining 1/3 crumbs on top. Freeze at least 6 hours or overnight. Serves 15.

*Esther Flora*

## Strawberry Rice Parfait

4 cups rice, cooked and sweetened*
4 Tbsp. sugar
1/2–1 pt. whipping cream

1–2 drops red food coloring
1/2 tsp. almond flavoring
1 pkg. frozen strawberries, thawed

Chill rice. Just before serving, whip cream. If desired, reserve 1/4 cup of whipped cream for garnish. Fold in coloring, flavoring, and remaining 2 Tbsp. sugar. Fold into rice. Fill serving dishes with alternate layers of rice and strawberries. Garnish with whipped cream and extra berries.

*To sweeten rice, add 2 Tbsp. sugar to rice cooking.

*Alice Mae Haney*

# Special No-Bake Desserts
MISCELLANEOUS

## Broken Window Glass Dessert

1 3-oz. pkg. lime
   gelatin
1 3-oz. pkg. orange
   gelatin
1 3-oz. pkg. cherry
   gelatin
4 cups boiling water
1 1/2 cups cold water
1 3-oz. pkg. lemon
   gelatin
1/4 cup sugar
1/2 cup pineapple
   juice
1 envelope whipped
   topping mix

Prepare first 3 gelatin
flavors separately,
using 1 cup boiling
water and 1/2 cup
cold water for each.
Pour each flavor into
a separate 8-inch
square pan. Chill
until firm. Combine
lemon gelatin, sugar,
and remaining 1 cup
of boiling water. Stir
until dissolved. Stir
in pineapple juice.
Chill until slightly
thickened. Mean-
while, cut the firm
gelatins into 1/2-inch
cubes. Prepare
whipped topping and
blend with thickened
lemon gelatin. Fold in
gelatin cubes and
pour into mold. Chill
at least 5 hours or
overnight.
Note:
This may also be
poured into a
graham cracker
crust.
*Edna Dutter*
*Susan Wray*

## Cheese Cake

Crust:
1/2 cup butter
32 graham crackers,
   crushed
1/2 cup sugar
Filling:
1 6-oz. pkg. lemon
   gelatin
1 cup hot water
1 8-oz. pkg. cream
   cheese
1 cup sugar
1 tsp. vanilla
1 2/3 cups whipping
   cream

Combine crust in-
gredients and line a
13x9x2-inch dish;
reserve some crumbs
for top. Dissolve gela-
tin in hot water and
let cool. Cream the
cheese, sugar, and
vanilla. Whip the
cream until thick;
add to cream cheese
mixture. Pour over
crumbs. Sprinkle re-
served crumbs on
top. Freeze or chill.
Serve very cold.
*Cora Eller*

## Chocolate Almond Delight

Crust:
1 1/2 cups graham
   cracker crumbs
   (about 10 double
   crackers)
1/4 cup sugar
1/4 cup butter or
   margarine, melted
Filling:
1 7 1/2-oz. milk
   chocolate almond
   bar
20 large marsh-
   mallows
1/2 cup milk
3 1/2 cups (9-oz. con-
   tainer) frozen
   whipped topping,
   thawed
1 1/4 cups (10-oz. pkg.)
   frozen strawberries,
   thawed and pureed

Combine crust ingre-
dients, and press into
foil-lined 8-inch
square pan. Finely
chop chocolate bar.
Melt marshmallows
in top of double
boiler over simmer-
ing water; remove
from heat. Add
chocolate pieces, stir-
ring until smooth.
Fold 2 1/2 cups
thawed topping into
chocolate mixture.
Pour over crumb
crust; cover and
freeze 1 hour. Com-
bine 1 cup pureed
strawberries and re-
maining 1 cup of
topping; spread over
frozen chocolate mix-
ture. Cover and freeze
several hours. Cut
into squares and
garnish with remain-
ing 1/4 cup puree.
Serves 9–12.
*Virginia Peters*

## Chocolate Dream Dessert

angel food cake, broken up
1 Tbsp. butter
2 pkgs. chocolate chips
4 eggs
1 pt. cream, whipped
chopped nuts

Place cake pieces in 13x9x2-inch pan. Melt butter and chocolate chips; add eggs one at a time, stirring after each addition. Cool mixture. Then, pour into whipped cream and blend. Spread over cake and garnish with nuts. Refrigerate at least 1 hour.
Variation:
Substitute pound cake for angel food cake.
*Bethel Hinkle*

## Chocolate Mallow Dessert

Crust:
whole graham crackers
1/4 cup butter, melted
Filling:
1/4 cup butter or margarine
1 cup powdered sugar
1/3–2/3 cup chocolate syrup
3 eggs, separated
1 pkg. whipped topping mix
1/2 cup nuts, chopped
12 large or equivalent amount miniature marshmallows

Line a 9-inch square pan with whole graham crackers; drizzle melted butter on top. Cream margarine and sugar together. Add syrup and yolks, blending well. Beat egg whites until stiff. Prepare whipped topping, and add to egg mixture. Stir in nuts and marshmallows. Pour over crust. Freeze and serve frozen.
*Anita Angle*

## Chocolate Ice Cream Dessert

Crust:
2 cups vanilla wafer crumbs
3 Tbsp. butter or margarine, melted
Filling:
1/2 cup butter or margarine
2 squares chocolate
2 cups powdered sugar
3 eggs, separated
1/2 cup nuts, chopped
1/2 gallon vanilla ice cream, softened

Grease 13x9x2-inch pan. Reserve 1/2 cup wafer crumbs. Combine remaining crumbs and melted butter. Pat on bottom of pan. Melt butter and chocolate together in top of double boiler. Add yolks and sugar; cook slowly until thick. Remove from heat. Beat whites and blend into chocolate mixture. Spread over crumbs; cool. Spread ice cream evenly over chocolate layer.

Sprinkle with reserved crumbs. Freeze until ready to serve. Cut into squares.
*Donna Rumble*
*Martha Gish*

## Mocha Dessert

1 10 1/2-oz. pkg. miniature marshmallows
1 cup strong hot coffee
1 Tbsp. instant coffee
2 cups whipped cream

Melt marshmallows with coffees in top of double boiler. Mix well; then cool until set. Add whipped cream. Pour into graham cracker pie shell or small baking dish lined with graham cracker crust. Chill. Freezes very well.
*Janet Rumble*

## Mint Dazzle

Crust:
2 cups vanilla wafer
  crumbs
1/2 cup butter, melted
Fillings:
1/2 cup butter
1 1/2 cups powdered
  sugar
3 eggs, slightly beaten
3 squares unsweetened
  chocolate
3/4 cup whipping
  cream
1 pkg. miniature
  marshmallows
1/2 cup peppermint
  candy, crushed

Blend wafer crumbs
and melted butter.
Press into 8-inch
square pan. Cream
butter and powdered
sugar. Add eggs. Melt
chocolate in top of
double boiler; add to
creamed mixture,
beating until light
and fluffy. Spoon
mixture over crumbs.
Freeze until firm.
Whip the cream and
fold in marshmallows.
Spread over frozen
mixture. Sprinkle
with crushed candy.
*Peggy Wise*
*Susan Young*
*Joan Swearingen*

## Tortoni Squares

Crumbs:
1/3 cup nuts, chopped
3 Tbsp. margarine,
  melted
1 cup vanilla wafer
  crumbs
Filling:
1/2 gallon vanilla ice
  cream, softened
1 12-oz. jar apricot-
  pineapple jam

Blend crumb ingredi-
ents. Reserve 1/4 cup
for topping. Press 1/2
remaining crumb
mixture into 9-inch
square pan. Spread
alternately with ice
cream, jam, and
crumbs until top
layer is jam. Sprinkle
reserved crumbs on
top. Freeze. Cut into
squares to serve.
*Janet Rumble*

## Velvet Cream

2 8-oz. pkgs. cream
  cheese, softened
1/2 cup sugar
2 tsp. vanilla
4 eggs, separated
1 bar sweet baking
  chocolate, melted
1/2 cup sugar
2 pkgs. whipped
  topping mix

Mix cheese, sugar,
and vanilla until well
blended. Beat egg
yolks and add to
cheese mixture.
Blend in melted
chocolate. Beat egg
whites to stiff peaks,
adding 1/2 cup sugar
gradually. Fold into
chocolate-cheese
mixture. Prepare
whipped topping
made with milk only
and fold into mixture.
Add chopped nuts.
Freeze.
Variation:
Also use chocolate
cookies on top and
bottom.
*Clara Meador*

Source: _____    Who Likes It: _____

Source: _____    Who Likes It: _____

Source: _____    Who Likes It: _____

## HEAVENLY RECIPE

*Take 1 cup of faith and spread generously through*
*Each lovely day God has given you.*

*Add 1 package of hope to every good deed.*
*And thank God for giving you graces you need.*

*Take 2 cups of charity, sift all around*
*To your friends, neighbors, anyone you've found.*

*Bake for a lifetime and ice it with love,*
*And you have the recipe for Heaven above.*

# In the Cookie Jar

*A loaded wagon creaks;*
*an empty one rattles.*
PENNSYLVANIA GERMAN SAYING

*God chose us*
*to be his very own,*
*through what Christ*
*would do for us;*
*he decided then*
*to make us holy*
*in his eyes,*
*without a single fault—*
*we who stand*
*covered with his love.*
EPHESIANS 1:4

# Bars

## BAKED

### Apple Bars 1

2/3 cup flour, sifted
3 tsp. baking powder
1/2 tsp. salt
2 eggs, beaten
1 1/2 cups sugar
3 tsp. vanilla
2 cups apples, pared and diced
1 cup walnuts, chopped

Sift dry ingredients except sugar. Beat eggs; add sugar and vanilla to eggs. Combine dry ingredients, egg mixture, apples, and nuts. Mix all together. Bake in large, greased baking dish for 45 minutes at 350°. Cool. Then sift powdered sugar on top. Cut into squares.
*Jennie Cowan*

### Apple Bars 2

2 eggs
1 1/2 cups sugar
1 cup flour
2 1/2 tsp. baking powder
pinch of salt
2 cups apples, diced
1 cup nuts, chopped
2 tsp. vanilla

Stir all ingredients together. Bake in 13x9x2-inch pan at 350° for 40 minutes. Note: Shortening is omitted.
*Mildred Davison*

### Apple Butter Bars

1 1/2 cups flour, sifted
1 tsp. baking soda
1 tsp. salt
2 1/2 cups quick oats
1 1/2 cups sugar
1 cup margarine, melted
1 1/2 cups apple butter
1/2 cup nuts, chopped

Sift together flour, baking soda, and salt. Add oats and sugar, mixing thoroughly. Add margarine and blend. Press 1/2 of mixture firmly into 12x8x2-inch pan. Spread apple butter evenly over top. Add remaining oat mixture lightly over top. Sprinkle nuts over all and lightly press smooth. Bake at 350° for 45 to 55 minutes. Cool and cut in squares.
*Sara Lee Switzer*

### Brown Sugar Bars

1 lb. brown sugar
4 eggs, beaten
1 1/2 cups flour, sifted
1 tsp. cinnamon
1 tsp. vanilla
1 cup walnuts, chopped

Mix all ingredients together and pour into well-greased or non-stick 13x9x2-inch pan. Bake at 300° for 30 to 40 minutes. Cut in squares when cool. These are very chewy.
*Dovella Boyd*

## Coconut-Apricot Bars

1 pkg. lemon cake mix
1/4 cup water
2 eggs
1/4 cup butter or
  margarine, softened
1/4 cup brown sugar
1 cup flaked coconut
1 cup dried apricots,
  chopped

Combine half the cake mix, water, eggs, butter, and brown sugar in mixing bowl. Mix thoroughly. Blend in remaining cake mix. Stir in coconut and apricots. Spread in greased and floured jelly roll pan. Bake 20 to 25 minutes at 375°. While warm, spread with *Lemon Glaze*.

Lemon Glaze:
1 cup powdered sugar
1/2 tsp. lemon peel,
  grated
1 tsp. lemon juice
2 Tbsp. milk

Beat glaze ingredients together until smooth.
*Clara Meador*

## Coconut Bars

Crust:
1/2 cup margarine
1/2 cup brown sugar
1 cup flour

Filling:
2 eggs, beaten
1 cup brown sugar
1 tsp. vanilla
2 Tbsp. flour
1 tsp. baking powder
1/2 tsp. salt
1 cup nuts, chopped
1 cup coconut, flaked

Mix crust ingredients together and press into 13x9x2-inch baking dish or pan. Bake at 350° for 10 minutes only. Meanwhile, mix filling ingredients. When crust is done, pour filling on top, spreading evenly. Bake at 350° for 20 to 25 minutes. Cool and cut into bars.
*Kathryn Beckner*

## Coffee Bars

1/2 cup butter
1 cup brown sugar
1/2 cup hot coffee
1 1/2 cups flour
1/2 tsp. baking soda
1/2 tsp. baking
  powder
1 tsp. cinnamon
1 egg
1/4 cup walnuts,
  chopped
1/2 cup raisins

Glaze:
1 cup powdered sugar
2 Tbsp. milk
1/2 tsp. vanilla

Mix together batter ingredients. Bake in flat 16x11x1-inch pan at 350° for 20 to 25 minutes. Combine powdered sugar, milk, and vanilla; pour over baked mixture while hot. Cool and cut into 1-inch bars.
*Marilyn Gish*

## Congo Squares

2 3/4 cups flour, sifted
2 1/2 tsp. baking
  powder
1/2 tsp. salt
3/4 cup shortening
2 1/2 cups (1 lb.)
  brown sugar
3 eggs
1 cup nuts, broken
1 pkg. milk chocolate
  chips

Mix and sift flour, baking powder, and salt; set aside. Melt shortening and add brown sugar, stirring until well mixed. Cool slightly. Add eggs, one at a time, beating well after each addition. Add dry ingredients, then nuts and chocolate chips. Pour into 8-inch square pan. Bake at 350° for 25 to 30 minutes. When almost cool, cut into 2-inch squares. Yields 48 squares.
*Fern Boyd*

## Dream Bars 1

Crust:
1/2 cup butter or
  margarine
1/2 cup brown sugar
1 cup flour

Filling:
2 eggs
1 cup brown sugar,
  firmly packed
1 tsp. vanilla
2 Tbsp. flour
1/2 tsp. salt
1 tsp. baking powder
1 1/2 cups coconut,
  shredded
1 cup nuts, chopped

Mix crust ingredients together. Pat into an 8x12x2-inch baking pan. Bake at 375° for 10 minutes. Cool.

For *Filling*, beat eggs, brown sugar, and vanilla together. Mix in 2 Tbsp. flour, salt, and baking powder. Blend in coconut and nuts. Pour onto baked crust and bake at 375° for 20 minutes. Frost with *Orange Butter Frosting*.

Orange Butter Frosting:
1/4 cup butter or
   margarine, softened
2 cups powdered
   sugar, sifted
1 tsp. vanilla
1 tsp. grated orange
   peel
2 Tbsp. orange juice

Cream butter and sugar. Add vanilla and orange peel. Work in orange juice, enough to make a little softer than you want the finished frosting. Frost and cut in squares.
*Betty King*

## Dream Bars 2

Crust:
1 cup flour
1/2 cup shortening
1/2 cup brown sugar
Filling:
2 eggs, well beaten
2 Tbsp. flour
1 1/4 cups brown
   sugar
3/4 cup coconut

Mix crust ingredients well. Pat into 13x9x2-inch pan and bake 10 minutes. Cool and spread with filling mixture. Bake at 375° for 20 minutes. Cut into bars while warm.
*Lois Bauman*

## Fruit Cocktail Bars

1 egg, beaten
1 cup flour
1 cup sugar
1 tsp. baking soda
1/2 tsp. salt
1 tsp. vanilla
1 cup fruit cocktail,
   drained
Nut Topping:
1/4 cup brown sugar
1/4 cup nuts, chopped

Mix all except topping ingredients until well blended. Pour into greased 13x9x2-inch pan. Cover with sugar and nuts. Bake at 350° for 30 minutes.
*Mary Howser*

## Gumdrop Bars

4 eggs
2 cups brown sugar
1 Tbsp. lemon juice
1 cup nuts, chopped
1 lb. gumdrops, cut up
2 cups flour, sifted

Beat eggs; cream in brown sugar. Add lemon juice and nuts. Combine gumdrops and flour. Add to creamed mixture. Pour into flat pan, lined with waxed paper. Bake at 350° for 40 minutes. Cool and cut in squares. Sprinkle with powdered sugar.

Note:
These are close to being a confection!
*Alice Kline*

## Lemon Bars 1

Crust:
1 cup flour
1/4 cup powdered
   sugar
1/2 cup butter
Filling:
2 eggs, well beaten
juice of 1 lemon, about
   1/4 cup
1 cup sugar
2 Tbsp. flour
dash of salt

Mix flour and sugar for crust; cut in butter until mixture is well blended. Pat into 9-inch square baking pan, building up slightly on the sides. Bake 20 minutes at 350°. Meanwhile, prepare filling, beating ingredients together. Pour filling over baked crust . Bake 25 minutes at 350°. When cool, sprinkle with powdered sugar. Cut into bars.
*Ruth Wise*

## Lemon Bars 2

Crust:
1/2 cup butter
1 cup flour
1/4 cup powdered
  sugar
Filling:
3 eggs, beaten
3 Tbsp. lemon juice
grated rind of 1 lemon
3/4 tsp. baking
  powder
1 1/2 cups sugar
3 Tbsp. flour

For *Crust:* Cream
butter; add flour and
sugar. Pat into
13x9x2-inch pan (use
metal for best results).
Bake 15 minutes at
350°. For *Filling:*
Combine eggs, lemon
juice, and rind. Add
baking powder, sugar,
and flour. Pour over
crust. Bake 25
minutes at 325°.
Cool. Sift powdered
sugar on top.
*Barbara Rumble*
*Dorothy Root*

## Lemon
## Cheese Bars

1 17-oz. pkg. lemon
  cake mix
1/2 cup margarine,
  melted
1 13 1/2-oz. pkg.
  lemon frosting mix
1 8-oz. pkg. cream
  cheese, softened
2 eggs

Mix cake mix and
melted margarine
until moist. Pat into
13x9x2-inch pan
greased on bottom
only. Combine frost-
ing mix and cream
cheese. Divide cheese
mixture in half. To
one half, add eggs
and beat 3 to 5
minutes. Spread egg
mixture over pan
crust. Bake at 350°
for 30 minutes. Cool
and spread with re-
maining cream
cheese mixture.
*Lois Cover*

## Cookie Nut Bars

2 Tbsp. butter
2 eggs
1 cup brown sugar
1 tsp. vanilla
5 Tbsp. flour
1 cup nuts, chopped
1/8 tsp. baking soda

Melt butter in 8-inch
square pan. Beat
eggs and sugar to-
gether. Add vanilla.
Sift flour and baking
soda; combine with
nuts. Fold dry ingre-
dients into egg mix-
ture. Pour over butter
in pan and bake at
350° for 15 to 20
minutes. Remove
from oven and let set
a few minutes. Turn
upside down and
sprinkle buttered
side with powdered
sugar. Cut in pieces.
Note:
If doubling recipe, use
a 13x9x2-inch pan
and bake longer.
*Margaret Bowman*

## Mrs. Graham's
## Best Nut Squares

3 eggs, separated
1 cup sugar
1 cup graham
  crackers, ground
1/2 cup nuts, chopped
1 tsp. baking powder
1 tsp. vanilla

Beat egg whites and
yolks separately. Add
sugar to beaten yolks;
then add ground
crumbs, chopped
nuts, baking powder,
and vanilla. Add
stiffly beaten egg
whites, folding in
gently. Pour mixture
into greased 8-inch
square pan. Bake at
325° for 40 minutes.
Cut in squares.
*Verna Kinzie*

## Nut Bars

2 cups brown sugar
1 cup flour
1/4 tsp. baking soda
1/4 tsp. salt
2 cups walnuts,
  coarsely ground
2 eggs, beaten
1 tsp. vanilla

Mix dry ingredients;
add nuts, beaten
eggs, and flavoring.
Mix well. Spread into
well greased 13x9x2-
inch pan. Bake at
325° about 25
minutes. Cut into
bars.
*Jeanette Scrivner*

## Orange Slice Bars

1 cup dates or raisins, cut up
1/2 cup sugar
3/4 cup water
2 Tbsp. flour
1 cup orange slice candy, cut up
1/2 cup nuts, chopped
1 cup brown sugar
2 Tbsp. milk
3/4 cup shortening
1 3/4 cups flour
1 tsp. baking soda
1/2 tsp. salt
1 tsp. vanilla

Cook dates, sugar, water, and flour until thick. Remove from heat; add orange candy and nuts. Cool. Cream together brown sugar, milk, and shortening. Beat well. Add flour, baking soda, and salt. Mix well; then stir in vanilla. Pour 1/2 of creamed mixture into greased 12x8x2-inch pan. Spread with date filling. Cover with rest of creamed mixture. Bake at 350° about 40 minutes. Cut into bars.
*Annabelle Gish*

## Peanut Butter Bars

1/2 cup shortening
1/2 cup sugar
1/2 cup brown sugar
1/3 cup peanut butter
1 tsp. vanilla
1 egg
1/4 cup milk
1 cup flour
1/2 tsp. baking soda
1/2 tsp. salt
1 cup rolled oats

Cocoa Frosting:
2 cups powdered sugar
1/4 cup cocoa
3 Tbsp. butter
2–3 Tbsp. boiling water
1/2 tsp. vanilla

Cream first 5 ingredients. Add egg and milk. Sift together flour, baking soda, salt, and oats. Blend into creamed mixture. Pour into 8-inch square pan. Bake at 350° for 20 to 25 minutes. Beat frosting ingredients until creamy. Frost cake when cooled.
*Jeanne Brubaker*

## Pecan Surprise Bars

1 pkg. yellow cake mix
1/2 cup butter or margarine, melted
1 egg
1 cup pecans, chopped
Filling:
2/3 cup reserved cake mix
1/2 cup brown sugar, firmly packed
1 1/2 cups dark corn syrup
1 tsp. vanilla
3 eggs

Grease bottom and sides of 13x9x2-inch baking pan. Reserve 2/3 cup dry cake mix for filling. In large mixing bowl, combine remaining cake mix, butter, and 1 egg; mix until crumbly. Press into prepared pan. Bake at 350° for 15 to 20 minutes until golden brown.

Filling:
In large mixer bowl, combine all ingredients and beat at medium speed for 1 to 2 minutes. (At high altitude, 5520 feet, decrease brown sugar by 1 Tbsp.) Pour filling over partially baked crust. Sprinkle with pecans. Return to 375° oven for 30 to 35 minutes until filling is set. Cool and cut into 36 bars.
Variation:
Sprinkle with coconut.
*Fern Boyd*

## Chewy Pecan Bars

1 cup white sugar
1 cup brown sugar
3/4 cup margarine, melted
1 tsp. vanilla
1 1/4 cups flour
1 cup pecans or walnuts, chopped
2 eggs

Mix all ingredients together and pour into greased and floured 13x9x2-inch pan. Bake at 350° for 30 minutes.
*Mary Boone*

## Six Layer Bars

1 cup butter
1 1/2 cups graham
  cracker crumbs
1 6-oz. pkg. chocolate
  or butterscotch chips
1 cup nuts, chopped
1 cup coconut, flaked
1 can sweetened
  condensed milk

Melt butter in
13x9x2-inch pan.
Sprinkle remaining
ingredients over the
top in layers. Bake at
325° for 30 to 35
minutes. Cool. Cut
into bars.
Note:
These taste better
several hours after
baking.
*Nelda Driver*

## Old-Fashioned Spice Bars

1 cup raisins
1 cup water
1/2 cup salad oil
1 cup sugar
1 egg, slightly beaten
1 3/4 cups flour
1 tsp. baking soda
1 tsp. nutmeg
1/2 tsp. cloves
1/4 tsp. salt
1 tsp. cinnamon
1 tsp. allspice
1/2 cup nuts, chopped

Bring raisins and
water to a boil and
remove from heat.
Stir in salad oil and
cool to lukewarm.
Stir sugar and egg
into raisin mixture.
Sift together dry in-
gredients. Combine
with egg-raisin mix-
ture. Add nuts. Bake
in a 13x9x2-inch pan
at 350° for 20
minutes. Cut into
bars.
*Darleen Layman*

## Yummy Bars

1/2 cup shortening
1/2 cup margarine
1 cup water
2 Tbsp. cocoa
2 cups sugar
2 cups flour
1/2 cup buttermilk
2 eggs, beaten
1 tsp. baking soda
1 tsp. vanilla
Boiled Icing:
1/2 cup margarine
4 Tbsp. cocoa
1 tsp. vanilla
6 Tbsp. milk
1 box powdered sugar
1 cup nuts, chopped

Boil first 4 ingre-
dients and then add
to remaining ingre-
dients. Pour into
16x11x1-inch pan
and bake at 400° for
20 minutes. While
cake is still hot, boil
ingredients for icing
and pour over cake.
Cut into bars.
*Nan Miller*

# Bars
NO-BAKE
## Dream Bars

18 whole graham
  crackers
1 cup margarine or
  shortening
1 cup sugar
1/2 cup milk
1 egg, slightly beaten
1 cup graham cracker
  crumbs
1 cup coconut,
  chopped
1 cup nuts, chopped
Butter Cream
Frosting:
1/2 cup margarine
2 cups powdered
  sugar
cream or milk to
  spread
1 1/2 tsp. vanilla

Line a 13x9x2-inch
dish with half of the
whole graham
crackers. Combine
1/2 cup margarine,
sugar, milk, and eggs.
Cook for 2 minutes
at full boil. Stir con-
stantly. Remove from
heat and add graham
cracker crumbs, coco-
nut, and nuts. Spread
mixture over first
layer of crackers.
Top with another
layer of whole
crackers. Combine
frosting ingredients
and spread on bars.
Chill and cut.
*Ruthanne Wise*
Variation:
Add 1/2 tsp. vanilla
to filling. For frosting,
omit vanilla and
margarine.
*Linda Lavy*

## Peanut Butter Cereal Squares

1 cup brown sugar
1 cup light corn syrup
1 cup peanut butter
6 cups crunchy cereal

Mix sugar and syrup and cook until bubbly. Remove from heat and add peanut butter. Mix well. Pour over cereal. Mix well and pour into buttered pan. Mash down firmly and cut into squares or spoon into mounds on waxed paper.
*Blanche Moore*
*Ruth Wise*

# Brownies

## Butterscotch Brownies 1

1/4 cup shortening, melted
1 cup brown sugar
2 eggs
3/4 cup flour
3/4 tsp. baking powder
1/2 tsp. salt
1/2 tsp. vanilla
1/2 cup nuts, chopped
small marshmallows

Frosting:
1 1/2 Tbsp. butter
1 1/2–2 Tbsp. hot water
1/4 cup brown sugar
1 cup powdered sugar

Combine all brownie ingredients except marshmallows. Bake in 9-inch square pan at 325° for 25 to 30 minutes. Remove brownies from oven; cover immediately with marshmallows and let melt.
Make *Frosting,* combining butter, water, and brown sugar. Stir in powdered sugar and beat. Then drizzle over marshmallows. Frosting will be thin.
*Ruth Balsbaugh*

## Butterscotch Brownies 2

1/3 cup shortening
1 cup sugar
2 eggs
3/4 cup flour
1/2 tsp. baking powder
1/2 tsp. salt
1/2 cup nuts, chopped
1/4 cup butterscotch bits

Cream first 3 ingredients together. Add the rest, blending well. Bake in 9-inch square pan at 350° 25 to 30 minutes. Cut into squares.
*Barbara Basore*

## Chocolate Brownies 1

1/3 cup shortening
1 cup sugar
2 eggs
1 tsp. vanilla
1/2 cup flour
1/4 cup cocoa
1/2 tsp. salt
1/3 cup nuts, chopped
small marshmallows

Frosting:
1 Tbsp. butter, melted
2 Tbsp. cocoa
1 1/2–2 Tbsp. hot water
1 cup powdered sugar

Combine all brownie ingredients except marshmallows. Bake in 9-inch square pan at 325° for 25 to 30 minutes. Remove brownies from oven; cover immediately with marshmallows and let melt. Make *Frosting,* combining butter, cocoa, water, and sugar. Then drizzle over marshmallows. Frosting will be thin.
*Ruth Balsbaugh*

## Chocolate Brownies 2

2 eggs
2 cups sugar
1/3 cup salad oil
1/2 cup margarine
2 cups flour
1/4 cup cocoa
1 tsp. baking soda
1/2 cup buttermilk
1 cup cold water

Beat eggs, adding sugar, oil, and margarine. Combine dry ingredients. Mix buttermilk and water together. Alternately blend dry and liquid mixtures into egg mixture. Beat thoroughly. Bake in greased jelly roll pan for 18 minutes at 400°. Cool. Make frosting. (See next page.)

Chocolate
Buttermilk Frosting:
1/2 cup margarine
1/2 cup cocoa
1/3 cup buttermilk
1 box powdered sugar
1/2 tsp. vanilla

Bring first 3 ingredients to a boil. Add powdered sugar and vanilla. Mix well and frost while warm.
*Marcele Jarboe*

## Chocolate Brownies 3

1/2 cup margarine
1 cup sugar
4 eggs
1 can chocolate syrup
1 cup plus 1 Tbsp. flour
1 tsp. vanilla
1/2 tsp. salt
1/2 tsp. baking powder
1/2–1 cup nuts, chopped

Combine all ingredients and pour into 9-inch square pan. Bake at 350° for 20 to 30 minutes. Cool. Make frosting.

Melted
Chip Frosting:
6 Tbsp. butter
6 Tbsp. milk
1 1/2 cups sugar
1/2 cup chocolate chips

Combine first 3 ingredients and boil for 30 seconds. Stir in chocolate chips. Cool until ready to spread.
*Carla Miller*

## Chocolate Brownies 4

1/2 cup butter or margarine
2 1/2 squares unsweetened chocolate
1/2 cup flour, sifted
1 tsp. baking powder
1 cup sugar
1 tsp. vanilla
1/2 cup nuts, chopped
2 eggs

Melt butter and chocolate in saucepan. Remove from heat, adding next 5 ingredients. Mix well and then add eggs. Beat thoroughly. Spread in greased 9-inch square pan. Bake at 350° for 30 minutes. Cool. Make frosting.

Creamy
Cocoa Frosting:
1 Tbsp. cocoa
1 cup brown sugar
1/4 cup cream
powdered sugar

Heat first 3 ingredients to *almost* boiling, but don't boil. Cool and add powdered sugar to desired thickness.
*Joan Benedict*

## Chocolate Brownies 5

6 rounded Tbsp. cocoa
1 1/2 cups flour
1 tsp. salt
3 cups sugar
4 eggs, beaten
1 cup shortening
3/4 cup milk
3 tsp. vanilla
1 cup nuts, chopped

Mix all ingredients well. Spread in 13x9x2-inch pan. Bake at 350° for 30 to 40 minutes. Cool and frost, if desired.
*Dorothy Moore*

# Cookies
DROP
Butter
## Basic Butter Cookies

1 cup butter or margarine
1 tsp. vanilla
1 cup sugar
2 cups flour
1/2 tsp. baking soda
pinch of salt

Cream butter, vanilla, and sugar. Add dry ingredients and mix well. Drop by teaspoon onto ungreased baking sheet. Bake 6 to 8 minutes at 350°.
Variation:
Add chopped almonds and almond flavoring, chocolate chips, or butterscotch chips to basic dough.
*Dorothy Moore*

## Chocolate
## Chocolate Chip Cookies

1 cup shortening
1/2 cup white sugar
1 cup brown sugar, firmly packed
1 tsp. vanilla
2 eggs, beaten well
2 1/4 cups flour
1 tsp. baking soda
1 tsp. salt
1 cup nuts, chopped
1 cup (6-oz. pkg.) chocolate chips

Cream shortening, sugars, and vanilla together. Fold in beaten eggs. Sift in dry ingredients. Add nuts and chips. Drop by teaspoon onto cookie sheet. Bake 10 minutes at 375°.
Variation:
Use butterscotch chips instead of chocolate chips.
*Phyllis Denlinger*

## Cocoa
## Drop Cookies

1 cup butter
1 3/4 cups sugar
1 cup cottage cheese
1 tsp. vanilla
2 eggs
2 1/2 cups flour, sifted
1/2 cup cocoa powder
1 tsp. baking soda
1 tsp. baking powder
1/2 tsp. salt

Cream butter and sugar until fluffy. Add cottage cheese and vanilla; beat thoroughly. Add eggs, one at a time, beating well after each addition. Sift flour, cocoa, baking soda, baking powder, and salt.

Gradually add to creamed mixture. Drop by rounded teaspoon onto greased cookie sheet and bake at 350° for about 12 minutes. Let stand a few minutes before moving from sheet. When cool, frost with a powdered sugar icing, if desired. Makes 6 dozen cookies.
*Carol Flory*

## Lemon
## Lemon Crisps

2 cups flour, sifted
3/4 tsp. baking soda
pinch of salt
3/4 cup shortening
1 cup sugar
2 3 3/4-oz. pkgs. lemon instant pudding
3 eggs, beaten slightly

Sift flour, baking soda, and salt together. Cream shortening, sugar, and pudding until light and fluffy. Add eggs, mixing with dry ingredients until well blended. Drop onto greased baking sheet about 2 1/2 inches apart. Flatten slightly with glass dipped in sugar. Bake at 375° for 8 to 10 minutes. Makes 4 dozen cookies.
*Arleen Peters*

## Molasses
## Ginger Creams

1/4 cup shortening
1/2 cup sugar
1 egg
1/3 cup molasses
2 cups flour, sifted
1/2 tsp. baking soda
1/2 tsp. salt
1 tsp. ginger
1/2 tsp. cinnamon
1/2 tsp. cloves
1/2 cup water

Cream together shortening and sugar; beat in egg. Stir in molasses. Sift dry ingredients and add alternately with water. Drop by teaspoon onto greased cookie sheet. Bake at 400° about 8 minutes. While slightly warm, frost with a powdered sugar icing. Makes 3 dozen.
*Edna Thompson*

## Old-Fashioned Molasses Cookies

2 cups brown sugar
1 cup shortening
3 eggs
1 cup molasses
6 cups flour
1 tsp. baking powder
1 tsp. ginger
1/2 tsp. cinnamon
1 tsp. salt
1 tsp. baking soda
1 1/2 cups hot water

Cream shortening and sugar. Add eggs and beat mixture thoroughly. Stir in molasses. Stir in dry ingredients, except for baking soda. Combine baking soda and water. Add to mixture and blend well. Drop by heaping teaspoon onto greased baking sheet. Bake at 375°. Ice with browned butter-powdered sugar icing. Sprinkle with chopped nuts or top with a walnut half.
*Freeda Beachler*

## Nut
## Aunt Sadie's Nut Cookies

2 cups brown sugar
1 cup butter or
  shortening, melted
3 eggs
2 1/2–3 cups flour

1 tsp. baking soda in
  4 Tbsp. warm water
1 cup nuts, chopped

Combine all ingredients and mix well. Drop by teaspoon onto greased cookie sheet. Bake at 350° for 10 to 15 minutes.
*Muriel Onkst*

## Peanut Crisps

1 cup shortening (part
  butter), softened
1 1/2 cups brown
  sugar, packed
2 eggs
2 tsp. vanilla
3 cups flour
1 tsp. salt
1/2 tsp. baking soda
2 cups salted peanuts

Mix first 4 ingredients thoroughly in bowl. Stir dry ingredients together in separate bowl and then combine with shortening mixture. Stir in peanuts. Drop dough by teaspoon about 2 inches apart onto lightly greased baking sheet. Grease the bottom of a glass; flatten each cookie by dipping glass in sugar and pressing on dough. Bake for 8 to 10 minutes at 375°. Makes about 6 dozen cookies.
*Denise Metzger*

## Pecan Crispies

1/2 cup shortening
1/2 cup butter
2 1/2 cups brown
  sugar
2 eggs, beaten
2 1/2 cups flour
1/4 tsp. salt
1/2 tsp. baking soda
1 cup pecans, chopped

Combine all ingredients, mixing well. Drop by teaspoon onto cookie sheet. Bake at 350° for 12 to 15 minutes. Makes 6 dozen small cookies.
*Anna Miller*

## Oatmeal Aggression Cookies

3 cups brown sugar
3 cups margarine
6 cups oatmeal
1 Tbsp. baking soda
3 cups flour
white sugar

Combine all ingredients, except white sugar, in a very large bowl and mash; knead and squeeze. Then form into small balls, midway between filbert size and English walnut size on an ungreased cookie sheet. Butter the bottom of a small glass, dip it into white granulated sugar, and mash the balls flat. Butter the glass bottom once or twice, but keep re-dipping it in sugar for each ball. Then bake at 350° for 10 to 12 minutes.
*Bethel Hinkle*

## Amish Cookies

2 1/2 lbs. lard
5 lbs. sugar
2 lbs. rolled oats
1 lb. peanuts,
  shelled and chopped
2 lbs. raisins
1 can molasses
1 qt. sour milk
12 eggs
1 1/2 tsp. salt
2 tsp. vanilla
6 lbs. or less flour
8 Tbsp. baking powder
8 Tbsp. baking soda
4 Tbsp. cinnamon
4 Tbsp. nutmeg
egg whites, beaten

Combine all ingredients, except egg whites, and mix well. Drop by teaspoon onto cookie sheet and flatten. Beat egg whites and spread over top. Bake at 350° for 20 to 25 minutes.
Note:
Feel free to cut the recipe by a third or even a fourth.
*Alice Mae Haney*

## Banana Oatmeal Cookies

1 1/2 cups flour
1/2 tsp. baking soda
1 tsp. salt
1 cup sugar
1 egg, beaten
1 cup bananas,
  mashed
1 3/4 cups quick,
  rolled oats
1/2 cup nuts, chopped
3/4 cup shortening
  (not oil)

Combine all ingredients and mix well. Drop by teaspoon 1/2 inch apart onto slightly greased cookie sheet. Bake at 400° for 10 to 15 minutes.
*Joan Cover*

## Butterscotch Oatmeal Cookies

2 eggs
1 cup shortening
3/4 cup brown sugar
3/4 cup white sugar
1/2 tsp. salt
1 tsp. vanilla
1 Tbsp. hot water
1 1/2 cups flour
1 tsp. baking soda
1 cup nuts, chopped
1 pkg. butterscotch
  chips
2 cups quick, rolled
  oats

Cream eggs, shortening, sugar, and salt. Add vanilla and then remaining ingredients. Drop by teaspoon onto cookie sheet and bake until light brown, 10 or 12 minutes at 350°.
*Edna Denlinger*

## Chewy Oatmeal Cookies

3/4 cup butter
1/2 cup white sugar
1 1/2 cups brown
  sugar, packed
2 eggs
1 tsp. vanilla
1 1/4 cups flour
1 tsp. baking powder
1/2 tsp. baking soda
1 tsp. salt
2 1/2 cups oats
1 cup nuts, chopped
1 cup raisins *or*
  coconut

Cream butter and sugars together. Add unbeaten eggs and vanilla. Sift dry ingredients and add to creamed mixture. Stir in oats, nuts, and raisins (or coconut). Drop by teaspoon onto lightly greased cookie sheet. Bake at 375° for 12 minutes.
*Betsy Yost*

## Coconut Oatmeal Cookies

1/2 cup white sugar
3/4 cup butter,
  softened
1 1/2 cups light brown
  sugar, packed
2 eggs
1 cup flour, sifted
1 tsp. baking powder
1/2 tsp. baking soda
1 tsp. vanilla
2 1/2 cups quick,
  rolled oats
1 cup coconut, flaked

Cream sugars and butter until light. Beat in eggs, one at a time. Add sifted dry ingredients, vanilla, and oats. Mix well and fold in coconut. Drop by teaspoon onto greased baking sheet. Bake at 350° for 10 minutes.
*Mary Heinrich*

## Crunchy Oatmeal Cookies

2 cups brown sugar
2 cups white sugar
2 cups margarine
4 eggs
4 cups flour
4 cups oats
2 tsp. baking soda
1 tsp. salt
2 tsp. vanilla

Beat sugars, margarine, and eggs thoroughly. Add remaining ingredients, mixing well. Drop by teaspoon onto lightly greased cookie sheet. Bake 10 minutes at 350°.

*Marietta Page*

## Sour Cream Oatmeal Cookies

1 cup white sugar
1 cup brown sugar
1 cup butter or margarine
1 cup sour cream
2 cups dates, chopped fine
1 cup nuts, chopped
2 eggs
2 cups quick, rolled oats
3 cups flour
1 tsp. baking soda
1 tsp. salt
2 tsp. vanilla

Mix all ingredients together. Drop by teaspoon onto greased cookie sheet. Bake at 325° for 12 to 15 minutes.

*Esther Flora*

## Oatmeal Cookie Mix

Ready Mix:
2 cups white sugar
2 cups brown sugar
2 tsp. baking soda
1 tsp. baking powder
3 cups flour
2 tsp. salt
2 cups shortening
6 cups quick, rolled oats

Blend all ingredients until mixture is crumbly. Refrigerate in an airtight container. To make fresh cookies, combine:

2 cups mixture
1 egg
1 tsp. vanilla

Drop dough by teaspoon onto greased baking sheet. Bake 10 to 12 minutes at 350°.
Variation:
Add 1/2 cup nuts, coconut, chocolate chips, or raisins.

*Miriam Mohler*

## Orange Gumdrop Cookies

1 cup white sugar
1 cup brown sugar
1 cup shortening
2 eggs
2 cups flour
1 tsp. baking powder
1 tsp. baking soda
1 cup coconut, flaked
2 cups rolled oats
5 Tbsp. water
1 cup orange gumdrops, chopped

Cream sugars and shortening together. Add eggs, flour, baking powder, and baking soda. Mix in remaining ingredients. Drop by teaspoon onto cookie sheet. Bake at 350° for 20 minutes or until done.
Note:
Put orange gumdrops in the water to keep them from gumming together.
Variation:
Candy orange slices may be used also.

*Lois Root*

## Persimmon

## Persimmon Drop Cookies 1

3/4 cup margarine or shortening
1 1/2 cups sugar
2 eggs
1 cup persimmon pulp
1 tsp. baking soda
1 tsp. vanilla
1 1/2 cups flour
2 tsp. baking powder
1/2 tsp. salt
1/2 tsp. nutmeg
1/2 tsp. cloves
1 tsp. cinnamon
1 1/2 cups quick, rolled oats
1/2 cup coconut
1/2 cup nuts, chopped

Cream together margarine and sugar; beat in eggs. Stir baking soda into persimmon pulp and add to creamed mixture. Sift dry ingredients and add with vanilla to creamed mixture; mix well.

Stir in oats, coconut, and nuts. Drop by teaspoon onto greased baking sheet. Bake at 375° about 12 minutes. Makes 6 dozen cookies.
*Marjorie Bauman*

## Persimmon Drop Cookies 2

1 cup persimmon pulp
1 tsp. baking soda, sprinkled over pulp
1 cup sugar
1/2 cup butter or margarine
1 egg
2 cups flour
1 tsp. cinnamon
1/2 tsp. salt
1/2 tsp. cloves
1/2 tsp. nutmeg
1 cup raisins
1 cup walnuts, chopped

Beat first 4 ingredients until frothy. Add remaining ingredients. Drop by teaspoon onto cookie sheet and bake 12 to 15 minutes at 375°.
Note:
These freeze well.
*Ethel Rumble*

## Persimmon Drop Cookies 3

1 cup sugar
1/2 cup shortening
1 egg
1 cup persimmon pulp
1/2 cup nuts, chopped
2 cups flour
1/2 tsp. baking soda
1/2 tsp. baking powder
1/4 tsp. cinnamon
1/4 tsp. nutmeg
1/2 tsp. cloves
1/2 cup raisins

Cream sugar and shortening; add egg and persimmon pulp. Sift dry ingredients and add to creamed mixture. Mix in nuts and raisins. Drop by teaspoon onto cookie sheet and bake at 375° for 10 minutes. Makes 5 dozen.
*Ruthann Orndoff*
*Mary Lou King*

## Pineapple Pineapple Cookies

2 cups sugar
1 cup shortening
4 eggs
1 tsp. vanilla
1 cup crushed pineapple, drained
4 1/2 cups flour
2 tsp. baking soda
1 tsp. salt

Combine sugar and shortening, beating well. Add eggs, one at a time; then add vanilla and drained pineapple. Combine dry ingredients and add to creamed mixture, mixing well. Dough will be stiff. Drop by teaspoon onto cookie sheet. Bake at 300° about 20 minutes or until golden brown.
*Virginia Peters*

## Glazed Pineapple Cookies

1/2 cup shortening
1 cup brown sugar
1 egg
1 tsp. vanilla
3/4 cup crushed pineapple, drained
2 cups flour
1 1/2 tsp. baking powder
1/4 tsp. salt
1/4 tsp. baking soda

Drain pineapple. Cream shortening and brown sugar; beat in egg. Add vanilla and pineapple. Add dry ingredients. Drop by teaspoon onto greased cookie sheet. Bake 18 to 20 minutes at 325°.
Cool and frost.

Frosting:
2 Tbsp. pineapple juice
1 cup powdered sugar

Beat juice and sugar together until smooth.
*Joan Swearingen*

## Pumpkin
### Pumpkin Cookies

2 cups sugar
2 cups shortening
1 16-oz. can pumpkin
2 eggs
2 tsp. vanilla
4 cups flour
2 tsp. baking powder
1 tsp. baking soda
1 tsp. salt
2 tsp. cinnamon
1 tsp. nutmeg
1/2 tsp. allspice
2 cups raisins
1 cup nuts, chopped

Cream sugar and shortening. Add pumpkin, eggs, and vanilla. Beat well. Add sifted dry ingredients to creamed mixture. Mix well and stir in raisins and nuts. Drop dough onto cookie sheets. Bake at 350° for 12 to 15 minutes. Cool and frost with vanilla icing. Freezes well.
Variation:
Use brown sugar instead of regular white sugar.
*Janice Root*

## Raisin-Nut
### Raisin-Nut Cookies

1 cup butter or margarine
1/2 cup white sugar
1/2 cup brown sugar, firmly packed
2 eggs
1 tsp. vanilla
2 3/4 cups flour
1/2 tsp. baking soda
1/4 tsp. salt
1/4 cup tomato catsup
1/2 cup raisins
1/2 cup walnuts, chopped

Combine all ingredients, mixing well. Drop by teaspoon onto greased cookie sheet. Bake at 375° for 10 to 12 minutes. Frost while warm with *Orange Glaze.*
Orange Glaze:
1 1/2 cups powdered sugar, sifted
2 Tbsp. orange juice
Combine and beat until smooth. If not thin enough, add a little more orange juice.
*Lillie Dunlop*

### Whole Wheat Cookies

1 cup butter or shortening
2 cups brown sugar
1 egg
2 tsp. baking powder
1/4 tsp. baking soda
1/2 tsp. salt
1 cup sour cream
4 cups whole wheat flour
1 cup raisins
1 cup nuts, chopped
nut halves, (optional)

Cream shortening, sugar, and egg. Add remaining ingredients. Drop small spoonfuls onto baking sheet. Place nut halves on tops of cookies, if desired. Bake at 400° for 15 minutes.
Variation:
Omit raisins.
*Mary Heinrich*

## FILLED
### Date-Filled Cookies

Dough:
3 cups quick, rolled oats
1 cup flour
1 cup lard
1/2 cup water
1 cup brown sugar, packed
1 tsp. baking soda

Combine dough ingredients, mixing well. Roll very thin, with additional flour on board. Cut into 2-inch circles. Bake at 350° for 10 to 15 minutes or until done. Cool. Spread *Date Filling* between cookies.
Date Filling:
1 1/2 cups sugar
2/3 cup water
1 1/2 cups dates, chopped
Boil ingredients and cool.
*Lillie Dunlop*

## Raisin-Filled Cookies

Dough:
2 1/4 cups flour, sifted
1/4 tsp. salt
2 tsp. baking powder
1/2 cup shortening
1 cup sugar
2 eggs, beaten
1/2 tsp. vanilla
1 Tbsp. milk

Raisin Filling:
1/3 cup sugar
1 cup raisins
1/3 cup hot water
dash of salt

Mix dough ingredients well. Roll out dough and cut into circles. Make raisin filling; combine ingredients, cook until thick, and cool. Place teaspoon of filling on half the circles. Keep it away from the edges. Cover with remaining circles and press together around the edges with tines of fork. Sprinkle with sugar. Bake at 375° for 12 minutes. Makes 2 1/2 dozen cookies.
*Sandra Switzer*

## MOLDED Butterscotch Cookies

1/4 cup butter or margarine
1/4 cup shortening
1/3 cup white sugar
1/3 cup brown sugar
1 egg
1 1/3 cups flour, sifted
3/4 tsp. baking soda
3/4 tsp. vanilla
1/3 cup walnuts, chopped

Melt butter and shortening. Add sugars and mix well. Add egg and beat until light colored. Sift together flour and baking soda; stir into egg mixture. Add vanilla and nuts. Chill. Roll into small balls. Bake on ungreased cookie sheet at 375° for 7 to 10 minutes. Remove at once. Makes about 4 dozen cookies.
*Edna Thompson*

## Chinese Almond Cookies

2 3/4 cups flour, sifted
1 cup sugar
1/2 tsp. baking soda
1/2 tsp. salt
1 cup butter, margarine, or lard
1 egg, slightly beaten
1 tsp. almond extract
1/3 cup whole blanched almonds, halved

Sift dry ingredients together into bowl. Cut in butter until mixture resembles cornmeal. Add egg and almond extract; mix well. Form into 1-inch balls. Place on ungreased cookie sheet about 2 inches apart. Flatten on cookie sheet with bottom of floured tumbler. Place almond half on each cookie. Bake at 325° for 15 or 20 minutes. Yields 50 cookies.
*Peggy Wise*

## Chocolate Macaroons

1/2 cup butter or margarine, melted
4 squares baking chocolate
2 cups sugar
4 eggs
2 tsp. vanilla
2 tsp. baking powder
2 cups flour

Mix butter, chocolate, and sugar; add eggs, one at a time, beating after each addition. Add vanilla. Then sift together dry ingredients and add to chocolate mixture. Chill well, preferably overnight. Grease hands well and form small balls. Roll them in powdered sugar. Bake on greased sheet 2 inches apart for 12 to 15 minutes at 350°.
Note:
Don't let butter boil while melting. Also, the tops crack and get a little crusty as they cool, while the insides stay chewy.
*Jan Cowan*

## Chocolate Crinkles

1/2 cup oil
4 pkgs. liquid chocolate
2 cups sugar
2 tsp. vanilla
4 eggs
2 cups flour
1 tsp. salt
2 tsp. baking powder

Mix oil, chocolate, sugar, vanilla, and eggs. Then add flour, salt, and baking powder; blend well. Chill overnight. Shape into balls and roll in powdered sugar. Bake at 350° for 10 to 12 minutes. Makes 5 to 6 dozen.
*Betty Lou Garber*

## Chocolate Snow Caps

5 squares unsweetened chocolate
1/2 cup oil
2 cups sugar
2 tsp. vanilla
4 eggs
2 cups flour
1/2 tsp. salt
2 tsp. baking powder
1 1/4 cups powdered sugar

Melt chocolate in top of double boiler. Remove and add oil, sugar, vanilla, and eggs. Beat. Sift dry ingredients and add to chocolate mixture; blend well. Chill overnight. Shape into balls and roll in powdered sugar. Bake for 12 minutes at 350°.
*Barbara Fall*

## Chocolate Thumbprints

1/2 cup shortening
1/2 cup sugar
1 egg, separated
1/2 tsp. vanilla
1 square baking chocolate, melted
1 cup flour
1/4 tsp. salt
finely chopped nuts

Combine all ingredients, except for egg white and nuts; mix well. Slightly beat egg white. Roll teaspoons of dough into balls and dip in egg white. Then roll in finely chopped nuts. Put on cookie sheet and press thumb in center firmly. Bake 10 minutes at 375°. Cool. Drop colored icing into cookie centers. Makes 3 dozen.
Variation:
Use 1/4 cup brown sugar instead of white; omit chocolate.
*Barbara Rumble*

## Crunch Cookies

1 cup white sugar
1 cup brown sugar
1 cup shortening
1 cup salad oil
2 eggs
1 tsp. baking soda
1 tsp. vanilla
1/2 tsp. salt
1 tsp. cream of tartar
3 cups flour
1 cup crunchy cereal, crushed
1 cup oats
1 cup nuts, chopped

Cream sugars and shortening together. Add oil, eggs, baking soda, vanilla, salt, and cream of tartar. Mix together flour, cereals, and nuts. Combine cereal and creamed mixtures, mixing thoroughly. Shape into small patties and flatten. Bake at 350° for 15 to 20 minutes or until done.
*Susan Fisher*

## Fruit Thumbprints

1/2 cup butter or margarine
1/4 cup sugar
1 egg yolk
1/2 tsp. vanilla
1 cup flour
1/4 tsp. salt
jelly, jam, marmalade

Cream butter and sugar. Add egg yolk and vanilla, mixing well; then add flour and salt. Shape the dough into small balls. Bake 5 minutes at 350°. Remove from oven, make a dent in each cookie, and return cookies to oven. Bake 12 minutes longer at 350°. Fill the dents with jelly.
*Joy Thompson*

## Ginger Cookies

3/4 cup shortening
1 cup sugar
1 egg
1/4 cup molasses
2 cups flour
1 1/2 tsp. baking soda
1 tsp. cloves
1 tsp. cinnamon
1 tsp. ginger

Combine all ingredients and shape into balls. Then roll in sugar. Bake at 350° for 12 minutes.
*Nancy Layman*

## Gingersnaps

2 cups flour
1 Tbsp. ginger
2 tsp. baking soda
1 tsp. cinnamon
1/2 tsp. salt
3/4 cup shortening
1 cup sugar
1 egg
1/4 cup molasses

Sift first 5 dry ingredients together; set aside. Cream shortening and sugar together; add egg and mix well. Then add molasses and mix. Add sifted dry ingredients. Shape into balls; then roll in sugar. Place balls on cookie sheet and bake at 350° for 12 to 15 minutes.
*Leah Garber*

## Kourabeides
(Greek Cookies)

2 cups butter
8 Tbsp. powdered
  sugar
4 cups nuts, chopped
4 cups flour
2 Tbsp. vanilla
2 Tbsp. ice water

Cream butter; then add powdered sugar, blending thoroughly. Combine nuts and flour; then add to creamed mixture. Add vanilla and ice water gradually until well blended. Form into teaspoon-shaped mounds, and place on ungreased cookie sheet. Bake 30 to 35 minutes at 350°. Sift sugar over top after baking.
*Annabelle Gish*

## Molasses Cookies 1

3/4 cup shortening
1 cup brown sugar
1 egg
1/4 cup molasses
2 tsp. baking soda
1/4 tsp. salt
1/2 tsp. cloves
1 tsp. cinnamon
2 1/4 cups flour
1 tsp. ginger

Mix first 4 ingredients thoroughly. Stir in the remaining ingredients. Chill dough. Roll dough into balls the size of large walnuts. Dip the tops in sugar. Place 3 inches apart on greased cookie sheet. Sprinkle each cookie with 2 or 3 drops of water for a crackled surface. Bake for 10 to 12 minutes, just until set, but not hard, at 375°. Makes about 4 dozen cookies.
*Doris Moore*

## Molasses Cookies 2

2 cups sugar
1 1/2 cups shortening
2 eggs
1/2 cup molasses
5 tsp. baking soda
4 cups flour
2 tsp. cinnamon
1 tsp. ginger
1/2 tsp. salt

Cream sugar and shortening; add eggs and molasses, beating well. Sift in dry ingredients. Roll into small balls and coat with sugar. Bake on greased cookie sheet at 375° until golden brown. Makes 7 to 8 dozen 3-inch cookies.
*Connie Reece*

## Molasses Cookies 3

3/4 cup shortening
1 cup sugar
1 egg
1/4 cup molasses
2 tsp. baking soda
1/2 tsp. salt
2 cups flour, sifted
1 tsp. cinnamon
3/4 tsp. cloves
3/4 tsp. ginger

Mix shortening, sugar, egg, and molasses well. Sift dry ingredients and add slowly to first mixture. Blend well. Form into walnut-sized balls. Place 2 inches apart on greased cookie sheet. Bake 10 to 12 minutes at 350°.
*Ella Huffman*

## Nut Nuggets

1/2 cup butter
2 Tbsp. sugar
7/8 cup flour, sifted
1 cup nuts, chopped
1 tsp. vanilla

Combine all ingredients. Shape into small balls. Place on greased cookie sheet. Bake at 350° for 15 minutes. Then roll in powdered sugar twice.
*Naomi Barton*

## Oatmeal Cookies 1

4 cups brown sugar
2 cups shortening
4 eggs
2 tsp. vanilla
3 cups flour
2 tsp. baking soda
2 tsp. baking powder
1 tsp. salt
6 cups quick, rolled oats

Cream together shortening and sugar. Add eggs and vanilla, beating well. Sift together dry ingredients and add to creamed mixture, blending well. Chill dough overnight. Mold into balls and roll in powdered sugar. Place on greased cookie sheet. Bake for 10 to 12 minutes at 350°. Makes 6 dozen.
*Bonnie Jamison*

## Oatmeal Cookies 2

1 cup shortening
1 cup white sugar
1/2 cup brown sugar
1 egg
1 1/2 cups flour
1 tsp. baking soda
2 tsp. cinnamon
1 1/2 cups quick, rolled oats
3/4 cups walnuts, finely crushed
1 tsp. vanilla

Cream shortening and sugars together; add egg. Sift together dry ingredients and add to first mixture. Then add oats, walnuts, and vanilla.

Chill 1 hour. Shape into walnut-sized balls and place on cookie sheet. Butter bottom of a small glass, dip in granulated sugar, and flatten cookies. Bake at 350° for 8 to 10 minutes.
Note:
Dough is very crumbly and has to be worked together with hands to get it to stick, but is worth all the trouble.
*Maralee Oyler*

## Peanut Blossoms

5 cups flour
3 tsp. baking soda
1 1/2 tsp. salt
1 1/2 cups sugar
1 1/2 cups brown sugar, firmly packed
1 1/2 cups shortening
1 1/2 cups peanut butter
3 eggs
6 Tbsp. milk
3 tsp. vanilla
100 chocolate kisses

Combine all ingredients, except candy, in large mixer bowl. Mix at lowest speed or blend by hand until dough forms. Shape dough into balls and roll in sugar. Place on ungreased cookie sheet. Bake at 375° for 10 to 12 minutes. Top each cookie with a candy kiss immediately after removing cookies from oven. Press down firmly so cookie cracks around edge.
*Dorothy Roesel*
*Connie Reece*

## Peanut Butter Cookies

1 cup brown sugar
1 cup white sugar
1 cup butter or
   shortening
1 cup peanut butter
1 tsp. vanilla
2 eggs, well beaten
3 cups flour
2 tsp. baking soda

Combine all ingredients. Shape into walnut-sized balls and flatten with a fork. Bake at 350° for 12 to 15 minutes.
*Betty King*

## Sugar Cookies

1 cup shortening
1 egg
1 cup sugar
2 cups flour
1/2 tsp. baking soda
1/2 tsp. cream of tartar
1/4 tsp. salt
vanilla
lemon flavoring
walnut halves,
   (optional)

Combine all ingredients, except walnuts, and shape into balls. Mash down with a glass dipped in a mixture of sugar and cinnamon. Top with 1/2 walnut in center before baking. Bake just until set, not brown, at 350°.
*Fern Boyd*

## Swedish Pastry

1 cup butter
2/3 cup powdered
   sugar
2 cups flour
1 cup nuts, chopped
1 tsp. vanilla

Cream butter and powdered sugar. Sift flour and add to creamed mixture, mixing well. Stir in nuts and vanilla. Roll into small balls and let stand for 30 minutes to 1 hour. Bake at 300° for 30 to 40 minutes until brown. Roll in powdered sugar.
*Mary Boone*

## Toffee Topper Cookies

2 cups flour
1 tsp. baking soda
1/2 tsp. salt
1 cup brown sugar,
   firmly packed
1/4 cup white sugar
3/4 cup butter,
   softened
1 egg
1 1/2 tsp. vanilla
   extract
4 3/4-oz. English
   toffee bars, crushed

In large mixer bowl, combine all ingredients except toffee candy. Blend well in electric mixer or by hand. Shape into walnut-sized balls. Place 3 inches apart on ungreased cookie sheet. Flatten with bottom of glass dipped in sugar. Cover center of each cookie with about 1/2 tsp. crushed candy. Bake at 400° for 8 to 10 minutes. Makes about 60 cookies.
*Denise Metzger*

## Walnut Frosties

2 cups flour
1/2 tsp. baking soda
1/4 tsp. salt
1 cup brown sugar,
   firmly packed
1/2 cup butter
1 egg
1 tsp. vanilla
Topping:
1 cup walnuts,
   chopped
1/2 cup brown sugar,
   packed
1/4 cup sour cream

Combine flour, baking soda, and salt; set aside. Cream sugar and butter in mixing bowl until light and fluffy. Add egg and vanilla, beating well. Combine dry ingredients with creamed mixture. Shape into 1-inch balls. Place 2 inches apart on ungreased cookie sheets. Make a depression in center of each cookie. Combine topping ingredients and place 1 tsp. topping in each depression. Bake at 350° for 12 to 14 minutes. Makes about 48 cookies.
Note:
If using self-rising flour, omit salt and baking soda.
*Jean Rumble*

## NO-BAKE
## Cereal Delights

1 16-oz. box chopped
  dates or 1/2 box
  raisins
1 cup margarine
1 1-lb. box light brown
  sugar
1 cup coconut, flaked
4 cups rice cereal
2 cups nuts, chopped
powdered sugar

Combine dates or
raisins, margarine,
brown sugar, and
coconut. Cook for 7
to 8 minutes, stirring
constantly. Pour over
cereal and nuts. Cool
slightly. Stir with
knife until mixed.
Shape into balls and
roll in powdered
sugar.
*Mildred E. Miller*

## Chocolate
## Cookies

2 cups sugar
1/2 cup butter
3 Tbsp. cocoa
1/2 cup milk
3 cups oatmeal
1/2 cup peanut butter
1 tsp. vanilla

Boil sugar, butter,
cocoa, and milk to-
gether for 1 minute.
Remove from heat
and add oatmeal,
peanut butter, and
vanilla. Drop by

teaspoon onto cookie
sheets and refrigerate
until hard, 1/2 hour
or so. Store in re-
frigerator.
*Janet Rumble*

## Chocolate-Peanut
## Butter Cookies

2 cups sugar
1/4 cup cocoa
1/4 cup butter
1/4 tsp. salt
1/2 cup milk
1 2/3 cups peanut
  butter
2 cups rolled oats
1 tsp. vanilla

Combine first 5 in-
gredients in sauce-
pan. Bring to rolling
boil. Stir constantly.
Remove from heat
and add remaining
ingredients. Drop by
teaspoon onto cookie
sheet or waxed paper.
*Mary Jane Root*

## Mosaic Cookies

1 6-oz. pkg. chocolate
  chips
2 Tbsp. margarine
1 egg, beaten
1 cup powdered sugar
4 cups colored
  miniature marsh-
  mallows
1 cup nuts, chopped
1 tsp. vanilla
graham cracker
  crumbs or coconut

Melt chips and mar-
garine in double
boiler. Add egg and
remove pan from hot
water. Add powdered
sugar, marshmallows,
nuts, and vanilla; mix
well. Then take 1/2 of
mixture and place on
waxed paper spread

with either crumbs
or coconut. Roll mix-
ture into log shape;
wrap in waxed paper.
Do the same with the
remaining dough.
Chill; then slice as
desired.
*Fanny Beachler*

## Peanut Butter
## Sticks

1 6-oz. pkg. semi-
  sweet chocolate
  chips
6 Tbsp. peanut butter
1 tsp. vanilla
1 cup wheat germ

Melt chocolate and
blend in peanut but-
ter and vanilla. Stir
in wheat germ. Press
into buttered 8-inch
square pan and chill.
*Linda Thompson*

## REFRIGERATOR
## Brown
## Butter Cookies

1 cup butter
2 cups brown sugar
2 eggs
3 cups flour
1 tsp. baking soda
1 tsp. cream of tartar
1/4 tsp. salt
1 cup pecans, chopped

Brown butter; then
add sugar. Mix well.
Add remaining ingre-
dients. Shape into
rolls; wrap in waxed
paper. Refrigerate un-
til firm. Slice very
thin. Bake at 375°
for 6 to 8 minutes.
*Sue Miller*

## Butterscotch Cookies

2 cups brown sugar
1 cup butter, melted
2 eggs
1 tsp. vanilla
3 1/2 cups flour
1 tsp. baking soda
1 tsp. cream of tartar

Combine all ingredients and mix well. Form into a roll. Let set overnight. Slice and bake on greased cookie sheet at 375° for 7 to 10 minutes or until done.
*Joann Cardin*

## Cinnamon Pinwheels

2 cups flour, sifted
3 tsp. baking powder
1 tsp. salt
1/3 cup shortening
3/4 cup milk

Filling:
2 tsp. cinnamon
1/2 cup sugar
2 Tbsp. butter or margarine

Sift flour, baking powder, and salt into bowl. Cut in shortening; add milk. Knead lightly. Roll dough to oblong shape, about 18x10 inches. Spread with butter. Sprinkle with cinnamon and sugar. Roll and slice. Place on greased cookie sheet. Bake at 425° for 12 to 15 minutes.
*Phyllis Denlinger*

## Date Pinwheel Cookies

1 lb. dates, chopped
1/2 cup white sugar
1/2 cup water
2 eggs
2 cups brown sugar
1 cup shortening
1 tsp. vanilla
1/2 tsp. salt
4 cups flour
1 tsp. cream of tartar

Cook dates, white sugar, and water over low heat until thick; let cool. Beat eggs; add brown sugar and shortening. Cream until light; then add vanilla. Combine dry ingredients; then add to creamed mixture 1 cup at a time. Beat until blended. Put last cup of flour mixture on dough board and knead into dough. Divide into 3 parts and roll about 1/4-inch thick. Spread with cooked dates and shape into a long roll. Chill or freeze before baking. Cut into slices and bake at 325° until light brown.
Note:
Can freeze and keep in freezer several weeks before baking.
*Edna Denlinger*

## Lemon Icebox Cookies

2/3 cup shortening
1 1/2 cups brown sugar
2 eggs
1/4 cup cream
3 1/3 cups flour
1 tsp. vanilla
1/2 tsp. lemon extract
1/4 tsp. salt
1 cup raisins
1 tsp. baking soda

Cream shortening and sugar; add eggs and cream. Beat well. Add rest of the ingredients. Shape into roll or pack into buttered ice tray pan or waxed paper. Chill 12 hours or overnight. Cut off thin slices. Bake for 10 minutes on greased cookie sheets at 350°.
*Alice Kline*

## Oatmeal Cookies

1 cup shortening
1 cup brown sugar
1 cup white sugar
1 tsp. vanilla
2 eggs, well beaten
1 1/2 cups flour
1 tsp. salt
1 tsp. baking soda
3 cups quick, rolled oats
1/2 cup chopped nuts *or* 1 cup flaked coconut

Cream shortening and sugars; add vanilla and eggs. Beat well. Add dry ingredients, oatmeal, and nuts or coconut. Shape into 2 or 3 rolls; wrap in waxed paper. Freeze. Bake when needed at 350° on ungreased sheet. Slice frozen. Good to have on hand.
*Mildred Moore*

## Northland Cookies

6 Tbsp. shortening
  (part butter)
1 cup brown sugar,
  packed
1 3/4 cups flour, sifted
1/2 tsp. salt
1 tsp. baking soda
1/2 tsp. cinnamon
1/4 cup cold water
1/2 cup nuts

Thoroughly cream
shortening and
brown sugar. Sift to-
gether dry ingredi-
ents and stir into
creamed mixture al-
ternately with 1/4
cup cold water. Blend
in nuts. Knead well
with hands. Shape
into a roll 8 1/2x2x1
1/2-inches. Wrap in
waxed paper and
chill until firm
(several hours or
overnight). Cut with
sharp knife into
slices 1/8-inch thick.
Place 1 inch apart on
ungreased cookie
sheet to allow for
spreading. Bake
about 6 minutes at
400°. Remove from
sheet immediately.
Makes about 6 dozen
cookies.
Note:
Use only 1/2 tsp.
baking soda if using
self-rising flour.
*Louise Root*

## Orange Refrigerator Cookies

1 cup butter
1/2 cup white sugar
1/2 cup brown sugar
1 egg
1/4 cup orange juice
1 Tbsp. orange peel,
  grated
1 tsp. vanilla
3 cups flour, sifted
1/2 tsp. salt
1/4 tsp. baking soda
1/2 cup walnuts,
  chopped

Thoroughly cream
butter and sugars;
add egg, orange juice,
peel, and vanilla. Beat
well. Sift together
flour, salt, and bak-
ing soda. Add to
creamed mixture;
mix well. Stir in nuts.
Shape into rolls 2
inches across or
smaller. Chill thor-
oughly. Slice very
thin, about 1/8-inch
thick. Bake on
greased cookie sheet
at 375° for 12 to 15
minutes. Makes
about 8 dozen.
*Ruth Wise*

## ROLLED Best-Ever Sugar Cookies

1/2 cup shortening
1/2 cup margarine
1/2 cup sugar
1 egg
3 tsp. vanilla
1/2 tsp. butter flavor-
  ing
3 cups flour, sifted
1/2 tsp. baking
  powder
1 tsp. salt

Cream together all
but last 3 ingredients.
Sift together flour,
baking powder, and
salt. Add to creamed
mixture. Mix well.
Chill dough 1 hour
or longer. Roll out
and cut with cookie
cutters or push
through cookie press.
Bake at 400° for 5 to
7 minutes just until
set and golden.
*Dorla Shuman*

## "To My Valentine" Oatmeal Cookies

2 1/2 cups flour, sifted
1 tsp. baking powder
1 1/2 tsp. salt
3/4 cup butter or
  margarine
3/4 cup sugar
2 Tbsp. milk
1 egg
1 tsp. vanilla
1 cup uncooked oats,
  quick *or* regular

Sift flour, baking
powder, and salt into
bowl. Add rest of
ingredients, except
oats. Beat until well
blended, about 2
minutes. Stir in oats.
Roll out on lightly
floured board to 1/4-
inch thickness. Cut
into heart shapes.
Bake on greased
cookie sheet at 375°
about 15 minutes.
Decorate with tinted
powdered sugar
frosting. Makes 3 1/2
dozen.
*Laura Belle Flory*

Source: _____ Who Likes It: _____

Source: _____ Who Likes It: _____

Source: _____ Who Likes It: _____

## THE COOKIE JAR

*A house should have a cookie jar*
*for when it's half past three*
*And children hurry home from school*
*as hungry as can be.*
*There's nothing quite so splendid*
*for filling children up*
*As spicy, fluffy ginger cakes,*
*and sweet milk in a cup.*

*A house should have a mother*
*waiting with a hug,*
*No matter what a boy brings home:*
*a puppy or a bug.*
*For children only loiter*
*when the bell rings to dismiss*
*If no one's home to greet them*
*with a cookie and a kiss.*

# Through the Sweet Shoppe

*A big wife*
*and a big barn*
*will never do a man*
*any harm.*
PENNSYLVANIA GERMAN SAYING

*Do you like honey?*
*Don't eat too much*
*of it, or it will*
*make you sick!*
PROVERBS 25:16

# Brittle

## Almond Brittle

1/2 cup butter
2 cups sugar
2 cups raw almonds
1/2 tsp. baking soda

Put butter, sugar, and almonds in large iron skillet. Stir continually over medium heat. When golden brown and sugar is melted (very syrupy), remove from heat. Stir in baking soda. Turn out on greased pan or marble slab. Crack when cool.
*Cora Eller*
*Bonita Gish*

## Cinnamon Candy

2 1/2 cups sugar
1 cup light corn syrup
1/2 cup water
red food coloring
1/2 tsp. cinnamon oil

Combine sugar, syrup, water, and enough coloring to reach desired color. Boil to hard crack stage, 295°. Immediately add cinnamon oil. Pour into medium-sized cookie sheet with sides. As candy begins to cool,
score with a knife into squares. Break into pieces.
*Mary Martin*
*Esther Huffman*

## Glass Candy

2 cups sugar
2/3 cup light corn syrup
1/3 cup boiling water
food coloring and
    flavorings of choice:
oil of cinnamon
    with red coloring
oil of sassafras with
    pink coloring
oil of lemon with
    yellow coloring
oil of orange with
    orange coloring
oil of sweet anise with
    red and green
    coloring to make
    black

Combine sugar, syrup, and water. Cook to 285°. Add coloring and a few drops of flavoring. Stir until well blended. Pour onto greased marble slab or greased griddle. Cut it with scissors into 1-inch wide strips when cool enough to handle. Then break into pieces like broken glass. Sprinkle with powdered sugar.

Note:
Keeps well in covered container. Purchase oils in small amounts from a drugstore.
*Mary Heinrich*

## Peanut Brittle 1

1/2 cup water
1 cup sugar
1/2 cup light corn syrup
1 cup raw peanuts
1 tsp. baking soda
1 tsp. butter

Cook water, sugar, and syrup to soft ball stage. Add peanuts and cook until mixture begins to turn color. Remove from heat. Add baking soda and butter; stir. Pour onto buttered cookie sheet and leave until cold. Break into pieces.
*Gladys Metzger*

## Peanut Brittle 2

2 cups sugar
1/2 cup water
1 cup light corn syrup
1 Tbsp. butter
2 cups raw peanuts
2 tsp. baking soda
1 tsp. vanilla

Put sugar, water, and syrup in heavy skillet or pan and cook to hard ball stage, 250°. Then add butter and nuts. Stir constantly and cook until a golden brown. Remove from heat. Add baking soda and vanilla. Pour at once into well-buttered cookie sheet. Cool; then break into pieces.
*Joan Howser*

# Cereal-Based

## Cereal Candy

6 cups corn flakes
4 cups rice cereal
1 can peanuts
1 cup sugar
1 cup cream
1 cup light corn syrup

Combine cereals and nuts; set aside. Boil sugar, cream, and syrup to medium hard ball stage. Pour over dry mixture and spread out on 13x9x2-inch pan. Cool and cut into squares.
*Bonnie Jamison*

## Cocoa Peanut Logs

1 6-oz. pkg. semi-sweet chocolate chips
1/3 cup peanut butter
2 cups chocolate-flavored rice cereal

Melt chocolate and peanut butter in heavy medium-sized saucepan over low heat, stirring constantly until well blended. Remove from heat. Add cereal, stirring until coated with chocolate mixture. Press mixture firmly into lightly buttered 9-inch square pan. Place in cool area or refrigerate until firm. Cut into log-shaped bars.
*Jane Rumble*

## Peanut Butter Clusters

1 cup maple-flavored corn syrup
1 cup sugar
1 12-oz. jar peanut butter, crunchy
5 cups crunchy cereal

Melt syrup and sugar; bring to a boil. Add peanut butter and melt; then add cereal. Drop by teaspoon onto waxed paper.
*Myrtle Bashor*

# Chocolate-Coated

## English Toffee 1

1 cup sugar
1/2 cup butter
1/4 cup water
1/2 tsp. salt
1 1/2 cups nuts, chopped (1 cup extra fine)
1 12-oz. pkg. chocolate chips

Cook first 4 ingredients to light crack stage, 285°. Add 1/2 cup chopped nuts. Pour into well greased pan and cool. Melt half the chocolate chips and spread. Sprinkle 1/2 cup finely chopped nuts on top; turn over. Melt last 6 ounces chocolate chips and spread. Sprinkle remaining 1/2 cup nuts. Cool; break or cut into pieces.
*Marie Haney*
Variation:
Use only 6 oz. chocolate chips, melt and spread on top only.
*Margaret Brubaker*

## English Toffee 2

1 1/3 cups butter
1 cup sugar
2/3 cup water
3/4 tsp. salt
1 1/2 cups almonds, chopped
1/2 tsp. baking soda
chocolate bars
finely chopped nuts

Combine first 4 ingredients in saucepan and cook over low heat, stirring constantly to boiling. Continue cooking to 236° without stirring. Add almonds. Continue cooking to 290°, stirring constantly. Remove from heat and stir in baking soda. Pour immediately onto greased cookie sheet. Place chocolate bars on top, spreading until melted; sprinkle with finely chopped nuts. Cool; break or cut into pieces.
*Marianne Bowman*

## Chocolate Nut Clusters

1/2 lb. sweet chocolate
1/2 can sweetened condensed milk
1 cup peanuts, almonds, or walnuts, whole or chopped

In top of double boiler, melt chocolate over hot water. Remove from heat. Stir in milk and nuts, covering nuts completely. Drop by teaspoon onto buttered cookie sheet. Refrigerate for several hours. Very good, not too sweet.
*Mary Howser*

## Glamorous Chocolate Rolls

Fudge Coating:
1 1/4 cups sugar
2/3 cup evaporated milk
1 cup (6-oz. pkg.) chocolate chips
2 1/4 cups powdered sugar, sifted
2 Tbsp. light cream
1 1/2 Tbsp. butter, softened
egg white

Filling Variations:
2 Tbsp. orange rind; peppermint extract and green coloring; pineapple juice instead of cream; 2 Tbsp. chopped Maraschino cherries

Topping Options: coconut, wheat germ, tinted sugar, chopped nuts, cereal flakes, chopped gumdrops

Combine sugar and milk; bring to full boil, stirring at boil for 3 minutes. Remove from heat and stir in chocolate chips. Divide mixture in half. Spread each into 12x4-inch strip on waxed paper. Chill. Choose filling flavor and blend with 2 cups powdered sugar, cream, and butter. Knead in 1/4 cup sifted powdered sugar. Divide in half and shape into two 12-inch rolls. Place each roll of fondant in the center of chilled strips of chocolate fudge. Roll up, sealing edges.

Wrap in waxed paper and chill. To decorate, remove waxed paper. Brush with egg white. Roll in topping of choice.
*Marjorie Bauman*

## Peanut Butter Cups

1 cup margarine
1 lb. smooth peanut butter
1 box powdered sugar
1 1/2 tsp. vanilla
10 oz. or more chocolate
1/4 block paraffin, melted

Melt margarine; stir in peanut butter, sugar, and vanilla. Beat with mixer until well blended and smooth. Chill 1/2 hour or longer. Form into little balls. Chill. Melt chocolate; add melted paraffin. Dip balls in chocolate and lay in cups or on waxed paper.
*Wilma Filbrun*

## Out-of-this-World Coconut Candy

2 boxes powdered
  sugar
1 can sweetened con-
  densed milk
1 cup margarine or
  butter, melted
2 cups coconut
2 cups nuts, chopped
3 6-oz. pkgs. chocolate
  chips
3/4 stick paraffin

Mix all ingredients
except chocolate and
paraffin. Roll into
small balls and chill
on waxed paper. Melt
chocolate chips with
paraffin. Dip balls in
chocolate and cool.
*Ruby Jamison*

## Fruited Apricot Candy

1/2 lb. dried apricots
2/3 cup evaporated
  milk
7 oz. flaked coconut
1 can toasted coconut

Put apricots through
food grinder or chop
small. Combine with
canned milk and
flaked coconut.
Shape into small
balls and roll in
toasted coconut.
Keep refrigerated.
*Joy Thompson*

## Chocolate-Caramel Apples

6 medium apples
6 wooden skewers
6 Tbsp. nuts, chopped
1 14-oz. pkg. caramels
2 Tbsp. hot water
1/4 cup semi-sweet
  chocolate pieces

Stick 6 wooden
skewers into stem
end of 6 medium
apples. Place 1 Tbsp.
chopped nuts in each
of 6 mounds, a few
inches apart on
waxed paper. In bot-
tom of double boiler,
heat about 1 inch
water to boiling.
Place other ingredi-
ents in top part of
double boiler. Set
over the boiling
water, stirring until
caramels and choco-
late are melted. Re-
move double boiler
from heat, keeping
top part over hot
water. With knife or
spatula, spread ap-
ples with chocolate-
caramel mixture.
Place each coated
apple on a mound of
nuts. If desired,
sprinkle any remain-
ing nuts around
skewers.
Note:
If caramel mixture
hardens during
spreading process,
place double boiler
over heat and bring
water to boiling
again.
*Denise Metzger*

## Fruit Balls

1 lb. figs
1 lb. dates
1 lb. raisins
1 lb. nuts
1 cup honey

Grind all together.
Shape into small
balls. Roll in ground
nuts or powdered
sugar or white sugar.
Or leave plain.
*Mary Filbrun*

## Yule "Apples"

3 cups dried apricots
1 cup salted almonds,
  ground
1 cup walnuts,
  finely chopped
2 slices drained pine-
  apple, ground
3 cups coconut
2 tsp. orange rind,
  grated
2 tsp. lemon rind,
  grated
1/4 cup lemon juice
whole cloves
powdered sugar

Wash and steam ap-
ricots in double
boiler for 5 minutes;
cool. Grind apricots
and add remaining
ingredients, except
cloves and powdered
sugar. Knead until
well mixed. If too
moist, work in small
amount of powdered
sugar. Shape into
3/4-inch balls and
roll in coconut. Place
a whole clove on each
one.
*Ethel Rumble*
Variation:
Roll in granulated
sugar. Omit almonds.
*Eunice Grover*

# Fudge

## "See's" Fudge

1 can evaporated milk
4 1/2 cups sugar
1 cup butter or
  margarine
3 6-oz. pkgs. chocolate
  chips
1 tsp. vanilla
1 8-oz. jar marsh-
  mallow cream
2 cups nuts, chopped

Boil milk and sugar
for 11 minutes. Add
remaining ingre-
dients and stir until
melted. Pour into two
13x9x2-inch buttered
baking dishes. Chill
before cutting.
*Betty Lou Garber*
*Nancy Bowman*

## Fudge 1

2 Tbsp. butter
6 tsp. cocoa
2 cups sugar
1 cup half-and-half
1 tsp. vanilla
2 cups nuts, chopped

Combine first 4
ingredients in sauce-
pan and cook to full
rolling boil, until a
little dropped in cold
water forms a soft
ball. Remove from
heat and cool to
lukewarm, setting
pan in cold water.
Add vanilla and nuts;
beat until thick. Pour
into 8-inch square
buttered dish. Chill
and cut into pieces;
serve when set.
Note:
Delicious served with
popcorn and apples.
*Joan Benedict*

## Fudge 2

3 3/4 cups sugar
1 1/4 cups evaporated
  milk
7 1/2 Tbsp. butter
1 jar marshmallow
  cream
1 12-oz. pkg. chocolate
  chips
1 1/4 cups nuts,
  chopped

Cook sugar, milk,
and butter to
medium soft ball
stage, 236°, stirring
often. Remove from
heat. Immediately
add marshmallow
cream, chips, and
nuts. Stir until all are
melted together. Pour
into 13x9x2-inch
buttered pan. Cool.
Yields 4 pounds.
*Leah Garber*

## Fudge 3

3 cups sugar
1/2 cup whipping
  cream
1/2 cup rich milk *or*
  half-and-half
1/2 cup cocoa
1 tsp. vanilla
1/2 cup butter
1 cup nuts, chopped

Mix first 4 ingredi-
ents well and place
over low heat, stir-
ring occasionally to
dissolve sugar before
boiling. Increase heat
and boil to 232°.
Remove from heat
and cool to quite
warm. Add vanilla
and butter. Beat until
candy starts to lose
its glossiness. Add
nuts and pour into
pan. Cut into
squares before cold.
*Lola Miller*

## Taffy Tan Fudge

2 cups sugar
1 cup milk
1 jar marshmallow
  cream
1 12-oz. jar crunchy
  peanut butter
1 tsp. vanilla

Combine sugar and
milk; bring to a boil.
Stir 5 minutes over
medium heat to soft
ball stage. Remove
from heat; stir in
marshmallow cream,
peanut butter, and
vanilla. Beat until
well blended. Pour
into 9-inch square
pan.
*Barbara Fall*

## Peanut Butter Fudge

2 cups sugar
2 Tbsp. cocoa
1 cup milk
2 Tbsp. butter
1 tsp. vanilla
1/2 cup peanut butter

Mix sugar and cocoa
in saucepan. Add
milk and butter; cook
to 225° or until it
forms a soft ball in
cold water. Remove
from heat; add
vanilla and peanut
butter. Beat until it
loses glossiness; pour
into buttered 8-inch
square pan. Cut into
squares.
*Esther Flora*

# Miscellaneous

## Caramel Candy

6 2/3 cups (2 1/2 lbs.)
   white or brown sugar
1 pt. light corn syrup
1/4 cup butter
1 pt. sweet cream
2 oz. paraffin
2 Tbsp. vanilla
chopped nuts,
   (optional)

Combine all ingredients except nuts, and cook to medium ball stage, 245°. Add nuts, if desired. Pour into buttered pans. When cool, cut into squares and wrap in waxed paper.
*Naomi Bauman*

## Divinity 1

Syrup 1:
1 cup sugar
2/3 cup water
Syrup 2:
2 cups sugar
1 cup light corn syrup
1 cup water

Start cooking both syrups separately but at the same time. Cook first syrup to soft ball stage or 234°.

2 egg whites
1/8 tsp. salt
1 tsp. vanilla
1 cup nuts

Beat egg whites and salt until soft peaks form. Pour first syrup slowly over egg whites, beating constantly. Let second syrup cook to hard ball stage or 254°. Add slowly to first syrup mixture, beating constantly until creamy. Then add vanilla and nuts. Pour quickly onto buttered, shallow baking pan. Cut into squares when cool. Makes about 4 dozen pieces.
*Marjorie Bauman*

## Divinity 2

4 cups sugar
1 cup water
1 cup light corn syrup
1/2 cup egg whites
1 tsp. vanilla
1 cup nuts, chopped

Cook sugar, water, and syrup to 262°. Remove from heat; cool. Meanwhile, beat egg whites very stiff. Pour cooked syrup over egg whites slowly with beater going on high. Beat until mixture begins to lose its gloss. Add vanilla and nuts. Pour into buttered 13x9x2-inch pan. Makes 3 pounds.
*Leah Garber*

## Divinity 3

2 1/2 cups sugar
1/2 cup water
1/2 cup light corn
   syrup
2 egg whites, beaten
   stiffly
1 tsp. vanilla
1 cup nuts, chopped
food coloring,
   (optional)

Cover sugar, water, and syrup and bring to a full boil until sugar is dissolved. Continue to cook to 250°. Then slowly pour into stiffly beaten egg whites, beating all the time. Add nuts, vanilla, and coloring as desired. Continue to beat until mixture starts to fudge. Pour into greased dish or drop by spoonfuls onto greased waxed paper.
*Lola Miller*

## Heavenly Hash Candy

1 1/2 cups cream
3 cups sugar
1 cup light corn syrup
pinch of salt
pinch of cream of
   tartar
1 cup nuts, chopped

Put cream, sugar, syrup, and salt into kettle; boil to hard ball stage. Remove from heat; immediately add cream of tartar. Beat until creamy. Add nuts and pour into buttered dish. Cut into squares when it begins to firm up.
*Mildred E. Miller*

## Molasses Taffy

2 cups molasses
1 cup sugar
3/4 cup water
1/4 cup butter
1/8 tsp. baking soda
1/2 tsp. vanilla

Combine molasses, sugar, and water; cook slowly, stirring steadily, until brittle in cold water. Remove from heat and add butter, baking soda, and vanilla. Pour into greased pan and cool enough to handle. Pull until light colored.
*Ruth Bauman*

# Candied Nuts

## Minted Walnuts

1 cup sugar
1/2 cup water
1 Tbsp. light corn syrup
6 marshmallows, cut up
pinch of salt
4 or 5 drops oil of peppermint
3 cups walnut halves

Boil sugar, water, and syrup until it spins a thread at 220°. Add cut-up marshmallows and salt. Stir until marshmallows are dissolved. Add peppermint and nuts, stirring until well coated. Turn onto ungreased waxed paper while coating still has a gloss. Cool; then remove. Good to double or triple this recipe.
*Grandma Colbert*

## Penuche Walnuts

1 cup brown sugar, firmly packed
1/2 tsp. salt
1/4 tsp. cinnamon
1 tsp. orange rind, grated
6 Tbsp. milk
1 tsp. vanilla
2 1/2–3 cups walnut halves

Combine sugar, salt, cinnamon, orange rind, and milk in saucepan. Cook, stirring frequently to 236° (soft ball stage). Remove from heat; add vanilla and walnut halves. Stir until mixture "sugars" and coats all the nuts. Turn out at once onto waxed paper and separate individual nuts. Makes about 3/4 pound.
*Lois Shirk*

## Sugar-Coated Nuts

1 cup sugar
6 Tbsp. milk
2 Tbsp. honey
1 tsp. cinnamon
1 tsp. vanilla
dash of salt
3 cups nuts, whole or halved

Boil sugar, milk, and honey to soft ball stage, 238°. Remove from heat; add other ingredients. Stir until creamy. Turn out quickly onto waxed paper and separate nuts. If desired, omit cinnamon.
*Emma Blickenstaff*

---

*MORNING PRAYER*

*When little things would irk me and I grow*
*Impatient with my dear ones, make me know*
*How in a moment, joy can take its flight*
*And happiness be quenched in endless night.*
*Keep this thought with me all the livelong day*
*That I may guard the harsh words I might say,*
*When I would fret and grumble, fiery hot,*
*At trifles that tomorrow are forgot—*
*Let me remember, Lord, how it would be*
*If these, my loved ones, were not here with me.*
*In Jesus' name I pray. Amen*

Source: _____ Who Likes It: _____

Source: _____ Who Likes It: _____

Source: _____ Who Likes It: _____

# The Snackery

*A man has
learned much who has learned
how to die.*
GERMAN PROVERB

*Jesus said,
"Take my yoke upon you
and learn from me,
for I am gentle
and humble in heart,
and you will find rest
for your souls."*
MATTHEW 11:29

# Snacks

## Christmas Chicken Feed

Sauce:
1 lb. butter, melted
1 tsp. onion salt
1 tsp. celery salt
1 tsp. Worcestershire sauce
1/2 tsp. garlic powder
1 tsp. Tabasco sauce
1/2 tsp. hot sauce

Mixture:
1 pkg. each of crunchy oat, wheat, rice, and corn cereals
1 lb. cashews
1 pkg. pretzel sticks
1 lb. blanched peanuts
1 lb. walnut kernels

Combine sauce ingredients and pour over *Mixture* ingredients, mixing well. Put in shallow pan and place in oven at 275° for 1/2 hour, stirring often. When partly cooled, store in tightly sealed containers.
*Mary Heinrich*

## Granola 1

2 lbs. rolled oats, raw
4 cups nuts, broken up
1 cup coconut
1 cup wheat germ
3/4 cup sunflower seed
1/2 cup flax seed
1/2 cup sesame seed
2 cups honey, heated

Mix dry ingredients together. Add honey to dry mixture. Put into 3 greased jelly roll pans. Bake at 350° (or less) for 1/2 hour. Stir every 10 minutes so it toasts evenly. Add raisins or dates before serving, if desired.
Note:
For backpackers and campers, this is great! Good as a snack or cold cereal. Store in tightly sealed container.
*Juanita Grover*

## Granola 2

5 cups regular rolled oats
1 cup almonds, chopped
1 cup unrefined sesame seed
1 cup wheat germ
1 cup sunflower seed
1 cup coconut, shredded (or flaked)
1 cup powdered milk
1/2 cup soy flour, (optional)
1 cup honey
1 cup vegetable oil (not olive oil)

Combine dry ingredients in large mixing bowl. Mix liquid ingredients in another bowl. Stir moist ingredients over dry mixture, using fingers to blend well. Spread on 2 cookie sheets and bake at 300° for an hour or until slightly brown. Stir often to prevent scorching. Store in small plastic bags. Serve with milk, adding raisins, cut-up dates or other dried fruit. No sugar is needed.
*Margaret Bowman*
*Suzie Beckner*

## Hi-Energy Trail Logs

1/2 cup raw or roasted cashews
1 cup walnut meats
3 dried figs
1/2 cup pitted dates
1/2 cup golden or dark raisins
1/4 cup dried apples
1/2 cup dried apricots
1 tsp. or more lemon juice
1 Tbsp. rum flavoring
enough honey to bind all together
powdered sugar or finely grated coconut

Run fruits and nuts through fine blade of food chopper and mix thoroughly with liquid ingredients. Roll into small logs about 2x3/4-inches. Roll in powdered sugar or coconut. Chill or freeze after wrapping each in foil.
Variation:
Use any other dried fruit or nuts desired.
Note:
These are handy for back packers and campers.
*Daisy Frantz*

## Popcorn Treat

1 cup brown sugar
1/2 cup light corn syrup
1/2 cup water
2 Tbsp. vinegar
2 Tbsp. butter
1/2 tsp. baking soda
12 cups warm popcorn, very lightly salted

Combine first 5 ingredients and cook to very hard ball stage. When nearly done, add baking soda. Pour syrup mixture over warm popcorn. Mix and bake in oven a little while, stirring often, until all kernels are evenly toasted. Spread out on buttered surface to cool.
Variation:
Add peanuts if desired.
*Sandra Switzer*

## Cracker Jacks

2 1/2 cups sugar
1/2 cup water
1/2 cup dark corn syrup
1/2 tsp. cream of tartar
1 tsp. baking soda
1/2 tsp. vanilla
12–14 cups popcorn
salt to taste

Fast boil all ingredients but baking soda and vanilla to hard crack stage; then add baking soda and vanilla. Pour over popcorn. Salt to suit your taste.
*Mary Heinrich*

## Popcorn Balls 1

1/3 cup butter
1/2 lb. (32 large) marshmallows
2 qts. popcorn, salted lightly

Combine butter and marshmallows in double boiler until marshmallows are melted. Add to popcorn. Butter hands for easier handling; shape popcorn into balls.
*Mary Gish*

## Popcorn Balls 2

3 cups sugar
3 Tbsp. vinegar
3/4 cup water
3/4 tsp. butter
3 Tbsp. light corn syrup
1 1/2 tsp. salt
8 or 9 qts. unsalted popcorn

Cook first 5 ingredients to hard crack stage. Add salt. Pour over popped corn and shape into balls.
*Gladys Metzger*

## Popcorn Balls 3

2/3 cup light corn syrup
1 1/4 cups molasses
1 Tbsp. butter
1/8 tsp. baking soda
4–5 qts. popped corn

Cook together syrup, molasses, and butter until syrup becomes brittle when dropped in cold water. Stir in baking soda; pour over popped corn and form into balls.
*Ethel Rumble*

## Soft Pretzels

1 pkg. cake yeast
1 1/2 cups warm
  water
3/4 tsp. salt
1 1/2 tsp. sugar
4 cups flour
1 egg, beaten
coarse salt

Preheat oven to 400°. Soften yeast in warm water in large bowl. Add salt and sugar. Mix in flour, kneading to make soft, smooth dough. Do not let rise. Cut immediately into smaller pieces. Roll into ropes and form pretzel shapes. Place on cookie sheet covered with foil and dusted with flour. Brush pretzels with beaten egg and sprinkle with coarse salt. Bake about 15 minutes or until light brown. Serve warm or cold, plain or with mustard. Makes from 3 to 6 dozen, depending upon size.
*Donna Switzer*

---

*RECIPE OF A FRIEND*

*3 cups trustworthiness*
*1 cup good humor*
*1 cup sympathy*
*1 cup hope*
*2 cups love*
*1 cup patience*
*1 strong shoulder to lean on*
*1 good listening ear*

*Combine all ingredients within one large heart. Serve in generous portions.*

_____
_____
_____
_____
_____
_____
_____
_____
_____

Source: _____ Who Likes It: _____

_____
_____
_____
_____
_____
_____
_____
_____
_____

Source: _____ Who Likes It: _____

_____
_____
_____
_____
_____
_____
_____
_____

Source: _____ Who Likes It: _____

## BAKING HINTS
## Making Tastier Cakes and Cookies

1. To make a finely textured cake, always add 2 Tbsp. of boiling water to the butter and sugar mixture.
2. Improve any cake by adding a teaspoon of lemon juice to the butter and sugar. This makes a cake very light and shorter. Fresh milk makes cake close-grained and more solid.
3. In creaming butter and sugar for a cake, add a little hot milk to aid in the creaming process.
4. Do not grease the sides of cake pans. Would you like to climb a greased pole?
5. For best results, use correct size pan. The time and the oven temperature should be adjusted to the type of pan being used. For shortening-type cakes, bake cupcakes at 375° for 18 to 20 minutes; layer cakes at 350° for 30 to 35 minutes, and loaf cakes at 350° for 40 to 45 minutes.
6. After using the oven, leave the door open until the oven is cool so that moisture will not condense and rust the metal.
7. When you do not want to heat your oven for a shortcake, make a thin batter for the biscuit dough with a little sugar added and bake in a waffle iron.
8. Make a good, quick frosting by boiling a small potato, mashing it, and adding powdered sugar and vanilla.
9. To decorate a cake without a decorator, cut a clean envelope from one of the top corners to the middle of the bottom and fill with frosting. Cut a little piece off the corner and decorate as desired.
10. For a nice decoration on white frosting, shave colored gum drops very thin and stick on. They will curl like little roses.
11. Do not discard rinds of grapefruit, oranges, or lemons. Grate the rinds first, put into a tightly covered glass jar, and store in the refrigerator. Makes excellent flavoring for cakes, frosting, and such.
12. To cut a fresh cake, use a wet knife.
13. An apple cut in half and placed in the cake box will keep the cake fresh several days longer.
14. To keep crisp cookies crisp, and soft cookies soft, place only one kind in a cookie jar.

## Avoiding Failures in Baking

FAILURES · CAUSES

1. *Yeast Breads:*
   (a) porous — (a) overrising *or* too low heat
   (b) dark, blistered crust — (b) underrising
   (c) no rising — (c) overkneading *or* using old yeast
   (d) streaked — (d) underkneading and uneven kneading
   (e) unevenly baked — (e) old, dark pans; too much dough in pan; crowded oven rack; too high heat

2. *Biscuits:*
   (a) rough texture — (a) insufficient mixing
   (b) dry texture — (b) too much handling; too low heat
   (c) uneven browning — (c) dark pan; too high heat; rolling dough too thin

3. *Muffins:*
   (a) coarse texture — (a) insufficient stirring; too low heat
   (b) tunnels; peaks in center; soggy texture — (b) overmixing

4. *Cakes:*
   (a) cracks and uneven surface — (a) too much flour; too high heat; starting with a cold oven
   (b) dry texture — (b) too much flour; too little shortening; too much baking powder; too low heat
   (c) heavy texture — (c) too much sugar; too short a baking period
   (d) sticky crust — (d) too much sugar
   (e) coarsely grained texture — (e) too little mixing; too much fat; too much baking powder; overly softened fat; too low heat
   (f) fallen cake — (f) not enough flour; underbaking; too much sugar; too much fat; not enough baking powder
   (g) uneven browning — (g) too high heat; crowding oven rack; dark pans
   (h) unevenly colored cake — (h) inadequate mixing

5. *Pies:*
   (a) crumbly pastry — (a) overmixing of fat and flour
   (b) tough pastry — (b) too much water; overmixing dough
   (c) unbrowned — (c) incorrect pie pan (for fruit or custard pies, use a Pyrex pie pan or an enamel pan, and bake at 400°–425° Fahrenheit kept constant)

## EMERGENCY SUBSTITUTIONS

| | |
|---|---|
| 1 Tbsp. cornstarch (for thickening) | 2 Tbsp. flour (approximately) |
| 1 whole egg | 2 egg yolks, plus 1 Tbsp. water (in cookies, etc.); 2 egg yolks (in custards and such mixtures) |
| 1 cup fresh sweet milk | 1/2 cup evaporated milk plus 1/2 cup water; powdered milk plus water (directions on package); 1 cup sour milk or buttermilk plus 1/2 tsp. soda (decrease baking powder 2 tsp.) |
| 1 cup sour milk or buttermilk | 1 Tbsp. lemon juice or vinegar plus enough fresh sweet milk to make 1 cup |
| 1 square unsweetened chocolate (1 ounce) | 3 Tbsp. cocoa plus 1/2 tsp. shortening |
| 1 cup honey | 3/4 cup sugar plus 1/4 cup liquid |
| 1 cup canned tomatoes | about 1 1/3 cups cut-up fresh tomatoes, simmered 10 minutes |

MEAT CHARTS

# BEEF
Meat Cuts and How to Cook Them

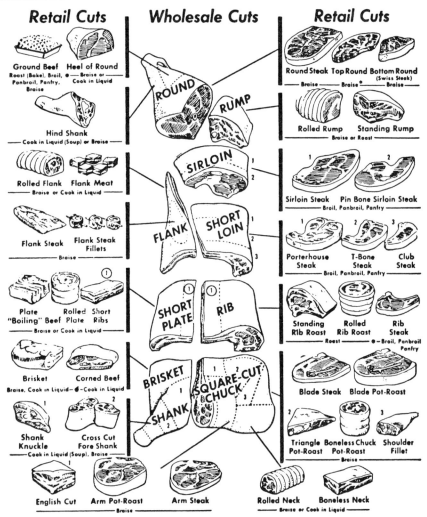

## Retail Cuts

**Ground Beef**
Roast (Bake), Broil, Panbroil, Panfry, Braise

**Heel of Round**
Braise or Cook in Liquid

**Hind Shank**
— Cook in Liquid (Soup) or Braise —

**Rolled Flank** **Flank Meat**
— Braise or Cook in Liquid —

**Flank Steak** **Flank Steak Fillets**
— Braise —

**Plate "Boiling" Beef** **Rolled Short Plate Ribs**
— Braise or Cook in Liquid —

**Brisket** **Corned Beef**
Braise, Cook in Liquid — / — Cook in Liquid

**Shank Knuckle** **Cross Cut Fore Shank**
— Cook in Liquid (Soup), Braise —

**English Cut** **Arm Pot-Roast**
— Braise —

**Arm Steak**

## Wholesale Cuts

ROUND
RUMP
SIRLOIN
SHORT LOIN
FLANK
SHORT PLATE
RIB
BRISKET
SQUARE-CUT CHUCK
SHANK

## Retail Cuts

**Round Steak** **Top Round** **Bottom Round** (Swiss Steak)
— Braise — / — Braise — / — Braise —

**Rolled Rump** **Standing Rump**
— Braise or Roast —

**Sirloin Steak** **Pin Bone Sirloin Steak**
— Broil, Panbroil, Panfry —

**Porterhouse Steak** **T-Bone Steak** **Club Steak**
— Broil, Panbroil, Panfry —

**Standing Rib Roast** **Rolled Rib Roast** **Rib Steak**
— Roast — / — Broil, Panbroil Panfry

**Blade Steak** **Blade Pot-Roast**

**Triangle Pot-Roast** **Boneless Chuck Pot-Roast** **Shoulder Fillet**
— Braise —

**Rolled Neck** **Boneless Neck**
— Braise or Cook in Liquid —

*Prime and choice grades may be broiled, panbroiled or panfried   **NATIONAL LIVE STOCK AND MEAT BOARD**

# LAMB
## Meat Cuts and How to Cook Them

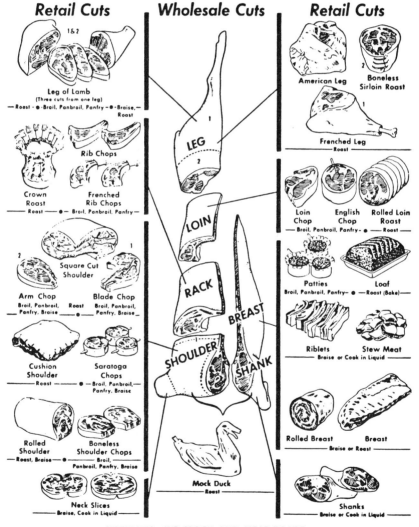

### Retail Cuts

**Leg of Lamb**
(Three cuts from one leg)
— Roast - ● -Broil, Panbroil, Panfry - ● - Braise,— Roast

**Rib Chops**

**Crown Roast**
— Roast —●—

**Frenched Rib Chops**
— Broil, Panbroil, Panfry —

**Square Cut Shoulder**

**Arm Chop**
Broil, Panbroil, Panfry, Braise

Roast ●

**Blade Chop**
Broil, Panbroil, Panfry, Braise

**Cushion Shoulder**
— Roast —

**Saratoga Chops**
●— Broil, Panbroil,— Panfry, Braise

**Rolled Shoulder**
—Roast, Braise— ●

**Boneless Shoulder Chops**
● Broil, Panbroil, Panfry, Braise

**Neck Slices**
— Braise, Cook in Liquid —

### Wholesale Cuts

LEG

LOIN

RACK

SHOULDER

BREAST

SHANK

**Mock Duck**
— Roast —

### Retail Cuts

**American Leg**

**Boneless Sirloin Roast**

**Frenched Leg**
— Roast —

**Loin Chop**

**English Chop**

**Rolled Loin Roast**
— Broil, Panbroil, Panfry - ● — Roast —

**Patties**
Broil, Panbroil, Panfry- ●

**Loaf**
—Roast (Bake)—

**Riblets**

**Stew Meat**
— Braise or Cook in Liquid —

**Rolled Breast**

**Breast**
— Braise or Roast —

**Shanks**
— Braise or Cook in Liquid —

**NATIONAL LIVE STOCK AND MEAT BOARD**

# PORK
## Meat Cuts and How to Cook Them

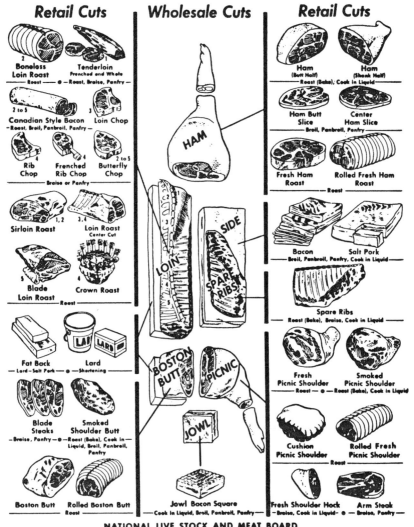

**NATIONAL LIVE STOCK AND MEAT BOARD**

# VEAL
## Meat Cuts and How to Cook Them

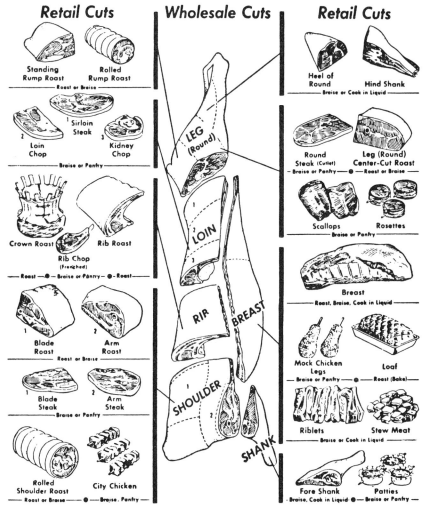

**Retail Cuts** — **Wholesale Cuts** — **Retail Cuts**

Standing Rump Roast · Rolled Rump Roast — Roast or Braise

Sirloin Steak · Loin Chop · Kidney Chop — Braise or Panfry

Crown Roast · Rib Roast · Rib Chop (Frenched) — Roast — Braise or Panfry — Roast

Blade Roast · Arm Roast — Roast or Braise

Blade Steak · Arm Steak — Braise or Panfry

Rolled Shoulder Roast · City Chicken — Roast or Braise — Braise, Panfry

LEG (Round) · LOIN · RIB · BREAST · SHOULDER · SHANK

Heel of Round · Hind Shank — Braise or Cook in Liquid

Round Steak (Cutlet) · Leg (Round) Center-Cut Roast — Braise or Panfry — Roast or Braise

Scallops · Rosettes — Braise or Panfry

Breast — Roast, Braise, Cook in Liquid

Mock Chicken Legs · Loaf — Braise or Panfry — Roast (Bake)

Riblets · Stew Meat — Braise or Cook in Liquid

Fore Shank · Patties — Braise, Cook in Liquid — Braise or Panfry

**NATIONAL LIVE STOCK AND MEAT BOARD**

## CALORIE COUNTER

| Beverages | Portion | Calories | Carbo* Grams | Cholesterol mg. |
|---|---|---|---|---|
| Coffee, plain | 1 cup | 0 c. | 0 | 0 |
| Tea, plain | 1 cup | 0 c. | 1/2 | 0 |
| Carbonated soft drinks | 8 oz. | 105 c. | 26 | 0 |
| Cocoa, all milk | 8 oz. | 235 c. | 20 | 62 |
| Lemonade | 8 oz. | 100 c. | 28 | 0 |
| Kool-Aid, pre-sweetened | 8 oz. | 90 c. | 1/2 | 0 |
| Beer | 12 oz. | 150 c. | 18 | 0 |

### Breads, Crackers, Grain Products

| | Portion | Calories | Carbo* Grams | Cholesterol mg. |
|---|---|---|---|---|
| Corn Bread | 2" sq. | 200 c. | 18 | 70 |
| French Bread | 1 slice | 290 c. | 55 | N/A |
| Protein Bread | 1 slice | 40 c. | N/A | Low |
| Raisin Bread | 1 slice | 75 c. | 13 | Trace |
| Rye Bread | 1 slice | 75 c. | 12 | Trace |
| White Bread | 1 slice | 65 c. | 12 | Trace |
| Whole Wheat Bread | 1 slice | 65 c. | 11 | Trace |
| Biscuits | 1 average | 123 c. | 18 | 0 |
| Rolls | 1 medium | 140 c. | 20 | Low |
| Saltines | 2" sq. | 25 c. | 3 | 0 |
| Soda Crackers | 2" sq. | 25 c. | 4 | 0 |
| Graham Crackers | 1 medium | 28 c. | 5 | Low |
| Matzoth | 1 | 75 c. | N/A | N/A |
| Egg Noodles | 1 cup | 185 c. | 49 | 213 |
| French Toast | 1 slice | 125 c. | 14 | N/A |
| Pancakes | 4" dia. | 75 c. | 8 | 54 |
| Macaroni - Spaghetti | 1 cup | 200 c. | 80 | 0 |
| Rice | 1 cup | 125 c. | 32 | 0 |
| Waffles | 1 average | 225 c. | 30 | 119 |
| Frankfurter Rolls | 1 average | 110 c. | 20 | Low |
| Hamburger Rolls | 1 average | 170 c. | 20 | Low |
| Nut Bread | 1 slice | | 11 | N/A |

### Cereals

| | Portion | Calories | Carbo* Grams | Cholesterol mg. |
|---|---|---|---|---|
| Cream of Wheat | 3/4 cup | 100 c. | 21 | N/A |
| Corn Flakes | 1 cup | 100 c. | 18 | 0 |
| Bran Flakes | 3/4 cup | 100 c. | 23 | 0 |
| Oatmeal | 3/4 cup | 100 c. | 18 | 0 |
| Puffed Rice and Wheat | 3/4 cup | 50 c. | 8 | 0 |
| Rice Krispies | 1 cup | 110 c. | 25 | 0 |
| Shredded Wheat | 1 cup | 100 c. | 36 | 0 |
| Wheaties | 1 cup | | 23 | 0 |

### Desserts, Sweets

| | Portion | Calories | Carbo* Grams | Cholesterol mg. |
|---|---|---|---|---|
| Angel Food Cake | 1 average slice | 110 c. | 24 | 0 |
| Chocolate Cake, 2 layer | 1 average slice | 400 c. | N/A | High |
| Cupcake, plain | 1 | 100 c. | 31 | Med. |

*Carbohydrate-grams

| | Portion | Calories | Carbo*<br>Grams | Cholesterol<br>mg. |
|---|---|---|---|---|
| Fruit Cake | 1 average slice | 300 c. | N/A | 7 |
| Shortcake with fruit | 1 average slice | 350 c. | N/A | N/A |
| Pound Cake | 1 average slice | 125 c. | 15 | High |
| Caramel Candy | 1 oz. | 250 c. | 8 | Med. |
| Fudge Candy | 1 oz. | 110 c. | 18 | Med. |
| Chocolate Cookies | 1 small | 18 c. | N/A | Med. |
| Chocolate Chip Cookies | 1 small | 22 c. | 7 | Med. |
| Oatmeal Cookies | 1 large | 100 c. | 16 | 0 |
| Chocolate Bar with almonds | 1 average | 260 c. | N/A | N/A |
| Chocolate Mints | 1 small | 41 c. | N/A | N/A |
| Doughnuts, jelly | 1 average | 250 c. | N/A | High |
| Doughnuts, plain | 1 average | 150 c. | 17 | High |
| Doughnuts, sugared | 1 average | 175 c. | 22 | High |
| Honey | 1 Tbsp. | 65 c. | 17 | 0 |
| Ice Cream | 1 cup | 400 c. | 28 | 85 |
| Ice Milk | 1 cup | 285 c. | 1/2 | 36 |
| Jello | 1/2 cup | 80 c. | 18 | 0 |
| Jellies, Jams | 1 Tbsp. | 50 c. | 14 | 0 |
| Pie, apple and other fruit | average slice | 330 c. | 50–54 | 0 |
| Pies, custard | average slice | 265 c. | 34 | 120 |
| Pies, cream | average slice | 400 c. | N/A | High** |
| Pudding, bread | 1/2 cup | 125 c. | 21 | |
| Pudding, tapioca | 1/2 cup | 140 c. | 16 | 80 |
| Pudding, vanilla | 1/2 cup | N/A | N/A | 18 |
| Pudding, chocolate | 1/2 cup | N/A | N/A | 15 |
| Sherbet | 1/2 cup | 120 c. | 28 | 0 |
| Sugar, granulated<br>and brown | 1 tsp. | 20 c. | 4 | 0 |
| Sugar, powdered | 1 Tbsp. | 90 c. | 8 | 0 |
| Syrup | 1 Tbsp. | 60 c. | 13 | 0 |

## Dairy Products, Fats, Oils, Dressings

| | Portion | Calories | Carbo*<br>Grams | Cholesterol<br>mg. |
|---|---|---|---|---|
| Butter | 1 Tbsp. | 50 c. | Trace | 35 |
| Cheese, American<br>processed | 1 oz. | 75 c. | 1/2 | 25 |
| Cheese, cottage | 1 cup | 240 c. | 6 | 48 |
| Cheese, farmer's, pot | 1 oz. | 25 c. | N/A | N/A |
| Cheese, Cheddar | 1 oz. | 100 c. | 1/2 | 28 |
| Cheese, Swiss | 1 oz. | 100 c. | 1 | 28 |
| Cream Cheese | 2 Tbsp. | 56 c. | 1/2 | 32 |
| Cream | 1 Tbsp. | 34 c. | 1 | 20 |
| Cream, whipped | 1 Tbsp. | 50 c. | 1/2 | Trace |
| Sour cream | 1 Tbsp. | 53 c. | 1/2 | 8 |
| Half & Half | 1 Tbsp. | N/A | 1 | 6 |
| Egg, whole | 1 large | 72 c. | Trace | 252 |
| white only | 1 large | 15 c. | Trace | 0 |
| yolk only | 1 large | 57 c. | Trace | 252 |
| Egg, boiled, poached | 1 medium | 75 c. | 0 | |
| Egg, fried | 1 medium | 100 c. | 0 | |
| Egg, scrambled | 1 medium | 125 c. | 1 | |
| Egg, omelet | 2 eggs | N/A | 1 | 526 |
| Milk, whole | 8 oz. | 165 c. | 12 | 34 |
| Milk, skim | 8 oz. | 85 c. | 13 | 5 |

*Carbohydrate-grams  **Depending on type of fruit

| | Portion | Calories | Carbo* Grams | Cholesterol mg. |
|---|---|---|---|---|
| Milk, 2% low fat | 8 oz. | 120 c. | | 22 |
| Buttermilk | 8 oz. | 72 c. | 13 | 5 |
| Margarine, oleo | 1 Tbsp. | 50 c. | 0 | 0 |
| Oils, cooking & salad | 1 Tbsp. | 100 c. | 0 | 0 |
| Salad Dressing, French | 1 Tbsp. | 100 c. | 2 | Low |
| Salad Dressing, Roquefort | 1 Tbsp. | 125 c. | 1 | N/A |
| Salad Dressing, Russian | 1 Tbsp. | 50 c. | 2 | Low |
| Salad Dressing, Italian | 1 Tbsp. | | 0 | Low |
| Salad Dressing, Mayonnaise | 1 Tbsp. | 93 c. | Trace | 8 |
| Vinegar and Oil | 1 Tbsp. | 130 c. | 0 | 0 |
| Salad Dressing, Thousand Island | 1 Tbsp. | 75 c. | 2 | Med. |
| | | (Most Dietary Dressings cut carbos 50%) | | |
| Yogurt | 1 cup | 165 c. | 10 | 17 |

## Meats & Poultry

| | Portion | Calories | Carbo* Grams | Cholesterol mg. |
|---|---|---|---|---|
| Bacon, fried crisp | 1 slice | 47 c. | 1/2 | 7 |
| Beef, hamburger, lean broiled | 3 oz. | 200 c. | 0 | 80 |
| Beef, roast, lean | 4 oz. | 210 c. | 0 | 90 |
| Beef, round steak | 2 1/2 oz. | 147 c. | 0 | 4 |
| Beef, sirloin steak | 3 1/2 oz. | 206 c. | 0 | High |
| Beef, liver with onions | 3 1/2 oz. | 248 c. | 8 | 438 |
| Bologna | 1 slice | 85 c. | 1/4 | High |
| Chicken, whole, broiled | 3 lbs. | | 0 | 542 |
| Chicken, fried | 1/2 | | 5 | High |
| Chicken, fried | thigh or leg | 135 c. | N/A | 47 |
| Chicken, fried | breast | 150 c. | N/A | 80 |
| Frankfurter | 1 (2 oz.) | 125 c. | 1 | N/A |
| Ham, smoked | average slice | 450 c. | 0 | High |
| Ham, baked | 3 oz. | 320 c. | 0 | High |
| Ham, canned, lean | 2 oz. | 170 c. | 0 | High |
| Meat loaf | average slice | 225 c. | 4 | High |
| Pork, roast | 3 oz. | 200 c. | 0 | 76 |
| Pork chops, fried | 1 medium | 325 c. | 0 | 76 |
| Pork chops, baked or broiled | 1 medium | 225 c. | 0 | N/A |
| Pork sausage | average patty | 170 c. | 0 | High |
| Veal cutlet, broiled | 3 oz. | 125 c. | 0 | 86 |
| Veal, roast | 3 oz. | 150 c. | 0 | 84 |

## Fish

| | Portion | Calories | Carbo* Grams | Cholesterol mg. |
|---|---|---|---|---|
| Catfish | average serving | 100 c. | 0 | Med. |
| Codfish | 3 1/2 oz. | 100 c. | 1/2 | 50 |
| Gefilte fish | average serving | 150 c. | 0 | High |
| Haddock, fried | 3 1/2 oz. | 250 c. | 4 | 60 |
| Halibut | 3 1/2 oz. | 200 c. | 0 | 60 |
| Perch | average serving | 100 c. | 0 | High |
| Salmon, canned | 1/2 cup | 160 c. | 0 | 35 |
| Salmon, fresh | 3 1/2 oz. | 160 c. | 0 | 47 |
| Trout, fried | 3 1/2 oz. | 220 c. | 0 | 55 |
| Tuna, canned | 3 1/2 oz. | 250 c. | 0 | 65 |

* Carbohydrate-grams

# Vegetables

| Vegetables | Portion | Calories | Carbo* Grams | Cholesterol mg. |
|---|---|---|---|---|
| Asparagus, canned | 1/2 cup | 25 c. | 3 | 0 |
| Avocado | 1 small | 425 c. | 12 | Med. |
| Beans, baked | 1/2 cup | 100 c. | 3 | Low |
| Beans, string | 1 cup | 25 c. | 10 | 0 |
| Beets | 1/2 cup | 35 c. | 8 | 0 |
| Broccoli | 1 cup | 45 c. | 8 | 0 |
| Brussels sprouts | 1 cup | 60 c. | 12 | 0 |
| Cabbage, raw | 1 cup | 25 c. | 10 | 0 |
| Cabbage, cooked | 1 cup | 40 c. | 10 | 0 |
| Carrots, raw or cooked | 1/2 cup | 25 c. | 5 | 0 |
| Cauliflower | 1 cup | 30 c. | 6 | 0 |
| Celery | 2 stalks | 10 c. | 1 | 0 |
| Corn, fresh or frozen | 1 cup | 140 c. | 16 | 0 |
| Corn, canned | 1/2 cup | 70 c. | 20 | 0 |
| Cucumbers | 1/2 cup | 10 c. | 2 | 0 |
| Lettuce, shredded | 1 cup | 10 c. | 3 | 0 |
| Mushrooms | 1/2 cup | 15 c. | 5 | 0 |
| Onions, raw or cooked | 1/2 cup | 25 c. | 9 | 0 |
| Peas, fresh, frozen or canned | 1 cup | 110 c. | 32 | 0 |
| Potatoes, baked or broiled | 1 medium | 125 c. | 21 | Med. |
| Potatoes, French fried | 6 average | 100 c. | 12 | Med. |
| Potatoes, mashed with butter & milk | 1/2 cup | 73 c. | 15 | Med. |
| Radishes | 7 | 15 c. | 3 1/2 | 0 |
| Sauerkraut | 1/2 cup | 25 c. | 3 | 0 |
| Spinach & other greens | 1/2 cup | 25 c. | 3 | 0 |
| Sweet potatoes, baked | 1 medium | 200 c. | 36 | 0 |
| Sweet potatoes, candied | 1/2 medium | 150 c. | 30 | N/A |
| Tomato, raw | 1 medium | 50 c. | 6 | 0 |
| Tomato, stewed | 1 cup | 50 c. | 10 | 0 |
| Tomato, juice | 1 cup | 50 c. | 10 | 0 |

# Fruit

| Fruit | Portion | Calories | Carbo* Grams | Cholesterol mg. |
|---|---|---|---|---|
| Apple, raw | 1 medium | 75 c. | 18 | 0 |
| Applesauce, sweetened canned | 1/2 cup | 100 c. | 25 | 0 |
| Bananas | 1 medium | 100 c. | 23 | 0 |
| Cantaloupe | 1/2 medium | 50 c. | 9 | 0 |
| Cranberry sauce | 1 Tbsp. | 34 c. | 18 | 0 |
| Fruit cocktail | 1 cup | 100 c. | 50 | 0 |
| Grapefruit | 1/2 medium | 50 c. | 14 | 0 |
| Grapefruit juice | 1 cup | 100 c. | 24 | 0 |
| Grapes | 1 cup | 85 c. | 16 | 0 |
| Oranges | 1 medium | 75 c. | 16 | 0 |
| Orange juice | 1 cup | 100 c. | 24 | 0 |
| Peaches, fresh | 1 medium | 50 c. | 10 | 0 |
| Peaches, canned | 2 halves | 93 c. | 24 | 0 |
| Pears | 1 medium | 75 c. | 10 | 0 |
| Pineapple, canned | 1/2" slice | 37 c. | 13 | 0 |
| Plums | 1 medium | 30 c. | 7 | 0 |

* Carbohydrate-grams

|  | Portion | Calories | Carbo* Grams | Cholesterol mg. |
|---|---|---|---|---|
| Prunes, cooked | 5 medium | 170 c. | 22 | 0 |
| Prune juice | 1/2 cup | 85 c. | 22 | 0 |
| Raisins, dried | 1/2 cup | 225 c. | 60 | 0 |
| Strawberries, frozen | 1/2 cup | 106 c. | 27 | 0 |
| Strawberries, fresh | 1 cup | 50 c. | 13 | 0 |
| Tangerines | 1 medium | 35 c. | 10 | 0 |
| Watermelon | 4" x 8" wedge | 100 c. | 29 | 0 |

## Miscellaneous

|  | Portion | Calories | Carbo* Grams | Cholesterol mg. |
|---|---|---|---|---|
| Ketchup, chili sauce | 1 Tbsp. | 25 c. | 4 | 0 |
| Olives, green | 7 large | 63 c. | 1 | 0 |
| Olives, ripe | 7 large | 63 c. | 2 | 0 |
| Nuts, cashews | 1/2 cup | 375 c. | 18 | 0 |
| Nuts, pecans | 1/2 cup | 375 c. | 8 | Low |
| Nuts, English walnuts | 1/2 cup | 375 c. | 4 | 0 |
| Peanut butter | 1 Tbsp. | 100 c. | 3 | 0 |
| Pickles, dill | 4" | 15 c. | 2 | 0 |
| Pickles, sweet | 1 medium | 25 c. | 5 | 0 |
| Pizza | 5" wedge | 225 c. | 23 | High |

*Carbohydrate-grams

# INDEX